Living with the Adirondack Forest

D1370027

Living with the Adirondack Forest

Local Perspectives on Land Use Conflicts

❦ Catherine Henshaw Knott

CORNELL UNIVERSITY PRESS
Ithaca and London

First published 1998 by Cornell University Press.

Printed in the United States of America

Cornell University Press strives to utilize environmentally responsible suppliers and materials to the fullest extent possible in the publishing of its books. Such materials include vegetable-based, low-VOC inks and acid-free papers that are also either recycled, totally chlorine-free, or partly composed of nonwood fibers.

Cloth printing   10 9 8 7 6 5 4 3 2 1

Library of Congress Cataloging-in-Publication Data
Knott, Catherine Henshaw.
    Living with the Adirondack forest : local perspectives on land use
conflicts / Catherine Henshaw Knott.
        p.   cm.
    Includes bibliographical references and index.
    ISBN 0-8014-3122-0 (cloth : alk. paper)
    1. Adirondack Forest Preserve (N.Y.)   2. Forest reserves — Multiple
use — New York (State) — Adirondack Forest Preserve.   I. Title.
SD428.A2N75   1997
304.2′7 — dc21   97-35390

to my grandmother
Wilma Henshaw Knott
who has always supported and encouraged a love of learning

and to the memory of my grandmother
Anna Dent Percy
who taught me to listen

Contents

List of Photographs

Adirondack Species Mentioned in the Text

Mammals

beaver	*Castor canadensis*
black bear	*Ursus americanus*
bobcat	*Felis rufus*
coyote	*Canis latrans*
eastern cottontail	*Sylvilagus floridanus*
fisher	*Martes penannti*
gray squirrel	*Sciurus carolinensis*
gray wolf	*Canis lupus*
lynx	*Felis lynx*
marten	*Martes americana*
moose	*Alces alces*
mountain lion	*Felis concolor*
porcupine	*Erethizon dorsatum*
raccoon	*Procyon lotor*
red fox	*Vulpes vulpes*
red squirrel	*Tamiasciurus hudsonicus*
river otter	*Lutra canadensis*
snowshoe hare	*Lepus americanus*
striped skunk	*Mephitis mephitis*
white-tailed deer	*Odocoileus virginianus*
woodchuck	*Marmota monax*

Fish

brook trout	*Salvelinus fontinalis*
brown trout	*Salmo trutta*
lake trout	*Salvelinus namaycush*
rainbow trout	*Salmo gairdneri*

largemouth bass   *Micropterus dolomieui*

largemouth bass	*Micropterus dolomieui*
smallmouth bass	*Micropterus salmoides*
pike	*Esox lucius*
sea lamprey	*Petromyzon marinus*
yellow perch	*Perca flavescens*

Birds

bald eagle	*Haliaeetus leucocephalus*
blackburnian warbler	*Dendroica fusca*
black-capped chickadee	*Parus atricapillus*
cedar waxwing	*Bombycilla cedrorum*
crow	*Corvus brachyrhynchos*
great blue heron	*Ardea herodias*
loon	*Gavia immer*
merganser	*Mergus merganser*
raven	*Corvus corax*
wood thrush	*Hylocichla mustelina*

Trees

American beech	*Fagus grandifolia*
American hornbeam	*Carpinus caroliniana*
black ash	*Fraxinus nigra*
white ash	*Fraxinus americana*
red maple	*Acer rubrum*
silver maple	*Acer saccharinum*
sugar maple	*Acer saccharum*
northern red oak	*Quercus rubra*
white oak	*Quercus alba*
pin (fire) cherry	*Prunus pensylvanica*
elm	*Ulmus americana*
eastern red cedar	*Juniperus virginiana*
northern white cedar	*Thuja occidentalis*
balsam fir	*abies balsamea*
larch (tamarack)	*Larix laricina*
black spruce	*Picea mariana*
red spruce	*Picea rubens*
white spruce	*Picea glauca*

eastern white pine	*Pinus strobus*
red pine	*Pinus resinosa*
eastern hemlock	*Tsuga canadensis*
quaking aspen	*Populus tremuloides*
bigtooth aspen	*Populus grandidentata*
shagbark hickory	*Carya ovata*
butternut	*Juglans cinerea*
yellow birch	*Betula alleghaniensis*
mountain paper birch	*Betula cordifolia*
paper birch	*Betula papyrifera*
gray birch	*Betula populifolia*
eastern hophornbeam	*Ostrya virginiana*

Organizations and Terms

Adirondack Association of Towns and Villages (AATV)
Adirondack Conservation Council
Adirondack Council (AC)
Adirondack Fairness Coalition (AFC)
Adirondack Landowners' Association (ALA)
Adirondack Local Government Review Board
Adirondack Mountain Club (ADK)
Adirondack Park Agency (APA)
Adirondack Planning Commission (APC)
Adirondack Solidarity Alliance
Association for the Protection of the Adirondacks
Board of Cooperative Education Services (BOCES): offers educational
	services
Citizens' Council: a property rights organization founded by Donald
	Gerdts
The Department of Environmental Conservation (DEC): manages the
	state-owned Forest Preserve and other environmental protection
	matters from two regional headquarters, at Raybrook and Watertown
Earthfirst!: a movement based on deep ecology principles, taking a
	"no compromise" position in environmental conflict
Empire State Forest Products Association
The Governor's Commission on the Adirondacks in the Twenty-first
	Century
National Audubon Society
The New York Blue Line Council, Inc.
New York State College of Environmental Science and Forestry (CESF)
People for the Ethical Treatment of Animals (PETA)
Residents' Committee to Protect the Adirondacks
Sea Shepherds
Sierra Club

Tupper Lake Shorefront Owners' Association: specializes in ownership, waterfront, and lake water quality issues, similar to other lake associations in the Adirondacks not listed here

Tupper Lake Woodsmen's Association

TERMINOLOGY

Towns: In the Adirondacks refers to a township. Most of the original large land purchases were divided into townships, which often bear little relation to today's towns.

Diameter breast height (dbh): refers to the diameter of a tree measured at approximately 4½ feet.

Preface

Walking through the brush in a ravine behind our house as I take a break from writing, I am reminded again of the importance of local knowledge, grounded in history and in a particular place. Whether one is considering the Oregon Coast Range or the Adirondacks clear across the continent, understanding ecological conditions means gaining a sense of place. My husband cut the alder and fir from this narrow ravine two years ago. Now the brush has crowded up again. It is dense, specific to the Coast Range and to the particular conditions here. From a distance I see the tall spires of purple and white foxglove that blanket the slopes, interspersed with stumps and dead trees peppered with woodpecker holes. Dark green clumps of sword fern and the lighter green of bracken fern interrupt this tapestry. But a closer look reveals other species taking back the ground: dutchman's breeches, clusters of wild iris, twinflower, nettles, clover, the ever-present salmonberry and native blackberry, thimbleberry, poison hemlock, wild cucumber, and watercress in the damp trickle of a stream. The Douglas fir trees my husband planted six months after cutting the timber are already two or three feet high, bristling with this year's growth. A dozen other species, with yellow flowers, tiny pink-striped flowers, white flowers, and mint or musk aromas burst from the grassy patches. Snake holes, gopher holes, and skunk trails abound.

The ridges stretching for miles around us are covered with a towering forest of dark fir and pale alder. A local preservation group is working to keep them that way. Yet is that their natural state? Forest Service photographs from 1940 show that these ridges were fern-covered at that time, and completely bare of trees. The Kalapuya Indians, living in nearby valleys until the 1830s, traditionally set fires to clear the brush for hunting. In the mid 1800s, before European settlers arrived, "the great fire" burned off almost all of the timber in this area. When the settlers arrived, the ridges were covered with ferns, thimbleberry, salmonberry, and dead trees. The few trees that were alive and standing were Douglas fir, some hemlock, red cedar. The open hillsides were attractive to settlers, and the native tree species reseeded themselves slowly. The settlers' angora goats kept down the brush and limited hardwood species until naturally seeded Douglas fir was well established.

Not many people today know about the fires. My husband knows because his family has been living on this particular piece of land since 1873 — 125 years of history and experience. When he was planting the new Douglas fir, a young cougar crouched at the edge of the clearing, watching him. The cougar — ready to leap back to the safety of the forest or into the brush to catch a rabbit — lives by the grace of the change inherent in ecosystems. The cougar is also a symbol of hope to me, hope that we can discover the right mixture of use and care — and how to let the wild be wild sometimes — by working together to learn about these places.

The issue of the balance of use and care, and of the role of disturbance, managed or natural, has again come to the forefront of the land use conflicts here in Oregon, in the Adirondacks, and elsewhere. In the spring of 1997 the Adirondack Park Agency was considering whether to allow shelterwood cuts of over twenty-five acres without special permits. A shelterwood cut involves removing the timber from a given area in two stages. At the time of the first cut, enough timber should be left to provide some wildlife habitat, to reseed the remaining ground, and to be resistant to windthrow. This remaining timber may be cut ten to fifty years later, when growth of new trees is well established. Forest researcher Dick Sage of the Adirondack Ecological Center argued in a hearing before the New York State Assembly that shelterwood cuts were an appropriate strategy for the Adirondack Park. He has maintained for years that shelterwood cuts provide adequate habitat for a more diverse population of wildlife, including more threatened species, than selective cutting, often preferred by environmental groups. Selective cutting of trees, while promoting a diversity of age groups in the forest, seems to provide good habitat for few species, since it offers neither old growth nor the abundant food supplies of disturbed sites. In addition, frequent entry into the forest may result in excessive road building and damage to the remaining stand. But to many people, selective cutting *looks* prettier. From an aesthetic point of view, a shelterwood cut may look just like a clearcut in two stages.

At the same time, large timber companies and private owners who have managed timber on their properties for many decades have found timber harvesting no longer profitable under current conditions. They are beginning to sell their holdings to developers, who will, to varying degrees,

diminish the open-space character of these large holdings. In the Adirondacks, the Whitney estate has negotiated with a developer who plans to
build large houses on multimillion-dollar estates. While this plan will only
minimally change the way Whitney Park looks from the road, it will make
an undeniable difference. Environmentalists have raised an outcry, yet
many fail to see the connection between the restrictive and time-consuming
permit system and the shift of timber interests away from the region. Other
causes are beyond the region's control: changing international timber markets, the rise of junk bonds, plantation forestry in the Southeast, and increasing mechanization, which works better on flat land than on the steep
and rocky slopes of the Adirondacks.

Meanwhile, the historian William Cronon's book *Uncommon Ground* has
opened a debate at the national level over whether nature and wilderness
are essentially human constructs imposed on a wide range of biological
realities. The journal *Wild Earth* replied with a dozen articles criticizing
Cronon and his colleagues' position as deconstructionist, and destructive of
the heart of environmentalism. As I discuss herein, I believe that we debate
the issue of land use and care in at least three different languages, depending on our beliefs and experiences. One is the language of aesthetics,
adopted by the mainstream environmentalists, and carried to a far extreme
by academics engaged in measuring statistically the relative values of "view-
sheds." The second, the language of ecology, attempts to define the needs
of ecosystems to reproduce themselves and their component species. But as
we are learning, there is more change and variability in these systems than
we had thought. And change is hard to measure. The third is the language
of zoning, used by administrators engaged in public planning as they attempt to respond to both aesthetic and ecologic concerns while bridging the
gap between human and natural systems. It is a most inexact and unsatisfac-
tory language, leaving gray areas and setting blanket conditions that rarely
respond to specific local ecological needs. A fourth language might be that
of local people recording local conditions. It was this language I listened
for, and its words that I have tried to bring to the surface of the discussion.
Those who speak it have much to say that is important.

This book grew out of an effort to learn about how people were living
with the Adirondack forest. My field research was completed over a period
of several years, culminating in a year of residence in the Adirondacks in
1990. The material was revised and updated after a visit to the Adirondacks
in 1994, and in phone interviews and research through early 1997. It is thus
limited to a specific time period in Adirondack land use history. Yet this

period, during and after the tenure of one of the most controversial land use commissions ever appointed in the United States, was a remarkable time. The commission's recommendations and the Adirondack Park Agency's management, in a park nearly three times the size of Yellowstone National Park, set precedents for both successful and not so successful management which are extremely relevant for the rest of the United States and the other nations of the world.

❧ Many people from many places contributed to the research for this book. Others have provided much-needed support during the writing phase. It has been a community effort in many ways, from the academic community in Ithaca, to the communities of the Adirondacks, to the community I live in now. It is impossible to thank everyone by name, and impossible to thank certain people enough.

Davydd Greenwood, James P. Lassoie, and Njoku Awa at Cornell University guided the dissertation research and writing that led to this book. Their support and insights have been invaluable. Peter Agree, editor at Cornell University Press, committed much time to thoughtful choice of reviewers and offered encouraging comments.

Numerous individuals and communities in the Adirondacks contributed to this research. While the research did not stress key informants, certain individuals helped me find woodspeople to interview, and steered me in the right direction many times. These people are friends as well as supportive advisers, and they deserve special mention. Lew Staats, State Extension Specialist for Maple Syrup Production, made extraordinary efforts to help with lodging, and put me in touch with many maple syrup producers, as well as providing a work space at the Uihlein Sugar Maple Research Station. Chris and Ida Moquin are personal friends who provided warm hospitality and helped with nearly everything. They also suggested a number of people to interview; their connections opened many doors for me.

Local people from every side of the land use issue shared their thoughts and their time with me, often inviting me into their homes. I am deeply grateful to all of them; each one added a valuable perspective to this work. I would like to mention by name the guide and fisherman Bill Freyne, who has since passed away, trapper and conservationist Nellie Staves, and logging camp cook and storyteller Rita Chiasson, each of whom extended an interview into a friendship, and continued to help me with the research in many ways.

Special thanks go to Breck Chapin and Mike Storey of the Visitor

Interpretive Center at Paul Smith's College, who included me in some of their conversations about preservation and teaching ecology. The staff of the Adirondak Loj in the High Peaks Wilderness Area helped me in many ways, and gave me a unique opportunity to meet wilderness travelers, Adirondack Mountain Club members, and preservation activists. The staff at the Adirondack Center Museum also gave me a special opportunity to meet folklorists working in the area, and to work with local experts in traditional occupations that rely on forest products. Laura Rappaport, reporter for the *Adirondack Daily Enterprise,* was friend, informant, and fellow investigator as we worked to understand the issues and the people involved. Janet Decker, research librarian for the Adirondack Collection at the Saranac Lake Library, became a friend, adviser, and kind supporter, inviting me to her home for a return visit to the Adirondacks. My heartfelt thanks go to the seven people who allowed me to include detailed accounts of their interviews.

Funds for the research came from the Kiekhefer Adirondack Fellowship, and a Sage Graduate Fellowship. In Oregon, the Hatfield Marine Science Center gave me a desk, their library staff helped with library research; and the staff of the Coastal Oregon Productivity Enhancement program generously allowed me to use their computers.

My children's unending patience helped a great deal. Susie Gilligan helped hold my baby daughter, cook meals, and revise sentences in the final days of editing. My deepest thanks go to my husband: his loving support and respect for my work enabled me to finish this book.

CATHERINE HENSHAW KNOTT

Corvallis, Oregon

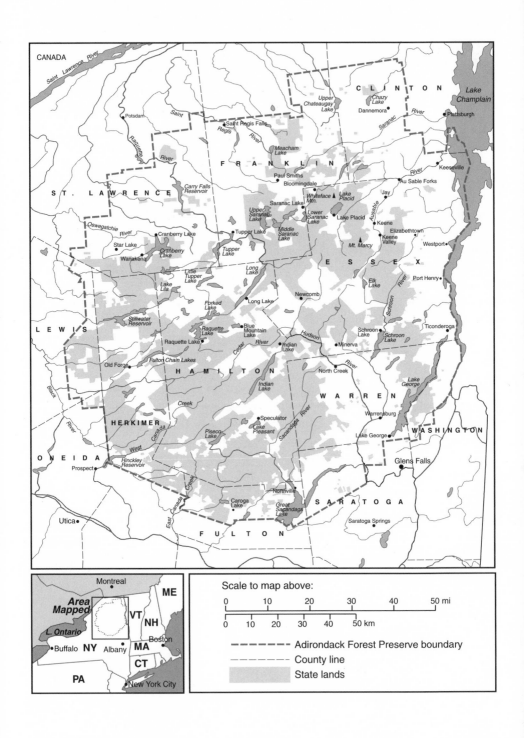

CANADA

CLINTON

Lake Champlain

FRANKLIN

ST. LAWRENCE

ESSEX

LEWIS

HAMILTON

WARREN

HERKIMER

WASHINGTON

ONEIDA

SARATOGA

FULTON

Potsdam

Saint Lawrence River

Raquette River

Saint Regis River

Upper Chateaugay Lake

Chazy Lake

Dannemora

Saranac River

Plattsburgh

Saint Regis Falls

Meacham Lake

Paul Smiths

Bloomingdale

Whiteface Mtn.

Lake Placid

Au Sable Forks

Keeseville

Carry Falls Reservoir

Saranac Lake

Upper Saranac Lake

Lower Saranac Lake

Lake Placid

Jay

Ausable River

Oswegatchie River

Cranberry Lake

Tupper Lake

Middle Saranac Lake

Mt. Marcy

Keene

Elizabethtown

Keene Valley

Westport

Star Lake

Wanakena

Cranberry Lake

Tupper Lake

Long Lake

Elk Lake

Port Henry

Schroon River

Lake Lila

Little Tupper Lake

Forked Lake

Long Lake

Newcomb

Stillwater Reservoir

Raquette Lake

Blue Mountain Lake

Cedar River

Hudson River

Indian Lake

Schroon Lake

Schroon Lake

Ticonderoga

Old Forge

Raquette Lake

Fulton Chain Lakes

Minerva

North Creek

Lake George

Indian Lake

Black River

Canada Creek

Speculator

Lake Pleasant

Piseco Lake

Sacandaga River

Warrensburg

Lake George

West Canada Creek

Hinckley Reservoir

Prospect

Caroga Lake

Northville

Great Sacandaga Lake

Glens Falls

Utica

East Canada Creek

Saratoga Springs

Montreal

ME

Area Mapped

VT

NH

L. Ontario

Boston

Buffalo

NY

Albany

MA

CT

PA

New York City

Scale to map above:

0   10   20   30   40   50 mi

0   10   20   30   40   50 km

– – – – – Adirondack Forest Preserve boundary

——— County line

State lands

Introduction

The debate over ecosystem management which came to the fore in the mid-1990s promotes collaborative landscape-level management across ownerships and political boundaries in the interests of promoting ecosystem health (Kohm and Franklin, 1997; Freemuth, 1996). The Adirondack Park has been working at the landscape level for over one hundred years; roughly 45 percent of the land within the Blue Line defining its boundaries is private, including large timber company holdings, private estates of several thousand acres, homes and farms of all sizes, and villages and hamlets. Designated as an International Biosphere Reserve in 1989, it provides critical lessons for other regions. These lessons include (1) case studies of both successful and unsuccessful public dialogue and collaborative land management processes; (2) insights into the underlying sources of land use conflict; (3) the results of restrictive timber-cutting policies, including sales of timber lands to developers and subsequent loss of open space; (4) administrative practices regarding public and private land categories and zoning practices relevant to current ideas about core and buffer zones in international parks, and the outcome of these practices over a quarter of a century; and (5) the role of local knowledge and participation in setting research agendas and the decision-making and implementation stages of land management.

Questions of "ecojustice" for marginalized people have risen to the surface of political discussion. Liberal democratic solutions that provide merely cosmetic solutions to the damage to ecosystems and the people dependent on them have come to be seen as insufficient. A more participatory, collaborative approach is called for, one that includes those people currently marginalized in the decision-making process (Plumwood, 1996). The Adirondack Park Agency's Board of Commissioners, which is designed to represent a wide range of interests, includes several influential area residents who were appointed to serve on this decision-making body. Western states are embracing stakeholder analysis and management, in a form of citizen advisory boards known as Province Advisory Councils for their large National Forest holdings. Forest Service staff choose local representatives of different interest groups, each of whom must be approved at the national level, to sit on these councils.

Yet international case studies are revealing the fallacies of these methods of addressing multiple claims and concerns. In part, the problem lies with assuming that we are all on a level playing field. First, the media are frequently controlled by the most empowered players with access to the greatest resources, especially education and money. The liberal media are "as much engaged in shaping public opinion as liberal democracy is in receiving popular input" (Plumwood, 1996. p. 145). This form of democracy results in a plethora of competing interest groups, which works against fairness to groups with less access to resources. Second, residents' stake in park areas is frequently tied to basic needs — livelihood and subsistence — while other interests are concerned with more diffuse societal goods or profits. Under cooperative management, government agencies and representatives of interest groups and residents administer a park or protected area through stakeholder analysis, often in the form of meetings and open hearings. Yet stakeholder analysis gives no attention to the difference in scale and immediacy of opposing stakes, nor does it take into account the ways in which nonresident parties got their stakes in the first place. In many cases these have been claimed at the expense of usufruct and historic access for indigenous and local populations (Brown, 1996). In stakeholder management, representatives of resident communities may achieve a place at the table, but will seldom be able to veto more powerful interests: "On the contrary, the majority of stakeholders may frequently overrule these local representatives on questions directly relevant to inhabitants' livelihoods" (Hughes, 1996, p. 37). Third, in the Adirondacks, the Pacific Northwest, and elsewhere, with some notable exceptions, residents are not allowed to choose their own representatives to serve on land use bodies; the model followed has been for the highest authorities of government, those most removed from the areas of conflict, to choose the representatives. Rejection of those chosen by popular opinion or by grassroots movements, or keeping them consistently in a minority, has historically led to open conflict.

Another part of the problem stems from confusion over the difference between "communities of place" and "communities of interest." In a passage critical to understanding rural community in land use conflicts, farmer and essayist Wendell Berry writes:

If the word community is to mean or amount to anything, it must refer to a place (in its natural integrity) and its people. It must refer to a placed people. Since there obviously can be no cultural relationship that is uniform between a nation and a continent, "community" must mean a people locally placed and a people, moreover, not too numerous to have a common knowledge of themselves and of their place. Because places differ from one another and because people will differ somewhat according to the characters of their places, if we think of a nation as an assemblage of many communities, we are necessarily thinking of some sort of pluralism.

There is, in fact, a good deal of talk about pluralism these days, but most of it that I have seen is fashionable, superficial, and virtually worthless. It does not foresee or advocate a plurality of settled communities but is only a sort of indifferent charity toward a plurality of aggrieved groups and individuals. It attempts to deal liberally — that is, by the superficial courtesies of tolerance and egalitarianism — with a confusion of claims.

The social and cultural pluralism that some now see as a goal is a public of destroyed communities. Wherever it exists, it is the result of centuries of imperialism. The modern industrial urban centers are "pluralistic" because they are full of refugees from destroyed communities, destroyed community economies, disintegrated local cultures, and ruined local ecosystems. The pluralists who see this state of affairs as some sort of improvement or as the beginning of "global culture" are being historically perverse, as well as politically naive. They wish to regard liberally and tolerantly the diverse, sometimes competing claims and complaints of a rootless society, and yet they continue to tolerate also the ideals and goals of the industrialism that caused the uprooting. They affirm the pluralism of a society formed by the uprooting of cultures at the same time that they regard the fierce self-defense of still-rooted cultures as "fundamentalism," for which they have no tolerance at all. They look with wistful indulgence and envy at the ruined or damaged American Indian cultures so long as those cultures remain passively a part of our plurality, forgetting that these cultures, too, were once "fundamentalist" in their self-defense.

4

> And when these cultures again attempt self-defense — when
> they again assert the inseparability of culture and place — they
> are opposed by this pluralistic society as self-righteously as
> ever. The tolerance of this sort of pluralism extends always to
> the uprooted and passive, never to the rooted and active.
> (Berry, 1993, pp. 168–70).

Communities of place are characterized by face-to-face interactions, a shared physical-geographical environment, and at least roughly similar access, or lack of it, to private and public infrastructure. Through years of living together in a place, the community shares births, deaths, celebrations, and the survival of natural forces such as storms, floods, and other disasters. "A community . . . lives and acts by the common virtues of trust, goodwill, forbearance, self-restraint, compassion, and forgiveness. . . . It has the power, that is, to influence behavior. And it exercises this power not by coercion or violence, but by teaching the young and by preserving stories and songs that tell (among other things) what works and what does not work in a given place" (Berry, 1993, p. 120).

Social scientists and others working on land use conflict issues have subverted some of the original connotations of "community" by referring to interest groups as "communities of interest" in contrast to traditional "communities of place." Yet the words of an eleven-year-old boy living in a rural area, referring to a self-identified "community of interest," make clear the profound difference: "They think that community means socializing and working with people who agree with you. In *our* community, community means helping each other even when we disagree." The not very pleasant tendency of communities of interest to exclude those with whom they disagree is obvious even to the very young.

Since my initial field study it has become increasingly clear to me that to balance collaborative land use planning, communities (and throughout this book the term will refer to communities of place) must have a greater role in decision making through participating in the creation of knowledge bases and choosing their own representatives to land use commissions. Participatory research and the international methodology of participatory rural appraisal can help to empower rural people by enabling them to share knowledge with those outside their community, and enhance their own analysis of trends and conditions in the local environment (Chambers, 1992). Internationally, there is an increasing recognition of the potential of community management of natural resources to address issues involving parks and protected areas, and many natural and social scientists are now documenting case studies (Western, Wright, and Strum, 1994). Yet grass-roots community-to-community transfer of stories of successful land use management will hold the most critical insights for ecosystem management and what follows.

When I started my field research in the Adirondack Park at the beginning of 1990, I planned to practice participatory action research, defined in anthropology circles as research that engages researchers and subjects together as active participants in setting the agenda and in finding solutions to problems uncovered in the process. Participatory research also implies an effort to understand the role of knowledge as a significant instrument of power and control. It honors local people's knowledge and experience and values the processes of genuine collaboration (Reason, 1994, p. 328). I discovered, however, during my first foray in participation, as a member of a park-wide Earth Day committee, that the various sides of the land use issues in the Adirondacks were so fiercely divided that if I "belonged" in any sense to a particular group, I might be denied useful access to other groups.

The Earth Day committee, made up of individuals from government and private conservation organizations, from the community college and the Adirondack Museum, and several citizen volunteers, voted to abstain from politicized issues in the hopes of creating a friendly context in which people could celebrate. But one angry member of the committee made an impassioned statement that this was destroying the meaning of the original Earth Day, which was intended as a challenge to politicians. Many other members were concerned about the potential for volatility, especially since we would be hosting public events. One event, in which a prominent preservationist would be speaking to a largely sympathetic audience, sparked a debate: Would angry local people storm the celebration? Should we have police guards? And when a photographer from the local paper took a picture of the Earth Day committee, a cooperative extension agent participating in the group refused to be in the picture, saying privately that being photographed in a group directed by an outspoken member of a leading preservation group, albeit in a nonpartisan context, could damage his relations with his local contacts. I quickly understood that even working with an allegedly nonpolitical group could jeopardize my research.

I realized that the position of an outside anthropologist would permit me to do more balanced research and to hear all sides of the land use issues than would belonging to any of the existing groups in the Adirondacks, or

6 trying, with an outsider's ignorance of local histories and contingencies, to start a new participatory research group. Thus, while maintaining a commitment to the values and direction of participatory action research, I employed more traditional anthropological methods. As a nonaligned outsider, I was permitted to ask questions, occasionally to be ignorant of the very obvious, and to make mistakes. Adirondack residents patiently explained to me the realities of their situations, the complex history of the Adirondacks, and ways to survive the long winters. As an interested researcher, I was not only allowed to question people about their lives and about their relations with the forests around them, but also heard the different sides of many land use issues. In some ways, because I was a relatively uninvolved outsider, and because I listened, I was able to act as an outlet; and in the process I gained more valuable information than I would have been able to elicit through direct questions. People talked, vented their frustrations, listed their grievances with the state agencies or the preservationists or the local people. Half-hour interviews stretched to two hours, and I learned a great deal. At the same time, hearing the personal histories and stories of conflict moved me from the realm of strictly objective, distanced observation toward a commitment to constructive resolution of the issues for all parties.

Researching land use issues challenged me to refine my understanding of anthropological theories and methods, and made me rethink my own beliefs. I had, and continue to have, sympathies on contrasting sides of many of the issues. As a longtime wilderness backpacker and canoeist, I share the preservationists' and others' appreciation of this wild, beautiful area for unique wilderness experiences. As a student of wildland and wildlife management and ethnobotany, as well as a former reforestation extension worker in the Sahel in West Africa, I know firsthand the importance of maintaining biological diversity, and the devastation to wild and human populations that follows its loss. Both Adirondack residents involved in using forest resources and preservationists inside and outside the Park perceive protection of biodiversity as an important issue.

At the same time, as an anthropologist and community worker, I have based my life and work on respect for local cultures and communities. Their survival depends on their ability to change to fit changing circumstances; it also depends on their ability to translate values and connections between individuals in the community from one set of conditions to another in such a way that these values and connections are not lost. Without the shared heritage of values and knowledge, the self-image of the community deteriorates, and its ability to sustain individuals in supportive networks deteriorates as well. Loss of traditional forest-based work in the Pacific Northwest has been tied to increases in substance abuse and the disintegration of families. Cultures and communities based on the use of natural resources suffer when they are cut off from these resources.

Because methods subsumed under participatory action research seemed a restrictive choice under the circumstances, I chose to follow more traditional anthropological methods, including participant observation, informal and formal interviews, attending key meetings, work opportunities, and use of a survey questionnaire, library research, and local publications. My family moved to the Adirondacks for a year and three months; we had already spent six to twelve weeks there during each of the three previous summers. Participation naturally included total involvement in Lake Placid village life, from making day care arrangements, to participating in the public schools, to getting acquainted with local politicians and business people, and becoming part of public gatherings from town meetings to Friday nights at the skating rink.

When I first arrived, I worked for two months with the Earth Day committee. During the spring I spent several days each month volunteering at the Adirondack Park Agency's Visitor Interpretive Center, getting to know the staff and the diverse volunteer group, as well as working with Adirondack schoolchildren. In the summer, as in previous summers, I spent time camping, hiking, backpacking, canoeing, and fishing in the Forest Preserve. In the fall I worked with the Adirondack Center Museum as a community liaison, bringing local people who had grown up within Adirondack craft, wildfood gathering, and storytelling traditions to the museum's annual Field and Forest Day. Through this association I worked with folklorists and staff, and met many craftspeople, trappers, and others who relied on forest resources for their trade. In late fall and winter I worked part-time for the Adirondack Mountain Club, where I became well acquainted with the staff and met several of the backcountry rangers. I had contact with many Adirondack Mountain Club members, with visitors to the Adirondak Loj, a popular wilderness facility, and with hikers and skiers in the High Peaks Wilderness Area.

I traveled widely in the Adirondacks, interviewing people from around Cranberry Lake in the west, Elizabethtown and Westport in the east, Old Forge and Lake George and Glens Falls to the south, and Peru and Chateaugay to the north. I focused my research, however, on the Tri-Lakes region in the northern half of the Park, and Newcomb, a small hamlet in the center of the Adirondacks. I conducted over 150 formal, prearranged interviews in different parts of the Park, starting each interview with a set of about thirty specific questions. Most interviews stretched well beyond the scheduled time, as people described their dreams, their anger, and their fears over land use issues in the Park.

I also conducted hundreds of informal interviews in the context of participating in Adirondack daily life, the jobs that I held, and the role of attending the unending meetings, presentations, and confrontational episodes that were part of the process of land use conflict. Often the meetings and confrontations were the source of intensive interactions; energy levels were high, and many people had come with concise formulations of their values and beliefs for the purpose of participating in the conflict. At larger events, including Tupper Lake's Woodsman's Days, Saranac Lake's Winter Carnival, conferences, crafts fairs, and so on, I was able to conduct rapid, single-issue interviews with many people. While these interviews lacked the in-depth focus on particular individuals that both formal and longer informal interviews allowed, they offered a way of checking the values and beliefs of a larger group of people. Often the most enlightening moments came when I was spending time with people on the job, or walking through forest land with them. Although I did not depend heavily on particular key informants, certain individuals helped me find woodspeople to interview and gave valuable suggestions.

These methods focused on individual differences rather than statistical norms; on specifics rather than generalizations. This research has been designed to bring out some of the complexities of land use conflict when seen through the eyes of many distinct individuals. At the same time, I looked for the roles of culture and community which brought the views of many into the restless, shifting harmony of diverse groups that defines the Adirondack land use conflict. As a means of examining the controversy and conflict as a process that involved individuals and groups at ever-changing levels of commitment, meetings became a rich source of data; they were both informational and expressive of subconscious relationships between the different groups. Above all, I listened for voices. I wanted to move my own anthropological framework beyond the academic interpretation of cultural norms and processes, divested of the individuals who spoke about them, to a place where I could begin to develop a sensitivity toward people's interpretations of their own cultural processes.

❧ The book's organization follows the connections between different levels of culturally based beliefs, knowledge, and processes in land use conflict in the Adirondacks. The first section addresses the attitudes, values, and beliefs behind the decisions in these controversies. Chapter 1 gives an overview of the Adirondack Park and the conflicts. Chapter 2 offers examples of human relations to wildlife in the Adirondacks to demonstrate the wide range of attitudes toward wildlife and as a partial reflection of the variety of attitudes toward the natural environment, or "nature," as a whole. Chapter 3 addresses the philosophical development of conservation and preservation through the history of events and individuals, and explores contemporary movements from Earth First! to Wise Use.

In the second section I look at the relationships of local communities to the forest, seen through the lives and thoughts of the people who act as reservoirs for indigenous knowledge, the "woodspeople" whose livelihoods bring them into daily contact with the forest. The chapters are arranged according to the individuals' particular livelihoods, and the kinds of relationships with wildland that those livelihoods foster. Chapter 4 deals with loggers and a town based on logging, a heavily extractive livelihood; Chapter 5 deals with craftspeople, trappers, and guides, whose levels of extraction are lower and more specific; Chapter 6 offers a closer look at how indigenous ecological knowledge functions among tree farmers and maple syrup producers, the group most likely to change the natural landscape at a complex qualitative level.

In the third section I examine the process of the conflict itself. Chapter 7, which consists of seven interviews with key players in the Adirondack land use controversy, taps the worldviews in which these individuals define their attitudes and the frameworks through which they interpret land use conflict. Chapter 8 explores the story of a small community's attempt to take charge of planning and zoning new development. Chapter 9 follows several actual controversies through the battles and bridge-building that characterize this process. And Chapter 10 poses the question, Why are local people and their indigenous knowledge left out of the process? and summarizes my findings. In the end, local people's participation in decision making seems to be the key missing factor that could shift the land use controversy from an unproductive, increasingly hostile cycle toward resolution. Discovering and validating the differences between the worldviews involved, and figuring out a way to incorporate participation at levels that

10 provide respect and justice to all participants, may be the steps that can move these conflicts beyond stalemate.

All names used in the text are pseudonyms, with the exception of state officials, citizens giving testimony in public hearings or meetings, Rita Chiasson, Lewis Staats, Ray Fadden, Laura Rappaport, Bill Frayne, Chris and Ida Moquin, and the seven interviewees in Chapter 7 who kindly allowed me to use their names. It is at times difficult to disguise the identity of interviewees through pseudonyms alone. I have tried to protect the privacy of individuals to the best of my ability. If there are instances in which some individuals are recognizable to friends, neighbors, or family, I beg their understanding, and hope with all due respect that the picture presented seems true and just.

The Human / Nature Relationship

Introduction

FROM THE AIR, IT LOOKS AS IF FIRE IS engulfing the Adirondacks. Fluorescent orange and yellow flames lick the slopes of the mountains; the fire burns hotter over the red maples, leaving scarlet tracks, heating the sugar maples and paper birches to sun color, stopping only at the line of spruce and balsam fir that marks the higher elevations. It is autumn in the Adirondacks, a season of change and slow, electrifyingly beautiful death. The branches let go the leaves glowing like embers; they fall to the ground, heaping in thick mats, until time and the snows cool the colors to the dull rich brown of new soil.

In the 1880s almost 150,000 acres of woods burned, sparked by sportsmen's campfires, farmers clearing land, and railways running through logging debris piles (White, 1985, p. 214). Concern over these fires, as well as lowered water volume in the Hudson River flowing from the Adirondacks, led to the designation of the state land as Forest Preserve and a larger area including private land as the Adirondack Park.

In 1989, when the governor of New York picked fourteen commissioners to write recommendations for additional regulations on private lands in the Adirondack Park, local residents threatened to set fire to the forests.

14   Stories circulated about a historic fire on Rockefeller forest land; it was rumored that local people had set it in anger back then. The fear of additional land use regulations suggested by the new commissioners, coupled with the lack of local participation in the process, struck a match that lit the tinder of discontent already lying thick in the hamlets and rural places of the Adirondacks.

The discontent was not uniformly spread across the landscape. Many, especially the more recently arrived, and those who had left cities to spend childhood vacations summering in the Adirondacks, favored additional regulations to protect what they saw as sacred wilderness or rich reserves of

Photo 1. A view of the forest. Photo D. Kuklok

biodiversity. But these views intermingled with the spreading patches of discontent. The frustration of local stakeholders at being left out of a political process affecting what they see as one of the bases of democracy — equal access to resources (Geisler, 1983) — has resulted in a stalemate in the state legislature, and a stalemate in the process of resolving land use conflict. For four years, legislation based on the recommendations of the Governor's Commission on the Adirondacks in the Twenty-First Century was brought to the legislature, and in large measure failed. The stalemate itself may affect the Adirondacks more than either the legislation's proponents or its opponents realize.

In 1991 someone did set fire to two barns belonging to Adirondack Park Agency commissioner and ecologist Anne LaBastille. Rumors spread that local people angry over the agency's increasing regulation of private lands within the Park had set the fire. Earth First! reported the event in the section of its journal devoted to encouraging members to take action; "monkeywrenching" and destruction by fire and other means are not unknown to Earth First! members. Would fire counter fire? These fires, too, will create change, and may have to burn until the cold snows signaling the death of an idea, a vision of a Park where wild and human communities can coexist, dampen the embers.

The fire tower in Pharaoh Lake Wilderness was pulled down. It had been a symbol for many local people of managing the environment for values of community — not just a human community or a wild community, but one in which the human and the wildland are integrated into a functioning whole. After the classification of the area as a wilderness, existing human structures were slated to be removed, including fire towers. The Department of Environmental Conservation had a mandate to take down the tower, but under pressure from neighboring communities to leave it, had stalled on setting an actual removal date. Then one night someone cut the legs of the fire tower, and it toppled. Locals suspected Earth First! or disgruntled DEC staff. An Adirondack woman who owns five hundred acres of forest nearby commented, "I liked to look up at the fire tower and know where I was. Now I really miss it."

Ending the idea of human communities coexisting with nature would be a loss for many in the Adirondacks, as well as for people living in other wild areas. The way the idea of human coexistence with the wild is formulated and decisions about land use are made and implemented will determine whether the Adirondacks become a blueprint for other regions or a model of failure. Will local communities continue to live with the forest,

16   or will a strict dichotomy between populated areas and wilderness prevail? To address these questions successfully, the governing and regulatory bodies must also address the issue of local participation and democratic representation in decision making, where inequalities of class, power, and voice prevail.

The Adirondack Park is not alone in the struggle between preservation of wildlands, support for livelihoods based on natural resources, and the protection of private property rights. Across North America, the relationship between human communities and wild communities is changing. The optimism which maintained that wilderness could be preserved in national parks and other federal and state lands, separate from the people who would visit for recreation and "leave only footprints" before returning to the cities, has dissipated. Many of the national parks are overused and under pressure at their borders from increasing development.

More and more the landscape represents a mosaic of human and wild communities, scattered in fragments across ecosystems and watersheds. The human communities depend on healthy ecosystems and watersheds to survive. Yet there is no longer room for these to be maintained solely in exclusively wild areas. Across the country, scientists and communities are searching for ways to integrate the human and the wild, while maintaining the integrity of each. The high mountains and desert areas that were largely unproductive for farming and other continuous human activity have been exploited or have become parks closed to resource extraction. Many of the remaining wild and semi-wild lands under scrutiny for preservation are the small mountains and foothills where human communities and the wild still coexist; the Adirondacks, Appalachia, the Ozarks, and the Coast Range of Oregon are among them.

Yet these areas also share a depressing history of resource colonialism. Each area experienced a period of heavy extraction of natural resources, including timber, water, and minerals which left the region as raw products, bringing relatively little income into the area. During this period regional political control came from wealthy, external administrators and landowners; these regions experienced direct political and economic control from outside, or no control other than exploitation. The period of heavy extraction was followed in each case by a period of resource impoverishment, leading to a "neocolonial" situation in which local leaders took over local and regional politics as scattered rural communities struggled and continue to struggle to extract leftovers: lower-quality wood, secondary forest products, and cropping that involves cheap human labor. External political controls operate behind the scenes, influencing local and internal regional administrators through the withholding or granting of economic support as these administrators cope with the problems of impoverished communities and diminished natural resource bases.

A third period of colonialism follows these other two. The regions have been entering this period in a trend from east to west and south to north. This is the period of tourist colonialism. In this phase most resources are severely diminished or unavailable, except for scenery and solitude. Remote locations are used for prisons or toxic waste sites. Many of the original local populations, dependent on subsistence and natural resources, dwindle, leaving mainly the poor, the elderly, retirees and second-home owners, and those who are able to make a living from what natural resources are still available. Many of these convert to providing low-wage seasonal labor for tourism. Outsiders migrate to the area as owners and developers of tourist facilities and services, taking advantage of the low-cost labor available. The latter stages of this period include cultural tourism as well as ecotourism. Appalachia provides a prime example of cultural exploitation, with everything from crafts to cultural heritage up for sale (Whisnant, 1983), priced for tourist dollars. Political control during this phase belongs increasingly to elites located both within and outside the region, and a wider base of interest groups focused on ecotourism — mostly outsiders, more recent arrivals, and locals with outside sources of income. Government control over land use increases through state and/or federal ownership of land and regulatory control over private lands. This regulatory control often overrides local interests in favor of the wider base of interest groups focused on tourism.

Ironically, the groups taking greatest advantage of the tourist opportunities in this third colonialism include those elites whose assets and wealth were developed during the period of heavy natural resource extraction, either in the same or other regions. These groups also include consumers of these resources in their post–value-added stage. Problems arise on the ethical front when these groups are unable or unwilling to take responsibility for their extraction and consumption levels. Heavily populated urban and suburban areas, which have become or are becoming wastelands virtually devoid of biodiversity, are deemed unreclaimable; the attention of the populations that created these areas shifts to other more distant and more pristine areas. The recognition of responsibility for this destruction is the missing piece in the wildlands management puzzle.

The Adirondacks, Appalachia, the Ozarks, the Coast Range, and other similar areas are thus part of a broader picture. The assumption of many Americans that we can destroy most areas so long as we preserve a few leads in part to the perceived dichotomy between human landscapes and wilderness landscapes which in turn drives land use conflicts. The possibility of an integrated landscape including human and wild communities, where people live *with* the forest rather than for or against it, is realizable only where each individual and community takes responsibility for its relationship with the natural landscape. The moral failure to take personal responsibility for how one lives — rather than how one vacations — with nature may have resulted in part from the modern shift from personal and local liability to corporate liability. It may also result in part from the decline of civic participation, or from a diminished sense of personal responsibility in large-scale systems. A diverse strategy is needed, one that protects existing parks, conserves and works with those human communities still living with the forest, and demands a greater accountability from those living in the cities and in industrial and suburban areas where the natural landscape has been erased almost beyond repair. In addition, innovative techniques for restoring these devastated landscapes should be given as much or more attention as protecting the more pristine landscapes.

Rural people, both as stakeholders and as those most intimately connected to these lands in their day-to-day lives, are demanding a voice in the political processes that determine land use management. Their knowledge — a localized, indigenous knowledge based on experience as much as education — can add to the general understanding of these ecosystems and watersheds and the possibilities for their management. Yet thus far these voices have remained largely unheard; their knowledge has been treated as illegitimate; and as individuals and communities, they have been left out of the decision-making process.

Because of the fundamental tie between access to natural resources and perceived access to the rights of citizenship in a democracy, the fire burns hot over these issues. It is more than a surface fire clearing a few years' supply of debris. This is a crown fire, the kind that consumes even the oldest trees, fueled by a hundred years of concerns about unequal access to resources in a system purporting to uphold equality. It is the kind of fire that, left unchecked, destroys whole forests.

1

The Adirondacks: A Case Study of Land Use Conflict

T HE ADIRONDACKS PROVIDE A WINDOW ON
the land use conflicts erupting across the United States and internationally. As a case of class struggle and rural-urban conflict over
values, this area is a hundred years ahead of the Pacific Northwest. As a
model in the search for the role of local participation and local knowledge
in the process of land use decision making, it highlights a history of science
and management subsumed in power struggles over zoning and aesthetics.
As an example of multiple stakeholders competing for a public voice, it
reveals wide gaps in communication between groups with different
worldviews, silent spaces amid the conflict where few really hear one another, and some voices are not heard at all.

When I first began research on the Adirondacks, I planned to learn
from the people whose lives involved both direct dependence on forest
resources and daily immersion in the forest environment — those who develop the most intensive relationships with the forest. I wanted to know, in
the context of a national forest land use crisis, how local people thought
about the forest, what they knew about it, and how they used their knowledge and beliefs to make decisions about managing the forest, either

20   through their own actions or by supporting the actions of others. I wanted to know how the forest fit into their lives, and how they fit into the forest.

Cultures and communities based on the use of the forests as natural resources, and groups or cultures whose involvement with the forests is based on recreation and aesthetic appreciation, have different views of the forest, which in turn stem from different worldviews. Anthropologists have defined worldviews as constructions of meaning based on divergent experiences. People base their views of the world on prior experiences, which usually take place in the context of a particular culture — their own. These views then focus and filter the experiences of the individual or group. New events that do not fit the worldview may lead to changes in the construction of meaning. Worldviews evolve, but even as they are evolving, they give birth to the attitudes, beliefs, and values that make individuals and groups behave as they do. Knowledge and experience both create worldviews and are shaped by them.

The attitudes, values, and beliefs stemming from these different worldviews, including varying constructions of the human relationship with nature, often lead to conflicts in decision making. Individuals' awareness of the conflicts in the Adirondacks colored my formal interviews with them and dominated many of our informal discussions. Because land use conflict was a part of the lives of the people who were my informants, it became a part of my research.

The current context of Adirondack land use conflict has had an enormous impact on the ways people make decisions about forest land use and which positions they support. The battles over Adirondack land-use have escalated to intense levels of conflict, including organized campaigning, litigation, even violence. As I listened, I sought to understand how the relationships between the different cultures and worldviews had developed and why the interactions had become so explosive. Each of the sides — and there are more than two — felt itself to be threatened at a level so deep that the life force itself, whether of a human or a wild community or both, was in danger. Value disparities are not resolved easily when the stakes are perceived to be so high.

❧ The Adirondack Park provides a unique case study for land use management in a wild forest setting. Six million acres in size, the largest park east of the Rockies, it encompasses public and private land under combined state and local regulation. The park supports a population of roughly 130,000 people, many of whom are indigenous to the area. By indigenous I mean groups which have lived there for more than one generation and often several, developing systems of knowledge and practices based on their experiences of living in the Adirondacks. When these systems of knowledge and practice are passed on to the next generation, they form the beginnings of a shared cultural tradition.

The Park supports the local population's subsistence and special forest products activities, as well as logging industries, mining, prisons, tourism, wilderness recreation, a growing second-home population, and a major north-south highway. Despite the patchwork of public and private, developed and undeveloped land, wild rivers and roadways, the Park has managed to provide a wild enough home for, among other species, bear, loons, recently reintroduced lynx, bald eagles, moose (who are reintroducing themselves), and, it is rumored, mountain lion.

The UNESCO Man and the Biosphere Program (MAB) has recognized the Park as part of the 10 million–acre Champlain-Adirondack Biosphere Reserve, the fourth largest biosphere reserve in the United States, and the most heavily populated of 337 reserves worldwide. The international network of biosphere reserves emphasizes regional and global issues requiring cooperation among scientists and institutions to develop perspectives on policy and action strategies. MAB intends that the reserves should demonstrate harmonious, long-lasting relations between human societies and ecosystems. Their plans include increasing recognition of the communities living within the boundaries of protected areas (Price, 1996 p. 648). As a wilderness park inhabited by humans as well as wildlife, the Adirondack Park offers a case study of a situation that is likely to become common internationally as human population continues to rise: people living adjacent to and in pockets within protected wildlands. The need for management plans that continue to preserve the ecosystems in these wildlands and at the same time preserve and sustain viable human communities makes the situation in the Adirondack Park even more important as a model for what, or what not, to do (see Appendix).

While there are many sides and many issues, I found that four basic positions emerged in any cross-section of Adirondack land use issues: those of the preservationists, the conservationists, the home-rule advocates, and the developers. The language of all four is indicative of their values and positions, and absolutely distinct. Preservationists talk about wilderness, conservationists talk about natural resources, home-rule advocates talk about private property, and developers talk about land; all four are referring to the Adirondack forests.

Each position has its own slogans. The preservationists use, among others, the phrase "In wildness is the preservation of the world" from Henry David Thoreau. The conservationists talk about "wise use of natural resources" from Gifford Pinchot. Home-rule advocates talk about the rights of private landowners, quoting from the Constitution. And developers recite "location, location, location." In essence, the Adirondack preservationists feel that they have a mandate to protect and preserve mountains, forests, waterways and wildlife in ways that generally preclude human interference and exclude extractive uses. Conservationists believe that their mandate is to promote ultimately sustainable uses of the mountains, forests, waterways, and wildlife, focusing on extractive and recreational uses, including limited mining and logging, as well as hunting, fishing, and trapping. The home-rule advocates believe that local people have the right to decide what happens on their land, and that state-level regulation of private land is inherently undemocratic. The developers believe that they have the right to build, with varying intensity, on any available land, removing and forever altering the forests on that land. These positions thus stand in contrast and opposition to each other.

Land in the Adirondacks falls into two major political categories, public and private. The "Blue Line," established in 1892, encircles the Adirondack Park on the state maps. Within this line, about 52 percent of the land is privately owned; the state owns the remaining 48 percent. All state land within Park boundaries becomes part of the State Forest Preserve and is designated "forever wild" by a legislative clause passed in 1895; the timber on Forest Preserve land may not be sold, removed, or destroyed (Brown, 1985, p. 201).

The state land is classified into nine categories: Wilderness, Wild Forest, Primitive, Canoe Area, Intensive Use, State Administrative, Historic, Scenic Vista, and Wild, Scenic, and Recreational Rivers. Each category supports different allowable uses, with Wilderness the most restrictive category. Public land in the State Forest Preserve is managed by the Department of Environmental Conservation. Private land within the Park boundary is regulated by the Adirondack Park Agency (APA), which has classified private land into six different categories according to the intensity of human use: Hamlet, Moderate-intensity Use, Low-intensity Use, Rural Use, Resource Management, and Industrial. "Hamlet" refers to the small villages where the majority of the human population of the Adirondacks lives.

An eagle flying over the Park would see different divisions in the forest.

The human presence on the land would separate into at least three major categories: large areas with no human impact on either private or public land; areas of partial disturbance or seasonal human impact such as state campgrounds and logging operations on private lands where the APA mandates a twenty-five–acre limit on clear-cutting; and areas of high year-round impact, including the hamlets and roadways. An eagle looking for a nesting site — and bald eagles are returning to this area (Adirondack Council Newsletter, Fall 1991) — might avoid the High Peaks Wilderness Area, where human traffic is heavy; up to two hundred hikers may be found on top of Mount Marcy on a summer day. Looking out over the great green blanket of forest, stippled and striped with lakes and villages, roadways and waterways, where the mountains throw deep shadows down slopes of balsam, hemlock, pine, and spruce, and clouds often hang over the bare rock peaks, the eagle might choose a nesting site on a mountainside next to an old clear-cut or in a wilderness area with a lake as yet undiscovered by tourists. The distinctions between public and private are human distinctions, and often have more to do with future possibilities than present realities. A bald eagle, a trout, or a red spruce might have a somewhat different definition of wilderness than we do.

Even within American cultural and legal definitions of wilderness there exist widely divergent perspectives. The 1964 Federal Wilderness Act defined it in these terms:

> A wilderness, in contrast with those areas where man and his own works dominate the landscape, is hereby recognized as an area where the earth and its community of life are untrammeled by man, where man himself is a visitor who does not remain. An area of wilderness is further defined to mean in this Act an area of undeveloped Federal land retaining its primeval character and influence, without permanent improvements or human habitation, which is protected and managed so as to preserve its natural conditions and which 1) generally appears to have been affected primarily by the forces of nature, with the imprint of man's works substantially unnoticeable; 2) has outstanding opportunities for solitude or a primitive and unconfined type of recreation; 3) is of sufficient size as to make practicable its preservation and use in an unimpaired condition; and 4) may also contain ecological, geological, or other features of scientific, educational, scenic, or historical value (78 Stat. 890, 16 U.S.C., sec. 1131 (c)).

This definition, while almost identical to the definition of wilderness in the New York State Department of Environmental Conservation's State Land Master Plan may vary substantially in practice with regard to acceptable levels of human intrusion and "the imprint of man's work." The State Land Master Plan notes, "At the time of the original enactment of this master plan, a majority of these areas contained some structures and improvements or were subjected to uses by the public or by official personnel that were incompatible with wilderness." In contrast to many of the federally designated wilderness areas in the West, the wilderness areas in the Adirondack Park had been substantially logged, opened with access roads, and even inhabited by the owners of scattered homesteads and summer homes. Preservation of wilderness areas in the Adirondacks has required reconstruction of wilderness as much as protection. Closing roads and allowing structures to crumble or be destroyed has played an active role in the re-creation of the Adirondack wilderness as well as in fanning the flames of local disputes. These are the forest lands that the preservationists, the conservationists, the home-rule advocates, and the developers are struggling to control.

Cultural Voices

The many different cultures of the Adirondacks speak in clear, distinct voices that blend together like the tributaries of a river as they are raised in discussion of the different issues facing the region. Local people, whether French-Canadian loggers, Native Americans, New England farmers, or long-term inhabitants of an Adirondack hamlet, frequently label themselves "Adirondackers." The term carries with it pride, a fierce sense of independence, and loyalty to an environment that is seen as both difficult and beautiful.

The French-Canadian lumberjacks have inhabited the Tupper Lake area since the mid-1800s. Though hard-pressed to recall elements of their culture beyond the French spoken by the oldest members of the community, the meat pies, and certain traditions of family prayer and holiday celebrations, these lumberjacks still define their logging practices within a context of independence, exhaustingly hard work, and keen observation of the woods.

Native Americans make up 4 percent of the population of Franklin County. The Mohawks retain a strong cultural identity and network of communication with other Native American groups. Ray Fadden, spokesperson and elder for traditional Mohawks, expresses attitudes that reflect current Native American philosophy about the Earth as Mother; his practice of leaving a little tobacco when he harvests wild plants derives from centuries of cultural tradition. Ironically, while preservationists often use Native Americans as an example of environmental sensitivity, the Mohawks' current, often violent struggle for sovereignty, and their efforts to resolve political divisions within their communities, parallel the home-rule struggles of the property rights activists in the Adirondacks, with whom the preservationists are in conflict. Indeed, the Mohawks argue that they have traditional rights to much of the Adirondacks.

The New England trappers and settlers who moved west into the Adirondacks represent another cultural tributary. Fiercely independent, relying on subsistence skills such as woodcutting, trapping, hunting, fishing, gathering, and gardening to support diversified household economies, they built communities rich in rural support networks. "Somebody's always going to stop and help if you are stuck on the side of the road, can't make it through the winter, get sick," one local man told me. Geographer Rutherford Platt (Platt, 1991, p. 138) notes that the characteristics of early settlements which shaped the evolution of the democratically run New England town included a common religious bond, a strong sense of independence, defiance of higher authority (other than God), an intractable terrain requiring cooperative effort for productive utilization, and fear of Indian attack. These conditions persist in Adirondack hamlets, except for the fear of Indian attack, though these days the fear of takeover by preservationist interests is a new unifying force. Platt notes that the town once served as a resource management entity as well, an idea that may have survived among those who support local control in the Adirondack land use controversy.

Many other ethnic and cultural groups have also contributed to the Adirondack social reality. This cultural diversity and cultural blending provide the anthropologist with a constant challenge. I frequently had to redefine what I had thought was a view particular to one group as one more widely held or adopted by another. Yet I felt while working, and still do, that the classification "rural American" is an oversimplification. It misses something essential about Adirondackers and their connection to this land of snow, mountains, forests, bear and deer, rocks and deep cold lakes.

I began to wonder again, as all anthropologists must, what culture *is*, and whether it is of necessity bound to a place. I was once asked in an exam whether a particular culture must be tied to a place. I answered with a qualified no, knowing the alienation from the land that is an unanalyzed assumption of urban academics, whose portable library of books and mementos becomes a second homeland. Now, however, I would state more clearly what I felt then: that, yes, land matters in the construction of culture. And *which* land matters a great deal. Although many cultural norms and values could arise in different places, the metaphoric language in which they are expressed, and the symbols that are used to imprint these values onto daily living, are uniquely bound to the environment in which the culture exists. And just as literary criticism has argued that content cannot exist apart from form, so I would argue that cultural norms and values cannot exist apart from the ecological reality that sustains their myths, metaphors, language, and symbols, and provides the physical materials for daily existence. The Haida of the Pacific Northwest would be a different people without the cedar and the raven. The Adirondackers would be a different people without the lakes and rivers and mountains, the harsh winters and sometimes impassable roads that paradoxically bind them together.

Some of the family and community cultural patterns of dominance, egalitarianism, independence, and tightly knit codependence derive in part from isolating factors in the landscape, physical barriers, difficulties of climate or terrain, or the fertility and transportation opportunities of river valleys. Yet within the variety of symbolic and structural possibilities offered by the landscape, each culture chooses its own lexicon and rules and creates its own interpretation of the natural and human cycles it witnesses.

Community and Conflict: The Role of Participation

Conflict often results from change, or the threat of impending change that may affect a community. Conflict also results from perceived threats to the boundaries of a community. By community I mean both a set of behaviors, such as people helping one another, which ties people together, and a symbol of shared identity. Community provides a sense of unity based partly on shared knowledge and common values, and partly on a recognition of the rights and responsibilities of the members. Rural sociologist Janet Fitchen writes, "Rural communities are presumed by their members to have individual identities" (Fitchen, 1991, p. 253). She identifies the rural community's self-concepts of uniqueness, commonality, connection between family and community, and security. In communities where many jobs are dependent on natural resources, work that members hold in common, such as logging, is closely tied to the identity of the community itself.

During periods of intensive change, social identity can stabilize around that occupation and the community as symbolic resources (Cohen, 1985).

Community members may perceive threats to logging or other natural resource–based jobs as threats to the very identity of the community. When outside groups do not recognize that identity or the knowledge, needs, and values of the community as important or legitimate, members may feel this as a transgression of the boundaries of their community. They may react strongly, using symbols of shared values to reassert their identity to outsiders. Bumper stickers and signs proclaim, "The Adirondacker — an endangered species." This reaction is exacerbated when the outsiders are perceived to have more power and influence than the locals.

Local participation in land use decision making in the Adirondacks has a clear role to play in affirming the importance of these communities and cultures. The lack of local participation, and the lack of attention to participation as a component of democracy, implies an equal lack of recognition for the validity of the communities' claims and concerns (Guba and Lincoln, 1989). Even when some of their concerns are taken into account, if local residents are not allowed to become part of the decision-making process, they feel that their knowledge and capabilities are being dismissed as invalid, and they respond as members of threatened communities. For them, issues of process must be resolved before differences of opinion over land use can even be discussed.

Participation provides the link between the knowledge a community member holds and using that knowledge to effect change. In a democracy it may seem obvious that all stakeholders participate, through democratic processes, in decision making (Guba and Lincoln, 1989). But in the Adirondacks, as in national politics, local people are feeling alienated and left out of the process. In *Who Will Tell the People: The Betrayal of American Democracy,* William Greider writes: "In a democracy, everyone is free to join the argument, or so it is said in civic mythology. In the modern democracy that has evolved, that claim is nearly meaningless. During the last generation, a 'new politics' has enveloped government that guarantees the exclusion of most Americans from the debate — the expensive politics of facts and information. . . . [O]nly those who have accumulated lots of money are free to play in this version of democracy" (Greider, 1992, p. 35). When participation is linked to the bureaucracy of regulatory agencies as well as the politics of contemporary democracy, the chances to play are even more limited.

Participation can take many forms. The word has been used euphemistically by groups with more power to mean that the groups with less power are allowed to listen, contribute labor, or voice their opinions without any assurance that their opinions will affect the final outcome. At the other end of the scale, groups interested in gaining ground have defined participation as equal access to information, equal ability to set agendas, voting to determine representatives for minority groups, and an elected representative in all decision-making (Young, 1990).

In contrast, more paternalistic models assume that the minority will be represented by the majority or by the elite group acting as guardian, as in the case of the Governor's Commission, or the group of scientists appointed by President Clinton to come up with options for managing the forests of the Pacific Northwest. The commissioners tried to take the claims and concerns of the locals into account, although neither appointed nor elected local representatives were there to voice their claims and concerns themselves.

Indigenous Knowledge and Community Management of Natural Resources

My initial assumption was that indigenous knowledge could be incorporated effectively into land use planning in the Adirondacks. As I became more aware of the deep levels of conflict over land use I realized that local people, especially those who were local experts in knowledge of the Adirondack forests, should play a greater role in decisions about land use than they do now. Why they were not already doing so was a factor of the complex relationships and historic class divisions between state agencies, outside interest groups, and the local population. My observations were based on the following premises.

Indigenous knowledge is a critical part of the construction of worldview in any culture; it both constructs and is molded by worldview. Adirondackers, including the French-Canadian trappers, loggers, and miners, Mohawks, and people of mixed European descent, have historically subsisted on farming, fishing, trapping, hunting, guiding, wild plant gathering, crafts, and other forest-based activities. Woodspeople, those who have adhered to these culturally sanctioned occupations which bring them into daily contact with the forests, act as reservoirs for indigenous knowledge. They are honored as experts in their own cultures.

This indigenous knowledge of the forests is largely ecological and relational in nature; taxonomy often takes second place. Ecological knowledge is based on observations not only of individual species but also of the interactions and information systems linking them. Ecological knowledge is hard to test by conventional methods; it is probably best represented by success in practical endeavors which require knowledge of a range of changing factors and ecological relations, such as trapping and maple syrup production. Those who possess this indigenous knowledge, along with other elements of the Adirondack population, hold a wide range of attitudes toward the environment, as demonstrated by their attitudes toward wildlife and forests. These attitudes, fed by the knowledge available to the indigenous cultures, operate to shape decision making with regard to the environment. But this decision-making capacity is often thwarted when outside forces — including special interest groups and state government — fail to recognize the value of this knowledge, preferring to rely on "experts" whom the outside groups have identified themselves.

The relationships between the local population, state agencies, and outside interests determine the nature of the processes that take shape in land use conflicts. Because the relationships are based on the unequal distribution of power and in power-motivated transactions, conflicts that threaten any party's values will escalate. The escalation spirals and gets stuck at standoffs and confrontation in part because the participants perceive the conflicts to be resolvable through fact-finding and bargaining. When conflict resides in differences between the value systems of different worldviews, resolution cannot occur before the different views are understood and respected.

Open communication is difficult between individuals and groups that do not have equal bases of power. Yet power differentials are exacerbated by the desire of the more powerful groups to control access to land and resources. These premises became clearer as I followed the land use conflicts in the Adirondacks and saw that effective local and indigenous knowledge is no guarantee of participation.

2

Wildlife: From Skins to Kin

THE BEAR PRINT GLEAMS, MUDDY AND blurred as the man's stubby fingers brush aside a damp mat of beech and sugar maple leaves. "It's a yearling," he says, kneeling and following with his eyes the faint smudged line of tracks disappearing into the forest. "Probably the same one we've seen up in the sugar bush. Look: you can just see, that left hind leg turns in a little. Not a big bear." He traces the outline with one finger. I look at the front paw prints, the size of my fist, the five toes barely distinguishable in the cold mud, the hind footprint longer, cleaner. I walk forward a few steps, trying to follow the tracks, barely more than a damp depression as they wander off the path. "Careful now, you'll be stepping on them," he says, grinning sideways at me. "There, next to your foot, that's one." It is clear to him from fifteen feet away; I can hardly distinguish it from any other irregularity in the surface. Yet I can almost feel the bear, the prints the tangible reminder of its presence.

"Look: over here, now that's deer. See the buck, and here's a doe," he says, pointing next to a clump of young maples.

"How can you tell it's a doe?" I ask.

"Well, the print is daintier somehow. She steps more lightly and picks up her feet more."

"Not just smaller deer?"

"No, no . . . I guess you just learn to see the difference, after a while." We walk slowly, beside the deer tracks. "That's a big buck," he says, meditatively. The prints are large, tear-shaped, sharp as if a stone had struck them out of the mud. "See how they are sunk in deep? He's heavy. Here he is starting to run. Dogs." A muddle of dog prints cuts in from the side.

"How did you learn all this about tracks?"

"Oh, just tracking, hunting. When I go out for two weeks in the fall, I usually go by myself. I just enjoy being out, alone, following the tracks. You learn to tell where they lay down, where they fed, where they bent twigs aside. Where their runs are. To tell the truth, I enjoy tracking them more than shooting them."

🐾 In the Adirondacks, wild animals are a part of daily life. Often when I ask people about the forest or wilderness, their first response is a bear story.

Photo 2. Bud Piserchia and bears at his taxidermy shop, Keene. Photo D. Kuklok.

Seeing bear, deer, fox, and even lynx is not unusual, yet the awe remains: stories of encounters with wildlife are savored and told again and again. The meaning of wilderness includes, for many people, a relationship with wildlife. The wild animals function within the human cultural context; threads of interaction with wildlife are woven into a complex fabric. And yet there is something more, something that resists analysis — an atavistic recognition of our relation to these other beings who look back at us from the wild places. Holmes Rolston III says it best in his essay "Beauty and the Beast: Aesthetic Experience of Wildlife" when he speaks of "kindred and alien life": "There is intrusion, intimacy, otherness. . . . [W]ith the fauna, especially the vertebrate, brained fauna, I meet a 'thou.' I see them; they also see me. . . . There is a window into which we can look and from which someone looks out" (Rolston, 1987, p. 190). Echoing and alluding to Aldo Leopold's seminal experience with a wolf he had shot, Rolston writes, "There is fire in those eyes" (Rolston, 1987, p. 190).

Wild animals in the Adirondacks, as elsewhere, operate in human cultures as symbols; as aesthetic standards for grace, movement, and beauty of form; as the dominated, as sources of fear, as trophies to be acquired; and on an economic plane as meat, fur, skin, and feathers. For some, including some of the Mohawks living in the Adirondacks and northern New York, wild animals are also considered relatives, both collectively and individually. Like human kin, they are given care, food, apologies, and respect, and their voices are listened to. Anthropological kinship diagrams do not often reflect the Native American recognition of kinship with wildlife, bound by Western intellectual traditions of a strict separation between "man" and "beast," curious as that dichotomy is in light of the intellectual community's general acceptance of the theory of evolution. In the confines of university seminar rooms, it is easy to think of wild animals functioning within human cultures solely as food or symbols or totemic signs, and to forget the immediacy of the deer veering away from the hunter, the fox trotting along the road, the bear in the backyard.

Wild animals form a part of the livelihood of many Adirondackers. Subsistence hunting and gathering from the forest is more widespread than is usually acknowledged (Ratner, 1984). There is some poaching of deer. Deer and fish are packed away in freezers along with blueberries and jam. Hunters (usually men) make sure that their nonhunting wives get tags too. One informant told me of several recipes she used to disguise venison as beefsteak or other beef products. Another served venison to nearly eighty people as the main course at her daughter's wedding. Guides count on wildlife sightings as an important part of the wilderness experience they package; nature photographers sell pictures of wildlife; artists and crafts-people in the Adirondacks frequently use animal motifs in their works. And these sell, both to tourists and to other Adirondack residents, one assumes because people relate to wildlife; the aesthetic pleasure of seeing wildlife is intertwined with recognition.

Recognition, curiosity, need, and appreciation lead to knowledge, and the indigenous knowledge of wildlife behavior and ecology leads to an understanding of how people relate to wildlife and what makes these rela-tionships work. Yet indigenous knowledge is elusive, quirky from a strictly scientific point of view, and sometimes as hard to track down as the shyest of big game. Americans are often more ready to accept that indigenous non-European cultures outside the United States possess such knowledge.

Is there a valid body of indigenous knowledge about wildlife and forests in the Adirondacks? I would argue that there is, but that it has more to do with relationships between species, between animals and birds and the forests, streams, and lakes they inhabit, than with genetic details. In other words, it is more about ecology than taxonomy, something that may make scientists, with their paradigmatically driven focus on specialization, slow to appreciate its depth.

While local knowledge develops among a group of individuals who live in a certain place, indigenous knowledge comes from the codification of that knowledge into a form that is passed on from one generation to the next. It binds a people to a place, giving individuals within that group a key to understanding the ecosystems on which the human system is overlaid. Acquisition of knowledge depends on utilitarian goals (Hunn, 1982), aes-thetics, and intellectual curiosity (Brown, 1985), perhaps in more equal proportions than proponents of one factor or another would like to believe.

Gary Nabhan, research director and cofounder of Native Seeds/ SEARCH, and environmental educator Sara St. Antoine propose four cross-cultural indicators of "biophilia," which they define as an innate ten-dency of all humans to focus on life and lifelike process:

1. Personal identification with the behavior and adaptive strate-gies of other creatures.
2. Positive valuing of wildness in the lexicon of a culture and its land management.
3. Continued oral traditions of storytelling about biota.

4. Interest in heterogeneity and diversity of any sort, but especially in environments and life forms unmanipulated by human handiwork. (Nabhan and St. Antoine, 1993 p. 247)

These indicators of biophilia, all of which I observed in interviews with local people dependent on natural resources, lead to knowledge of the environment, a knowledge that becomes indigenous when it is passed on from generation to generation. Our attitudes inspire us to seek knowledge; increased knowledge then circles back to influence our values, beliefs, and attitudes toward wildlife.

A value is a principle, standard, or quality considered worthwhile or desirable. The value I am talking about here is not how much a beaver skin is worth but what the beaver is *for* in human terms. Beliefs — either that the beaver exists for human use, or that it has a right to exist in and of itself, or that it does not matter whether or not there are beavers — can derive from values or give birth to them. Attitudes refer to feelings or emotions toward a fact or state, in a frame of reference such as a belief system. Together, values, beliefs, and attitudes about wildlife, mingled with those about other subjects, lead to the behaviors and decisions about human relations with wildlife that have become so controversial in the Adirondacks.

❧ Wildlife management researcher Stephen Kellert uses various terms to describe prevalent attitudes toward wildlife: naturalistic, ecologistic, humanistic, moralistic, scientific, aesthetic, symbolic, utilitarian, dominionistic, and negativistic (Kellert, 1987). He found in several studies that from 1900 to 1975 there was a decline in utilitarian valuations of wildlife and in overall levels of fear, hostility, or indifference to animals. At the same time, he found that negativistic and utilitarian perceptions of wildlife remain very common, "particularly among lower socioeconomic, elderly, rural, and natural-resource-dependent groups" (Kellert, 1987, p. 223). I noted, through observation, participation, discussion, and interviews that the main difference between Kellert's definitions, which apply easily to urban tourists, and the attitudes of the rural or semi-rural Adirondack residents lay in their complexity. The tourists, frequently from large cities, or suburban areas, often hold fairly streamlined attitudes toward wildlife, either the naturalistic attitude of birdwatchers, the humanistic attitude of those who focus on large, appealing animals with anthropomorphic associations, the moralistic attitude of animal rights activists, or the dominionistic attitude of sportsmen on a hunting vacation. Generally, as with Kellert's findings, one attitude seems to dominate, linked strongly to a particular hobby or behavior that operates outside the daily urban lifestyle.

In contrast, residents of the Adirondacks, people who spend their lives among wildlife from fieldmice to bald eagles, from trout to lynx, and who frequently must deal with wildlife issues affecting their communities, hold attitudes that are often complex and pluralistic. For example, many hunters who are dominionistic and utilitarian toward deer during the fall hunting season are moralistic and humanistic in the winter, when they feed the deer and learn to identify them affectionately as individuals. Nellie Staves, a professional trapper and president of the Franklin County Federation of Fish and Game Clubs, hunts in the fall. "But in the spring," she says, "if I come upon a doe or a fawn, I don't look at those big eyes and think of hunting then."

In the November 26, 1991, issue of the *Hamilton County News* are two photos of hunters and one of members of the Long Lake Fish and Game Club feeding deer. The same local deer hunters who feed the deer often have negative attitudes toward coyotes (which they believe threaten deer herds), alongside naturalistic attitudes, which Kellert defines as a "primary interest [in] and affection for wildlife and the outdoors," as demonstrated in their pursuit of knowledge about the outdoors well beyond what is necessary to bag a deer. One man in his eighties, nut brown and lanky, who has hunted everything from rabbit to bear and is also a water diviner, told me that he spends all day from sunrise to sunset in the woods "about 300 days a year." Other hunters as well as nonhunters are ecologistic, with "a primary concern for the environment as a system" (Kellert, 1987, p. 224).

Fishermen and women, as well as trappers, spend many days outdoors on the wild lakes and streams where they troll or fly-fish. The fishermen I interviewed, including several guides, fish for food or aesthetic pleasure, or, if they are guides, as a vocation. One guide spent his life teaching several very wealthy and well-known people who own summer homes in the Adirondacks the finer details of fly-fishing. He learned his early skills from his father, who was also a guide. Although he relished fresh trout, he also heaped scorn on those who do not know how to release a fish unharmed. Another fisherman, a regular hunter and eater of venison, practices catch-and-release fishing because he does not like to eat fish. Several times I fished with him and his wife where pike lurk among the reeds along the edge of the lake. His thumb on the jaw of a pike is as delicate as the touch of a father with a newborn child, as he removes the hook from the lip and sets the flailing, shark-mouthed creature back into the water. One day when I was fishing with him, I saw him wince when one fish didn't make it; he watched, frowning, as it floated belly up, just below the surface.

Another fisherman, a guide and owner of a sporting goods store, practices catch and release because he is concerned about the low levels of trout and other wild game fish in local lakes and streams. The guide's knowledge, gleaned from experience, books, magazines, television programs, fish and game clubs, and other fishermen, is founded on a recognition of the interconnectedness in nature.

❦ Kellert defines the ecologistic attitude as "directed at a systematic conceptual understanding of the interrelationships of species in the context of ecosystems" (Kellert, 1989, p. 6). Many Adirondack fishermen and women, hunters and trappers, express their knowledge of wild game through its relationships within an ecosystem. Bill Frayne, a well-known guide who guided for fifty-odd years, spoke of knowing the right time to start trout fishing in the spring. For lake trout it must be 55 or 56 degrees Fahrenheit for a few days so that the fish rise to the surface, occupying a thermocline, a darker blue strip of water from two to two and a half feet in depth. As the water warms, the lake trout go deep. In Lake Placid, this can mean a depth of up to two hundred feet.

It is crucial to know which lakes, rivers, and streams have the best fishing and what gear to use. Fly-tying for a professional guide requires knowing what the fish eat and what they are likely to snap at during different seasons and times of the day. Bill was well known in town for his "muddlers." After he gave me one of his specials, a friend caught two rainbow trout in half an hour at a spot where we had tried with no luck several times before. Bill also made careful note of the weather and carried a barometer with him. If it was rising and the wind was right, he was optimistic; if it was falling, he figured he might as well stay home. He kept notebooks in which he jotted down careful records of the temperature, weather conditions, fishing gear used, and his catch for every day he went fishing. Later he studied them, looking for patterns and trends. He commented many times to me, as others did, on the decline of trout, and especially native brook trout, in the past few years. He was also worried by the decline in size, and the increase, especially in Lake Champlain, of deformities, cancerous growths, and other ailments, including, in Bay Pond, a lice epidemic among brook trout.

One Adirondack couple I interviewed provide an example of the richly interwoven attitudes that constitute the basis of their relationships with wildlife. They work full-time making rustic furniture and baskets, and act as caretakers for a large private property, where they live surrounded by nine hundred acres of forest. Ted came to the area many years ago to attend forestry school; he changed course but continues to read texts on ecology and silviculture. He spends many days collecting materials for his furniture from the forest; he often has to travel the breadth of the Adirondacks for a particular kind of wood. Joan was born and raised in the Adirondacks in a family of caretakers. Her work has given her a sophisticated understanding of different plant species. She also manages the couple's business.

Their brown house blends into the woods, a visual reminder of the connection between humans and wild nature. The adjacent corral holding a white pony demonstrates their ability to negotiate with the forest for their own uses. The living room is a clutter of baskets and strips of pounded bark and wood set among comfortable armchairs. Wild animals, stuffed, carved, painted, and mounted on walls and bookshelves, fill the room with suspended motion and watchful eyes. Ted and Joan have taught their daughter, at thirteen, to recognize the tracks of all the animals nearby and to interpret contexts in tracking: "To Aurora, a duck on the river is not just a duck, it's a merganser. She has a love for the earth; she doesn't just see the beauty, she sees the whole picture," Ted says. Her parents contrast this attitude, and their daughter's awareness of the presence of violence and death in nature, with the humanistic attitude of many of the tourists and summer visitors they encounter, some of whom they find trespassing on the land they caretake. "People definitely come up here with stars in their eyes. . . . People from the city . . . think nobody should ever kill a deer, and chipmunks are the most beautiful thing in the world," Ted tells me. Ted and Joan believe that wild animals have the right to exist. They also believe in their own right to exist in the forest environment they love, knowing that they are displacing some of those animals.

❧ While individual interviews most clearly illustrate the depth of these attitudes and their interrelationships, the attitudes crystallize for communities around specific issues. Most Adirondack communities are involved with decisions about human-wildlife relations every year through action committees, local fish and game clubs, or town planning boards. The Department of Environmental Conservation for Region 5, located in Ray Brook next door to the Adirondack Park Agency, must make numerous management decisions about wildlife; in the more controversial ones they are often assisted by citizen advisory boards. The most interesting and controversial issues debated during the past few years have included both those subject to current legislation or regulation changes and those under philosophical discussion in anticipation of change, or perhaps those meant to provoke change. Deer hunting, use of the pesticide rotenone, fish stocking, lampricides, leghold traps, protection of loons and coyotes, blackfly spraying, feeding pigeons, deer, or bear, the reintroduction of lynx, wolves, moose, and possibly mountain lions all inspire heated debates, and reveal much about the balance of attitudes toward wildlife within a community.

These issues mirror the relationships among human beings, as individuals and communities, and wild animals as individuals and populations or members of ecosystems. As the significant other, wildlife fascinates and preoccupies people. As Claude Lévi-Strauss (Lévi-Strauss, 1962) pointed out, as symbols, animals are also "good to think." The DEC, more practical, lists ten broad categories of human values that determine wildlife management: positive values of (1) existence, (2) information and education, (3) observation, (4) hunting, (5) trapping, (6) direct use and sales, (7) related income; and negative values of (8) disease, (9) damage, and (10) nuisance and problems associated with users of wildlife resources. Many wildlife management issues have to do with the last category; like a photographic negative, the nuisance species reveal the boundaries of these values most starkly.

❦ The blackfly is probably the smallest wild creature visible to the naked human eye that most visitors to the Adirondacks meet. This tiny fly breeds in small, swift streams. In May, when the dogtooth violets bloom, the adult flies emerge in swarms in the woods. About two weeks after their appearance, they begin biting. Human beings and wild animals alike provide blood meals for the females. The small bite, not particularly painful, often bleeds freely because of the anticoagulant injected by the flies. The bites itch annoyingly for several days and, on soft tissues such as eyelids and ears, often cause swelling and tenderness. The main problem is that the flies attack in such numbers, and can wriggle beneath most protective clothing, that they are enough to keep many people out of the woods for the month of June. I unfortunately cured one of my son's friends of all interest in camping after he was bitten so badly one rainy night that one eye was swollen shut for three days; it was as black and blue as if he had been hit with a baseball bat.

For years Adirondack residents permitted aerial spraying to reduce

blackfly populations. Spraying of large areas with Dibrom-14 and malathion eventually engendered a controversy over the safety of these
chemicals for humans and the environment. Duflo-Spray Chemical, Inc.,
the sole spray company operating currently in the Adirondacks, used
first DDT, then Dibrom-14 (naled), and now Scourge, whose active in-
gredients are resmethrin and piperonyl butoxide. The labels on these pesticides read:

> PRECAUTIONARY STATEMENTS HAZARDS TO HUMANS &
> DOMESTIC ANIMALS. Harmful if swallowed. Avoid breathing
> vapor or spray mist. This product is toxic to fish and birds. Do
> not apply to lakes, streams, or ponds. (Scourge)

> PRECAUTIONARY STATEMENTS HAZARDS TO HUMANS &
> DOMESTIC ANIMALS. Causes irreversible eye and skin dam-
> ages. May be fatal if swallowed, inhaled or absorbed through
> the skin. This pesticide is toxic to fish, aquatic invertebrates,
> and wildlife. Do not apply directly to water or wetlands
> (swamps, bogs, marshes and potholes). This product is highly
> toxic to bees. (Dibrom-14)

> PRECAUTIONARY STATEMENTS HAZARDS TO HUMANS AND
> DOMESTIC ANIMALS. This product is toxic to fish and aquatic
> invertebrates. Drift and runoff may be hazardous to aquatic or-
> ganisms in areas near application site. This product is highly
> toxic to bees. (malathion) (Grayson, 1990)

At a hearing held by the town of Webb, concerned citizens from as far
away as Lake Placid and Keene packed the meeting room to protest the use
of chemical sprays. Ostensibly a presentation of an update to a 1983 Northern New York Programmatic Environmental Impact Statement to approve
use of the pesticides by Duflo, the meeting quickly became a citizens' forum.
Speaker after speaker stepped up to the podium to document the hazards
of the pesticides and to decry their use in the Adirondacks. A science
teacher from Old Forge, who had worked three years in a neurotoxicology
lab, demonstrated that piperol used as a liquid carrier acted synergistically
with the spray to increase its toxicity. He stated that the major problem was
the toxicity to the aquatic environment, especially since the smaller streams
were not mapped, and the spray would drift from the intended path in
winds as low as three miles per hour.

A physician's assistant who worked in the emergency room of an area hospital said that there was a flood of asthmatics and emphysemics at the emergency room at the time of spraying each year. The kerosene base of the pesticides causes acute respiratory irritation, especially in those with respiratory ailments. He talked about chronic toxicity in relation to repeated exposure to the pesticides over long periods of time, and the possibility for symptoms of acute poisoning to arise as the fat-soluble toxins become concentrated in the body. He presented a letter from seventeen doctors and physician's assistants supporting his statements. Blackfly bites don't kill, he added.

Gary Randorf, then director of the Adirondack Council, called the environmental impact statement inadequate. He presented data collected by council member and naturalist Greeney Chase, who had been keeping track of communities where the pesticides were used, and had found that the bird, owl, and small mammal populations were all down. Randorf suggested that citizens finding violations (where the spray had reached water bodies) should take legal action: "Duflo will be held responsible, as will the local governments," he warned, and reminded the audience that the New York State Department of Health no longer pays for a.part of the cost for spraying because it does not consider blackflies a health threat.

A scientist from the highly regarded Atmospheric Science Center, located halfway up Whiteface Mountain, talked about the very long range transport of droplets: "I myself have observed [pesticide] being sprayed on water bodies, many times. . . . [S]hortly after spraying we have seen signs of pesticides in water bodies." The audience was shocked into momentary silence when he had a fit of coughing in the middle of his presentation, and excused himself, murmuring, "I'm an asthmatic."

A representative from Vector Tech, Inc., described an alternative biological agent, *Bacillus thuringiensis israeliensis* (Bti), which her company markets and applies. Bti kills only blackflies, mosquitoes, and midges. The process is labor-intensive, requiring hand placement in streams, where the agent kills the larvae. She argued that Bti is nontoxic except to the target species, results in a greater reduction of the blackfly population than with aerial sprays, and provides local people with work opportunities. Several of the other citizen speakers wanted to know why Bti had not been considered or recommended as an alternative.

What emerged from the hearing was an active, knowledgeable group of citizens who had become informed and set out to inform others about the ecological and health hazards of chemical blackfly spraying. They expressed highly ecologistic attitudes, offering example after example of the effects that the toxins have on a wide range of interconnected ecosystems and organisms. Their ecological and scientific knowledge several times appeared to overwhelm the certified environmental professional who had prepared the one-sided environmental impact statement. She was unable to answer several of the citizens' criticisms of her statistical methods and her scientific deductions.

Naturalistic attitudes surfaced in several of the testimonies. Yet the leading statements, including the rejection of the toxic sprays and the support of Bti as a safe, effective alternative, were at base representative of an anthropocentric worldview, at least with regard to blackflies. While defending the rights of the fish, birds, and amphibians who would be affected, no one defended the right of the blackfly to exist. This faceless, charmless denizen of nature had evidently earned the status of nuisance — an unwanted species. Only a handful of people seemed to believe that nothing should be done, and that the sprays were ineffective anyway. Wayne Failing, the president of the New York State Outdoor Guide Association, felt that it was courting disaster to interfere with natural processes. But no one felt sorry for the blackflies or spoke out against the assumption of the human right to exterminate as many of them as possible. By fall 1996 all towns had ceased spraying. Several are now using Bti; the Adirondack Council, the most visible preservation group in the park, supports its use (Adirondack Council newsletter, July 1991).

🍂 The coyote is another nuisance or "weed" species (botanists define weeds as aggressive invaders), in at least some people's view. The DEC, in its "Summary of Public Input on Wildlife Management Needs," described the input from a series of twelve public meetings across the state and from mailed written comments on coyotes:

> There [were] . . . concerns regarding coyotes depressing rabbit, grouse, turkey, and deer populations. One attendee noted that coyotes were pushing deer out of the Speculator/ Whitehouse area. One person called for a bounty on coyotes funded by hunters, while another wanted protection removed from coyotes. Others stated that the coyote problem was not as bad as some people perceived, while some asked for more information on coyotes and suggested that we need input from university researchers rather than hunters. A couple of letters

expressed their interest in greater protection for coyotes on the basis of their esthetic values and ecological role as a natural predator of deer. (DEC, 1989)

In a draft for public review and comment, the DEC stated that coyotes are widely distributed in New York, with a secure and stable population, adding that "they appear to regulate their own population density through territorial behavior." Discussing human values for the coyote, the assessment describes a similar range of attitudes:

> The Eastern coyote is a protected furbearer at present but its pelts have recently declined in value with other long-haired furs. Its trophy value is increasing among hunters and trappers. In northern New York, this species continues to be the center of controversy over its suggested negative impact on white-tailed deer populations. . . . [C]oyotes are sometimes seen near residential areas which causes some alarm among residents. The Eastern coyote has a very positive value to amateur naturalists for a variety of reasons relating to its conspicuous and interesting behavior, including vocalization. Its incidental observation is often highly valued. (DEC, 1989, p. 55)

Hunters frequently brought up the coyote in our conversations as an example of poor wildlife management; many believed that there should be a year-round season on coyotes, a bounty set, or even an eradication program. Several said that coyotes were much more prevalent than DEC reports suggested, and that they were often seen running in packs, much like wolves. Many hunters believed that these packs attacked deer, and several feared that they could be dangerous to solitary hikers or children. Hunters and others regularly came across their tracks in the woods, often fairly close to towns. The hunters' negative attitudes toward coyotes derived not from fear for themselves but from their desire to protect the deer, as well as women, children, and unwary city dwellers, from rapacious attacks. One wildlife biologist confided to me that control programs made no difference because coyotes seemed to adjust litter size to their current population density; that is, if the population declined, the coyotes produced much larger litters.

By 1994 the DEC had held meetings in the four corners of the Adirondacks, only to find that there was no clear-cut consensus on whether or not to permit year-round hunting of coyotes. Concerned livestock owners felt that there must be other, better ways to control them. But, as one DEC official who preferred not to be identified commented, "There are a few dyed-in-the-wool sportsmen who think coyotes should be eliminated."

❧ In the case of "trash fish" species (such as yellow perch) introduced into certain lakes, where they force out the naturally occurring and more desirable wild trout, decisions about their management have been swifter. The DEC applies rotenone to the affected water body. Rotenone kills all the fish, as well as amphibians and some invertebrates, and then dissipates after several days; the DEC then reintroduces the desirable fish species. Many residents and nonresidents have objected to this practice, but sport fishermen generally support it wholeheartedly. The Adirondack Mountain Club, a conservation group which includes members from many states, originally opposed the use of rotenone in the High Peaks Wilderness Area. Eventually the staff succumbed to pressure from its members and to concerns about the wild trout species, and changed its position.

❧ The sea lamprey, a nonnative parasite in Lake Champlain, "is having a major impact on the salmon, brown trout and steelhead populations and sport fisheries" according to a DEC draft environmental impact statement (DEC, 1987). In 1990 and 1991, the DEC began a program to reduce sea lamprey abundance in Lake Champlain through the use of two lampricides, TFM (applied to tributaries) and Bayer 73 (applied to five delta areas). Adirondack residents had raised questions about the effectiveness of the lampricides, their effects on other wildlife, and the possibilities for using other methods to control the lamprey population (DEC, 1987, Appendix A). The lampricides are known to kill some species of fish, some amphibians, and some invertebrates. When the stream treatments started, a small group of concerned residents and two Earth First! activists showed up to protest. The rest of the local population either supported the program, were unaware of it, or were not so concerned about the fate of an unattractive parasite and an indeterminate number of other fish, amphibians, and invertebrates.

❧ These four examples exemplify the interrelatedness of wildlife characteristics that shape people's attitudes toward them: nativeness versus nonnativeness; threats to humans; threats to other desirable species; and aesthetic, symbolic, or naturalistic interest to humans. The blackfly is a native pest with a roughly stable population. The coyote is a native species expanding to fill a niche left by the absence of other deer predators. The accidental "trash fish" are nonnatives that threaten the existence of more desirable native species. And the sea lampreys are nonnative, parasitic, and just plain ugly.

How do people draw the line between what they value in wildlife — its aesthetic qualities, existence value, and symbolic representation of wilderness — and what is simply considered a nuisance, a "weed"? How do people decide how much of any wild species is enough? Can there be such a thing as a nuisance or "weed" species in a wild environment? Or is "weed" a purely human concept? Would populations in the wild self-regulate? And what does that mean? Are coyotes like lemmings, or are they invaders? In other words, these debates over blackflies and coyotes all pose the question, Where do human beings fit in? Do human beings belong in a wild community? And if so, then how: As managers? As caretakers or stewards? Or simply as another species?

❧ When Mike Story, a naturalist for the APA, designed the trails at the Visitor Interpretive Center at Paul Smith's College several years ago, he planned around the beavers. Walking the trails with him, I listen to his description of the views he wanted to capture: from Barnum Brook, winding through a forest of many species, including birch, hemlock, sugar maple, beech, pine, balsam, spruce, down to a scenic pool widening out onto the marsh. He designed a platform at the pool, where beautiful shots of the changing seasons were taken for the visitor center's slide show. Another platform looks out over the marsh toward the beaver lodge.

Now, shaking his head with a rueful laugh, he says that the beavers are changing things. They have dammed the brook in several places, even using the fish ladder, jamming it full of peeled sticks. Several large birch trees have fallen, gnawed in half. The water level in the pool has dropped almost two feet. Soon, he suspects, after building a few more dams, they will abandon this part of Barnum Brook and head for a fresher food supply. I ask whether he will try to refill the pool, or manage the brook at all, to keep the fit with the elaborate wooden bridges and platforms, or reroute the trail. No, he says, it's all part of nature. As human beings, we just watch what happens. If he interfered, it would no longer be truly wild.

Increasingly, beaver activity competes with human activity. In 1994 an eleven-member group of farmers, landowners, planners, and others was formed after "more than 200 attended meetings to complain about flooding caused by beaver dams" (*Watertown Daily Times*, September 25, 1994, p. B2). The citizens' task force is developing an action plan to deal with the beaver. Beaver populations have been labeled nuisances to public highways. In addition, the animals have cut down ever larger numbers of trees on private and public land. Of all mammals, beaver seem most human-like in their drive to manage and change their environment.

The increased populations appear to be the result of the dropping prices for beaver pelts. The DEC is now considering setting up "beaver nuisance zones" in which shooting and trapping would be allowed at any time of the year. Should more beaver be killed? Balancing nature when nature is no longer in a position to balance itself becomes a tricky act of manipulation.

🐾 In Saranac Lake, for weeks the newpaper runs stories and letters to the editor about a man who has built a platform to feed pigeons. Some town residents have complained and tried to stop him, saying that he attracts more pigeons to the downtown area, where they are a nuisance. Others defend his right to enjoy birds in his own way. Are the pigeons part of nature and as such essentially wild? Are they legitimate members of an urban community? Or are they merely weeds, an aggressive species invading another species's territory? Are any animals who move into human communities still wild and a part of nature? Falcons and even snowy owls are nesting on skyscrapers in cities. Deer are overpopulating the suburbs. Raccoons dine out of garbage cans. Should humans be feeding them, interfering with their "natural" food gathering from the refuse and litter they find in the streets?

The Long Lake Fish and Game Club members feed the deer in winter. Many people feed birds in their yards in winter. Ray Fadden, for more complex reasons, feeds perhaps thousands of birds and over a hundred bears in the woods behind his house. Driving up to Ray Fadden's house, I feel rather than hear the sudden shift in the symphonic sounds of the forest. The soughing of the pine boughs and hidden rustlings and twig crack of a small bird here and there suddenly erupt into a raucous chorus of ravens, the whistling and chirping of hundreds of songbirds, and the deeper, unpredictable sounds of bears moving in the shadowy spaces beneath the boughs. Ray Fadden, blue-eyed elder of the Mohawk Indians, lives in Onchiota, where he runs the Six Nations Indian Museum, a small building filled with artifacts of Mohawk life. His house sits across the road.

I park and hold my baby son up to hear the sounds of the animals. Ray comes and stands in the porch doorway, a small bony figure with wide shoulders under his flannel shirt, soft white hair, skin the color of the tannin-stained brooks. His gaze is direct. "I was watching you with the baby," he says, and grins. I am glad I have brought Daniel.

I follow Ray inside. The living room evokes middle America: stuffed chairs and couch, large television set, shelves of symbolic items, family pictures. But the magazines tell a different story: *Utne Reader, Mother Earth News.* And when I take a second look at the family pictures, I see a young boy in full Mohawk ceremonial dress, animals in the picture. The animal motif is everywhere. A drawing of a fox's head looks at me from a glass frame propped against the wall. A large piece of twisted wood is decorated with small plastic and wooden figures of wild animals. I remember the stories of the forty-pound porcupine that lived with Ray and his wife. And all the time I can hear the raucous calls of crows and ravens and jays feeding out back.

For traditional Mohawks, people and animals form a continuum of living creatures. They speak of the two-legged and four-legged peoples, the flying people and the swimming people. All creatures, plants, and natural objects have spirits. "The woodchuck has as much right to exist as I do," says Ray. His philosophy predates Aldo Leopold's similar claim in his essay, "The Land Ethic" in his classic *Sand County Almanac,* yet Native Americans get little credit for the modern extension of ethics to include animals and other natural subjects (cf. Callicott, 1987).

Totemism has been a way of thinking, doing, and being for the Mohawk and other Native Americans for centuries (Lévi-Strauss, 1962). Animals figure in myths, rituals, dreams, and observations as alter egos, parts of the personality, messengers from the spirit world, or carriers of traditional beliefs. In thought, animals act as symbols that can be manipulated to create complex reflections on the culture itself. They provide the lexicon for the metaphysical structure at the core of a people's beliefs and behaviors. The Iroquois divide themselves into clans that cut across local bands. Each clan has "a totemic animal, plant, or other natural object, of which it is guardian, interpreter, and representative" (Shepard, 1985, p. 209). Among the Iroquois, including the Mohawk and Seneca, the clans or societies include the Bear Clan, a powerful medicine society which incorporates many healing songs and dances into its rituals. Suppressed at the time of Handsome Lake (a Seneca prophet from 1799–1815), these societies have become important again among contemporary Indians who follow traditional teachings (Parker, 1968).

Anthropologists have made extensive studies of totemism, animal mythology, and the use of animals as signs, symbols, and motifs in the rituals of traditional peoples. They have paid much less attention to the importance of individual living animals to individual living members of these cultures, and the interactions between them. Ray Fadden feeds the birds and the bears because he believes that they are in danger, starving in an environment weakened and depleted by the white man's destructive behavior. At the local meeting where a Duflo-Spray employee was promoting the use of Scourge, dibrom-14 and malathion, Ray asked if these chemicals killed bees. The answer was yes. Ray responded: "If this kills bees, how are you going to have any more pollination? How are you going to have any more apples, strawberries, raspberries, chokecherries, blueberries, huckleberries, and a thousand other plants? If this kills other insects, what are the birds supposed to eat? And the frogs, the toads, the salamanders, the fish, the spiders? . . . Everything was put here for a reason. Even the blackflies are necessary."

Ray tells me about the rapid loss of topsoil in the last hundred years, acid rain, global warming, pollution, overdevelopment, destructive logging practices, mining. "They are skinning Mother Earth like a muskrat," he says. He has watched the gradual diminution in numbers of birds, bears, and other wildlife and attributes it to all these factors, which add up to loss of habitat and inadequate or poisoned food supplies. "I haven't seen whippoorwills for years. There used to be flocks of cedar waxwings, hundreds. . . . I haven't seen one this year. You go back in the woods a mile — it's *silent.*" The birds, bears, and other creatures are his brothers and sisters, he says. He feels obligated to feed the individuals who come to him, as he would a kinsperson. "I get scraps from the butcher and the baker in town. . . . Lately they haven't had enough. I've got to get more. I've got two mothers with three kids each." One wounded bear came back every day for weeks and finally allowed Ray to touch him before he disappeared, Ray thinks, to die.

One day I arrive with both of my boys in time to see Ray feeding the bears. He warns us to stay close to the back of the house and to keep quiet. "These are wild bears," he says softly. Carrying a torn packing box overloaded with strips of fat and scraps of meat, he enters the gloom of the forest behind the house. We see them coming, four or five shadowy black shapes, moving toward Ray. He sets the box down and backs away, slowly. The bears come in to feed, and the green space under the trees seems suddenly electrified by their presence.

Members of the preservation community in the Adirondacks honor Ray and ask him to speak at yearly Earth Day celebrations. The Department of Environmental Conservation staff privately shake their heads over his bear-feeding activities. They are less concerned with maintaining individual bears than with sustaining a viable breeding population. To the DEC staff, feeding the bears may make them dangerous, and risks altering their wild character. When the Long Lake landfill was about to be closed, town supervisor John Hosley drew national attention when he proposed creating troughs for household food waste to feed the bears who had been entertaining people at the landfill. Tourists enjoy stopping at Bud Piserchia's taxidermy shop to see the bears and other animals stuffed so that they stand, leap, or run in lifelike postures. The preservationists, Ray Fadden, the DEC, landfill watchers, tourists, and hunters all have radically different attitudes toward bears. Yet these attitudes, the knowledge they spawn, and the behavior they engender together add up to a complex set of relationships between bears and humans.

❦ Adding "totemistic" to Stephen Kellert's list of attitudes toward nature would cover not only the values of many traditional Native Americans but also the more subconscious values of many other Americans. Naturalist Paul Shepard writes: "The use of animals in childhood as the heralds of thought and self-knowledge is universal. It accounts for the fascination animals have for all children, a kind of mental food, at first an orderly mechanics of ideal organization and grouping, and then the separation and representation of qualities and traits, and at the same time protagonists of folktales and fairy tales that externalize elements of the child's inner life and give him the means of coping with the conflicts and uncertainties of the developing personality" (Shepard, 1985, p. 208).

As American children reach adulthood, on the surface these animal symbols or mentors are discouraged. We treat fairy tales and folktales, Uncle Remus stories, Aesop's fables, *Winnie the Pooh* and *The Wind in the Willows* as children's fare. Yet by adulthood we have internalized the basic symbolic/totemistic/metaphoric structure that allows us to use animals in our thinking. Our language employs rich animal symbolism even though most of the population lives in cities. She eats like a bird, a bear, a horse. Wolfing his food, he growled. Birdlike, tigerish, elephantine, eagle-eyed, owlish: it permeates our vocabulary and expressions so thoroughly that the loss of even a single element could make us stumble. Could someone be as hungry as a bear if there were no bears?

At some level we identify with particular animals, and think of others as identified with other animals. Almost everyone identifies with a particular animal species. By making these private thoughts known to friends and family, we can ease personal relationships, giving others an inside perspective through shared understanding of our "animal logic."

❧ Deer hunting, which would seem to fall entirely within Kellert's categories of dominionistic and utilitarian attitudes, may have a deeper connection with totemism than is usually acknowledged. Deer hunting is informally ritualized, requiring special clothing and immersion in a wild environment apart from civilization, generally in groups of close male friends or family members. Male bonding may be an important sociological side effect of hunting; human-animal bonding may be an even more fundamental aspect of hunting, often overlooked because of a seeming incompatibility with the act of killing. But it is possible that through killing, and at times refraining from killing (Faulkner, 1940), some men feel closest to the life spirit of wild animals. Following animal scat and tracks, walking along deer runs, discovering the hollows where animals bed down, sharing their wild environment, its scents and sounds, views and weather, the touch of leaves, and finally observing an animal, watching its movements, even meeting its eyes, all create a sense of connection to the wild creature and its environment, paradoxically linked to killing it. Men mark one another with the blood of the deer, eat the meat, hang up the racks, and sometimes the heads, in their living rooms or dens. Are these racks merely trophies, or are they a synecdochic link to the experience of connectedness to another living creature? Psychologist Miriam Miedzian describes a deer hunting ritual common in Mississippi and other parts of the South as the closest we come to initiation rites for boys. She quotes from an interview with a hunter: " 'Your first deer is a big deal. It signifies you have done something significant approaching manhood.' Blood from the deer is smeared all over the boy's face and photographs are taken and often displayed on family mantelpieces" (Miedzian, 1991, p. 87).

From these totemistic origins within our logic and cultures, wild animals acquire great generative power as symbols. The function of certain wild animals as symbols heightens concerns over their protection or reintroduction in the Adirondacks. Certain animals also deepen the emotional and spiritual content of human relations with wildlife. Loons, wolves, moose, bald eagles, lynx, and mountain lions all connote wilderness, and as such are connected to the vision of an American national character formed in a struggle with nature, as well as with values of purity, spirituality, power, and solitude (Nash, 1982). The DEC describes the values associated with loons: "There is enormous public interest in loons due to their visual attractiveness, their haunting calls, and their symbolic identification with wilderness. Visitors to the Adirondacks gain special enjoyment from the presence of loons" (DEC, 1989, p. 15).

Part of the loons' symbolic identification with wilderness is based in biological fact. They are the most primitive birds living today, and are extremely sensitive to lake acidification and to motor activity on lakes, which disturbs their low-lying nests. This makes them a symbol of the purity of wilderness to many people. Their beauty, strangeness, and wild ululations make them aesthetically satisfying subjects for paintings, carvings, and other art. The Adirondack Council features them in its logo; loon emblems preside on mailboxes, wind socks, pillows, ornaments, photographs and paintings in many Adirondack homes. Bald eagles similarly support an identification with wilderness, as well as with American patriotic values. Their increasing presence in the Adirondacks seems to validate the region's wild character for many people.

This positive attitude toward animals associated with wilderness is not adopted by everyone, however. In 1987 the State University of New York's College of Environmental Science and Forestry (CESF) began a lynx restoration effort in the Adirondacks, releasing eighteen lynx in the High Peaks region in 1989 (DEC, 1989). Reactions were mixed. Some hunters and trappers I spoke with were concerned about the effect of the lynx on the population of snowshoe hare, their primary prey. In general, however, the local newspapers reflected a high level of public interest and curiosity regarding the lynx, especially when several were seen near Saranac Lake and one lynx kitten turned up in someone's backyard. Unfortunately, few of the lynx survived the experiment, and those that did were inclined to migrate out of the region.

Moose, quietly reintroducing themselves into the Adirondacks as the vegetation reaches a climax forest stage in areas adjacent to wetlands, also meet with mixed reactions. Almost everyone in the Adirondacks has heard the amusing story of a moose that tried to woo a cow in Vermont; they have also heard of serious motor accidents in Vermont involving moose. Moose are the largest land animals in New York State, and they provide a thrilling "wilderness experience" when observed. They are also a potential game animal.

In August 1992 the APA voted by a margin of one to allow funding for moose restoration, but local residents shot down the DEC's moose reintroduction proposal. After fifteen public meetings, eight of which were held in northern New York, the DEC found that the general flavor was negative from a variety of views. People were concerned about moose-vehicle collisions, the cost of speeding up a reintroduction that was happening naturally, and at downstate meetings, anti-hunting segments were against classification of moose as a game animal.

The moose evoked strong reactions for complex reasons, however. "The moose was the straw guy, the windmill people were charging because of anti-government feeling," one DEC official who was present at the meetings told me. Wildlife becomes a synecdochic link to the total wilderness experience, and their "print," whether photo, trophy head, or footprint, becomes a symbol of that experience. Equally, government manipulation and regulation of wildlife has become for some a symbol of government's manipulation and regulation of people.

Wolves arouse polarized feelings as well. Some Adirondack residents view their possible reintroduction with nothing less than horror, seeing the wolf as a menace to humans and livestock. Hunters worry about the potential effect on the deer population. Wilderness advocates, however, enthusiastically promote the restoration of wolves as both a symbolic and a biological achievement for wilderness recovery in the eastern half of the United States. A small group has initiated a formal "Wolf Project," even as controversy swirls around the reintroduction of wolves in the West in Yellowstone National Park.

Earth First! has adopted the wolf as its totem. While camping near an Earth First! group one rainy spring evening, I listened to their human howling reverberating through the wet trees as they attempted, symbolically and physically, to reestablish their connectedness with "brother and sister wolves."

🌿 Another large mammal that symbolizes wilderness for many people, the mountain lion or cougar, awakes both fear and awe. Proving the existence of mountain lions in the Adirondacks is as difficult and elusive as proving the existence of a body of indigenous knowledge. No sighting of a wild mountain lion in the Adirondacks has been verified, but rumors abound. Reiner Brocke, professor of wildlife biology at SUNY Syracuse, insists that it would be impossible for mountain lions to become established in the Adirondacks. He argues that the bigger mammals need large areas not bisected by busy roads. The presence of humans alone does not seem to bother cougars, he says, and in fact, they like areas with a mix of wilderness and an old clear-cut or shelter wood cut because of the greater diversity and abundance of prey species. Roads seem to inhibit mountain lion travel, however, and the Adirondacks, Brocke says, have enough cross-cutting roads to restrict mountain lions to territories too small for their wide-ranging search for food. Some local people disagree. Several reports of mountain lion sightings have surfaced in the northern part of the park. Nellie Staves, trapper and hunter, president of the Tupper Lake Rod and Gun Club and the Franklin County Federation of Fish and Game Clubs, and at one time of the Adirondack Conservation Council, believes that she has seen a mountain lion twice along a road in the northern section. "Just like the movies," she told me. Dark tan and moving like a silent streak of lightning, it jumped into a dense thicket near Barnum Pond. Another woman told me that her husband and son had seen mountain lion tracks on their land.

Finally, I had to look for myself. I studied the tracking guides, memorized the prints of bear, bobcat, lynx, and cougar, the sizes of each and the distances between prints both walking and running, the gestalt of a lumbering bear, a trotting bobcat, a running cougar. I followed Nellie's advice. I walked to the end of the visitor center trails and left them, bushwhacking along the edge of the marsh looking for tracks. The temperature, a damp 32 degrees, was holding the snowfall of the early morning intact. About an inch had fallen, fresh and blue-white over the grayer, packed, thawed-and-then-frozen snow of the day before. Chickadees "Here petey"-ed, two red squirrels scuttered along the branches of a hemlock, and the snow made soft crushing noises under my boots, but the rest was a cool silence, filled with the tension of watching. A tiny, chilly wind brushed my bare hands and the boughs of the white pines, too faint to rustle them. Beside the outflow of the brook I saw the soft-edged, splattered prints of a snowshoe hare, beside it the curiously petite prints of a fox, like someone hopping on a peg leg. The hare had veered off across the fragile ice and mud of the marsh; the fox had veered into the woods. I decided to follow the snowshoe hare's tracks. Perhaps the cougar, if there were one, would consider it for dinner. I walked out over the flat, empty snow.

And suddenly I was upon them, big blue prints carved deep into the snow. Bigger than my fist, running in almost a straight line beside the snowshoe hare tracks, sometimes crossing them, two and a half feet between each print. I plunged on, once breaking through the thin ice over the stream. And then, seeing the big prints heading for the bare red branches of the alder thicket, I headed straight across to the thicket, until I was touching the branches, peering inside its dim shadows. The prints disappeared into the thicket. I bent the first branches down, then stopped, startled into a realization: the mountain lion—myth, symbol, totem, wishful thinking, or a snarling reality of blood, bone, and tissue—might quite possibly be waiting there.

3

History of Land Use Philosophies in the Adirondacks

FROM THE TOP OF MOUNT MARCY, WHERE we are hiking, we can see only thick gray mist. Shrouds of mist whip past about a yard in front of us. Beyond that, nothing. We are in a cloud.

The top of Mount Marcy, the highest mountain in the Adirondacks, is often hidden in cloud. But on a clear day the summit gives a view of the Adirondacks from Lake Champlain to the western forests. People who have made decisions about land use in the Adirondacks have acted on the images that this view carved into their imagination — and on what their imagination created from the view — as they stood on this wind-bruised rock. The Iroquois and the Algonquin, surveyor Verplanck Colvin, Ralph Waldo Emerson, Teddy Roosevelt, Gifford Pinchot, Bob Marshall, and others all stood here looking out over the Adirondacks — and all saw different views.

From the perspective of Colvin, the Adirondacks served as the watershed for the Hudson River. For Emerson the Adirondacks were a fit setting for his philosophical and poetic musings. For the Native Americans they were hunting grounds. For the outdoorsman Marshall, the mountains were a great outpost of freedom from civilization. For Pinchot they were prime forests for productive timber management. And for Roosevelt the Adirondacks were all of these things.

Today the clouds are creeping down the mountains, and a chill wind blows. It is no longer clear what function these mountains serve for people, or even whether they should be "for" people at all. The confusion over land use, and the conflicts between the different worldviews that determine actions taken in the name of the Adirondacks, have obscured the view of the forests for everyone.

The Adirondack Mountains are part of a national debate on the relationship between humans and nature. To some extent the national debate was forged and the battle lines drawn in the Adirondacks in the 1890s, a conflict that still reverberates all over the United States in the 1990s. Because the conflict over land use in the Adirondacks stems in part from a confrontation between groups holding different philosophies of the human/nature relationship, unearthing a little of the history of these philosophies will help in digging out the roots of the conflict.

Photo 3. View of the High Peaks. Photo D. Kuklok

Foundations of Controversy: From 1776 to 1976

Ravens croak in the chill air. We can hear them even as our boots push through the wet spring snow, stumbling over the boulders on Avalanche Pass, the divide between the Hudson and Ausable rivers. It is hardly a path, an aisle between columns of birch and hemlock and spruce, through steep rock walls like the nave of a cathedral open to the sky, an aisle built of boulders. We clamber over them going up, and then clamber down, even climbing down two ladders put in by the trail crew where the going is too steep. Then we are edging Avalanche Lake itself, center of the High Peaks area and emblem of the controversy over land use and preservation. The lake is cold, deep, maybe two hundred feet, with sheer rock cliff walls falling into black water. The ravens are calling back and forth, an eerie sound that echoes across the stillness. One imagines canoeing around the lake, unable to land because there are no shores, only the cliffs rising abruptly. But at the far end a narrow gravel beach meets the waters on the other side. There hikers and ravens alike can rest and listen to the wind — and to the different voices in the controversy over this land.

In *Wilderness and the American Mind* (1982), Roderick Nash traced European-Americans' attitudes toward the wilderness, from atavistic responses of fear, awe, and kinship to the Judaeo-Christian desire for control and dominance over nature. Early settlers brought deeply ingrained religious values that defined wilderness, in both the Old and New Testaments, as a howling wasteland, though it could also provide refuge from oppressors. The pioneers were ambivalent toward the wilderness they passed through and attempted to tame. Some believed that the dark forests where they battled storms, fires, and wild animals were strongholds of chaos and evil. Nash gives examples of military metaphors used at the time: wilderness was represented as "an 'enemy' which had to be 'conquered,' 'subdued,' and 'vanquished' by a 'pioneer army'" (Nash, 1982, p. 27). Later writers disagreed with Nash's presentation as one-sided and cited examples of journals in which both men and women recorded feelings of awe and aesthetic pleasure; at the same time, they felt it was their duty to clear the land, impose their own order upon it, and make it productive on their own terms (Boag, 1992).

In the eighteenth and nineteenth centuries, as the wilderness receded inland from the eastern states, American city dwellers picked up from Europeans themes that granted positive values to wilderness. In Europe, aesthetic appreciation of the wilderness had increased with the theories of the sublime and the picturesque. According to historian Philip G. Terrie, "the chief attribute of sublime scenery was its incomprehensible greatness" (Terrie, 1985, p. 18); the sublime in nature reflected God's infinite powers and could draw the viewer into contemplation of them. The picturesque valued gentler, more bucolic scenery.

Deism, which took the relationship of God and wild nature as the basis for religion, and primitivism, whose proponents believed that people were happier living simpler, more "primitive" lives close to nature, increased the appreciation of nature among writers, artists, scientists, and the upper classes in America. Leading primitivists included Jean-Jacques Rousseau, Alexis de Tocqueville, and Lord Byron. Popular primitivism in America made heroes of "wild men," from hermits to the "noble savages" of James Fenimore Cooper's novels to Daniel Boone. Admiration of the "wild man's" supposed qualities of exceptional strength, hardiness, innocence, and nobility led to the concept of retreating to the wilderness in order to recover one's physical, moral, and spiritual strength (Nash, 1982).

Romanticism included an appreciation of the sublime, of deism and primitivism. It grew out of the Enlightenment understanding of nature as a manifestation of God; and yet the attributes that Romanticism valued differed qualitatively from those the Enlightenment valued. The Romantics rejected the ordered gardens of the Enlightenment in favor of the strange, remote, solitary, and mysterious qualities of wilderness landscapes (Oelschlager, 1991).

By the mid-nineteenth century, wilderness retreats became a necessity for philosophers, writers, artists, and others. The Adirondack region, up until then considered largely uninhabitable because of its impenetrable forests and mountains and its long, cold winters, became celebrated as a retreat from crowded civilization. Where only a few hardy trappers, hunters, and subsistence farmers had ventured to live (Native Americans used the Adirondacks for hunting and fishing but did not establish any permanent camps there), soon wealthy tourists visited, and began to build lavish summer camps. Joel T. Headley's 1849 book *The Adirondack: or, Life in the Woods*, describing the pleasures of vacationing in the Adirondacks, went through several printings (Terrie, 1985), as more and more urban dwellers discovered the area.

Yet the Romantics' true feelings for wilderness were often ambivalent. They experienced this ambivalence on two levels, the perceptual and the relational. Their perceptions of wilderness, educated by the aesthetics of Edmund Burke emphasizing grandeur, balked when they ran up against wilderness landscapes that Burke had not described. Prepared to accept cliffs, mountains, and gorges as sublime, the romantics did not know what to think of bogs, marshes, or dense undergrowth, and often reacted with repugnance. Writer and traveler A. B. Street, referring to small, isolated lakes west of Upper Saranac in the Adirondacks, wrote, "The shores . . . were low, belted with swamp and disfigured with dead, ghastly trees" (Terrie, 1985, p. 57).

The American Transcendentalists, including Ralph Waldo Emerson and Henry David Thoreau, were among the visitors to wilderness areas. The Transcendentalists believed in the existence of a reality higher than the physical and held that there was a correspondence between the higher realm of spiritual truth and the lower one of material objects. Nature was the perfect medium for this transcendence; Emerson called nature "the symbol of the spirit" (Nash, 1982, p. 85).

But Emerson, who visited remote Follensby Pond in the Adirondacks on a retreat with a group of intellectuals and artists, also expressed ambivalence toward wilderness. When, in the middle of his return to nature and its Transcendentalist virtues, he received news of the transatlantic cable, he relegated nature to its proper place, declaring that "the lightning has run masterless too long" (Emerson, 1867 p. 21; Graham, 1978). Thoreau also expressed ambivalence toward wilderness. He loved wild nature, as in the quiet woods surrounding Concord, yet was shocked by the harshness of the wild landscape surrounding Mount Katahdin in Maine. This ambivalence has persisted in attitudes toward wilderness in this century.

At the same time, others found uses for the American wilderness, including the Adirondacks, besides scenic appreciation and vacations. Scientists had discovered in wild nature a biological richness that provided a living laboratory for botanists, ornithologists, biologists, and others. Logging operations in the Adirondacks began to remove the huge white pines, and later the red spruce. Archibald McIntyre set up iron mines in North Elba, Adirondac and Tahawus in the early 1800s (Fennessy, 1988). Small farming communities started to grow. Over the next fifty years Saranac Lake became a center for tuberculosis sanatoriums; the balsam-laden air of the Adirondacks reputedly had healing properties. Tourism spawned hotels, inns, guides, and suppliers. And the wealthiest visitors, many of them well-known families, including the Durants and the Litchfields, built increasingly luxurious "camps" within thousands of acres of private forestland, where the upper class could enjoy roughing it in the privacy of their own preserve. These multiple views of the proper uses of the Adirondacks, twisting perception of its resources one way and another, formed the basis for the controversy over land use in the region.

This controversy burned on, with fuel supplied by a national debate over the management of wilderness and wilderness forests. Influential political, scientific, and cultural leaders, including the painter George Catlin, Francis Parkman, and George Perkins Marsh, began calling for the preservation of wilderness areas. In 1872 public support brought about the establishment of Yellowstone National Park.

As logging continued in the Adirondacks, and intensified with the introduction of pulp and paper mills, which took logs of small dimensions, and the charcoal and tanning industries, which used hemlock bark, the public became increasingly concerned about the destruction of the Adirondack forests. Although logging had not yet depleted the forests, the brush left by the logging operations contributed to destructive wildfires.

In 1864 George Perkins Marsh published his influential book *Man and Nature*, which underlined the economic importance of the Adirondack forests in protecting and regulating the watershed of the Hudson. New York businessmen, in addition to being outdoor enthusiasts, became concerned about protecting the Adirondacks when prominent journals outlined the possibility of low water levels in the Hudson and threats to transportation waterways.

At the same time, two men, writing vastly different accounts of the Adirondacks were attracting attention to the wilderness area, helping to generate dedicated popular support for maintaining its wild features. W. H. H. Murray, a minister from Boston, popularized camping in the Adirondacks with glowing descriptions in his book *Adventures in the Wilderness*. A best-seller in 1869, it attracted large numbers of tourists to the Adirondacks. Many were unprepared for the harsh conditions, the blackflies, and the rain; yet many others returned, and gradually enough hotels, guides, and amenities sprang up to accommodate the taste for comfort in the wilds.

The other, Verplanck Colvin, was commissioned by the state of New York to produce a survey of the Adirondacks. He wrote annual reports that gave romantic and yet naturalistic reports of his wilderness experiences in the Adirondack Mountains. In 1872 he discovered the source of the Hudson, a small, high lake below Mount Marcy, which he named Lake Tear of the Clouds. His enthusiasm for the Adirondacks, which gave him a "strange thrill of interest and of wonder at what may be hidden in that vast area of forest" (Terrie, 1985, p. 79), imbued his writings with a perspective that was at once romantic, naturalistic, and conservationist. Yet ultimately Colvin looked at the Adirondacks with a utilitarian eye. He proposed a continuous timber yield to the state and suggested a huge aqueduct scheme which would have altered substantially the character of the forests. Like many others of his time, he believed that man stood apart from nature and superior to it (Terrie, 1985). Colvin and Murray both advocated the use of the wilderness area for the benefit of the public.

❧ Thousands of tourists hike up the slopes of Mount Marcy each year; in summer the figure may reach close to a thousand a day. But the day my family and I hike Marcy in the fog, there is almost no one else. Descending on a steep trail, we pass a junction to other peaks. Beyond the junction, our feet sliding in the soggy ground, we reach a small pond. Its surface is still, opaque, misted; a few stunted and barren tree branches hang over it. It is Lake Tear of the Clouds, the source of the Hudson.

❧ On the regional and national level, philosophies of the human/nature relationship were broadening and becoming more diverse than the Calvinistic-romantic dichotomy. Frederick Law Olmsted was designing a wild yet ordered retreat, Central Park, in the center of a great metropolis; and concerns over the careless destruction of Yosemite had led to its classification as a national park.

John Muir, one of the prominent voices in the struggle to protect Yosemite from further degradation, was fast becoming the hero of a new brand of wilderness appreciation: wilderness for wilderness' sake. Born in Scotland, he came at a young age to Wisconsin, where his family farmed near the wild forests. Rejecting his father's stern Calvinist doctrine, he embraced nature as the home of true religion and the purest expression of God. Yet from that point he departed from the Romantic tradition. While calling the wilderness his "temple," he employed rigorous scientific scrutiny, and studied geology and other natural sciences. He proposed the theory of Yosemite's formation by glaciers, in contradiction to contemporary scientific notions. His observations led him to formulate his own version of wilderness philosophy. In a philosophical shift regarding the relationship between humans and all else, he foreshadowed Aldo Leopold's argument for the rights of other species: for him, even the tarantula had a right to exist.

But while Muir was raising the public consciousness about the value of wilderness for wilderness's sake through his popular books, the question of preserving the Adirondacks was arising largely for utilitarian reasons. In

1872 a State Park Commission was created in New York to look into preserving the watershed of the Hudson as a public park. Verplanck Colvin was appointed secretary of the commission. The press, while noting the recreational possibilities of such a park, supported the idea that the Adirondack forests should be preserved primarily for their role in maintaining the steady flow of the Hudson (Graham, 1978; Terrie, 1985). The commissioners recommended that they be managed by professional foresters as they were on the Continent, and that some mining be allowed. When sportsmen, tourists, and aesthetes observed the continuing destruction of the forests by mining, logging, and fires (frequently sparked by trains), and the depletion of fish and wildlife, they too supported the preservation of the Adirondacks (Graham, 1978).

In 1883 the legislature voted to withdraw from further sale all state-owned lands in the Adirondacks, though much of this land had already been logged or burned (Terrie, 1985). In 1884 Charles Sprague Sargent, a professor of arboriculture at Harvard, and one of the leading proponents of scientific forestry, led the government-appointed Sargent Commission in recommending the establishment of a Forest Preserve, which "shall be forever kept as wild forest lands" (E. Brown, 1985, p. 22). The law did not protect the timber, which could be sold through individual contracts with timber companies; a three-member Forest Commission was appointed to apply scientific forest management principles to provide a sustainable timber harvest and protect the area from forest fires (Terrie, 1985; White, 1985). The Forest Commission also agreed to pay taxes to the affected counties equal to those on comparable private lands (White, 1985). The economic definition of "comparable" has been an issue ever since in those counties.

At this time the public and the press were largely supportive of continued timber harvesting, so long as it was done according to sound scientific management principles. But an almost immediate outcry arose when Theodore Basselin, a Lewis County lumber baron, was appointed as one of the commissioners; collusion between the public commission and the lumber industry was suspected (Terrie, 1985). The *New York Times* and professional foresters (including Bernard Fernow, director of the College of Forestry at Cornell University, who himself came under fire for allowing thousands of acres of college land in the Adirondacks to be clear-cut) criticized the Forest Commission to such an extent that public opinion began to turn not only against the commission but also against any form of logging in the Adirondacks.

In 1892, the same year that Muir founded the Sierra Club, the legislature voted to establish the Adirondack Park, defined by the "Blue Line," a border drawn around some 2.8 million acres. The Forest Commission called for the state to acquire the land within the Blue Line in "one grand unbroken domain," yet stated that park purposes could be achieved by interspersing public with private lands. The commissioners apparently considered lumbering on state lands to be an appropriate use, but believed that continued lumbering on private lands, presumably by less scrupulous means, would be detrimental (E. Brown, 1985).

By 1893, the commission had reported that it did *not* intend to acquire all lands inside the park boundary, and it became obvious that it would be financially impossible for the state to do so at that time (E. Brown, 1985). The issue of state acquisition of lands and whether or not the state and private interest groups have a hidden agenda of eventually acquiring all the land within the Blue Line remains a heated subject among Adirondack residents today. In 1994 the state tried to acquire Follensby Pond, but the owner withdrew from negotiations. Preservationists were disappointed, though many others felt that the remote pond would be better preserved under continued private ownership. Their concerns are echoed elsewhere: across the United States citizens are challenging the notion that public ownership preserves land better than private ownership and management. Even the national park system has been challenged, particularly where it does not allow indigenous subsistence uses (Joanne Enter-Wada, pers. comm. 1995).

As the public became more aware of the continuing devastation caused by extensive logging for the paper mills and by fires resulting from the brush piles left behind by loggers, as well as the continuing problem of timber theft from state lands (White, 1985), there was increasing agitation for something more to be done to protect the Adirondack forests. The Board of Trade and Transportation of New York City, which had been involved in Adirondack conservation issues ever since its members realized the impact that destruction of the forest could have on the waterways, came up with the idea of protecting the Forest Preserve through the state Constitution (E. Brown, 1985). At the 1894 New York State Constitutional Convention, David McClure, a leader in the New York City bar, sponsored an amendment, Article 7, section 7 (later Article 14, section 1): "The lands of the State, now owned or hereafter acquired, constituting the forest preserve, as now fixed by law, shall be forever kept as wild forest lands. They shall not be leased, sold, or exchanged, *nor shall the timber thereon be sold, removed or destroyed*" (E. Brown, 1985, p. 201). The state had reversed its

policy concerning timber harvest on state lands within the Adirondack
Park. Philip Terrie writes, "The language abandoned faith in the lumberman and reflected apocalyptic fears concerning man's capacity to alter the
landscape and threaten his own well-being" (Terrie, 1985, p. 104).

❧ Hiking up the side of Mount Algonquin in a rocky streambed, we duck
under the branches of red spruce, their thin needles pricking our wrists.
Reaching its bare domed top, we can see for miles. Today the clouds ride
high, leaving the view clear. Far below are Heart Lake and Colden Lake.
Gazing across, we see ridge upon ridge, the shoulders of giants cloaked in
heavy forest. This is the forest that grew under "forever wild" and that
cannot be sold, removed, or destroyed.

Professional foresters, as well as Adirondack lumbermen, were disturbed by the removal of state lands from the timber harvest, and the
long-range implications of the "forever wild" clause (Terrie, 1985). Gifford
Pinchot, thirty years old, was already on the leading edge of the advocacy
of scientific forest management. As a boy of thirteen he had visited the
Adirondacks, where he had enjoyed fishing and camping in the wilderness.
In 1892 he returned to survey a large private tract owned by Seward Webb
in the western Adirondacks. His management plan for Webb's estate argued
that it was possible to create a sustained yield of profitable spruce by cutting
the older trees that were shading the new growth (Graham, 1978). He
hoped that his sustained yield management plan would be a model for all
Adirondack landowners, including the state (Terrie, 1985). When the "forever wild" amendment passed, Pinchot opposed it bitterly; the prohibition
on timber harvest struck him as the antithesis of progressive and enlight-
ened use of natural resources.

In 1896 Pinchot and Muir met. The idea of the forests as wood factories
and the idea of the forests as wilderness temples coalesced, clashed, and
moved apart. The National Forestry Commission, with Pinchot as secretary,
traveled west. John Muir joined the group, acting as guide and member ex
officio (Graham, 1978). Pinchot and Muir, two tall, lean men of the forests
and mountains, became close companions. When the others retired to their
hotel, Pinchot and Muir sneaked off to sleep on beds of cedar boughs in
the forest, where Pinchot listened to the older Muir's tales by the firelight.
"It was such an evening as I never had before or since," Pinchot wrote later
(Graham, 1978, p. 139).

Both Muir and Pinchot subscribed to the idea of multiple use, at least
in theory. But for Pinchot, timber harvest held primary importance, while

for Muir, spiritual valuation of wilderness was most important. Although the public recognized timber, wildlife, watershed, aesthetic, and health and recreation values for wilderness, neither the social sciences nor the forestry schools had yet figured out a way to formulate management for multiple use. Land management decisions appeared to be made on an ad hoc basis. In Seattle, Pinchot told sheep ranchers that he saw no harm in letting sheep graze in the federal reserves. Muir, arriving in Seattle on his way back from Alaska, read Pinchot's comments in the newspapers and confronted him. He hated the destruction sheep caused to mountain flora. Pinchot had to own up to his quoted remarks.

"Then I want nothing more to do with you," Muir said, and stalked off (Graham, 1978, p. 141). It was the end of their friendship, and their break split the American conservation movement in two: the preservationists went one way and the utilitarian, resource-oriented conservationists another. Each side of the movement adopted its own credo. The preservationists took Thoreau's famous words, "In wildness is the preservation of the world"; the conservationists used Pinchot's motto, "the wise use of natural resources." This split has affected land use issues in the Adirondacks ever since.

❧ Aldo Leopold (1886–1948) took the philosophy of the rights of nature and wilderness to exist one step further; looking at the relationship scientifically, he began to change the definition of that relationship to encompass a sense of balance and interconnectedness (Nash, 1989). Leopold studied forestry at Yale during a time when the forestry profession was flourishing under Pinchot and the government conservation work that Theodore Roosevelt encouraged (Meine, 1987). He went on to work for the Forest Service in the Southwest, specializing in game management. At that time he participated in and encouraged wolf extermination campaigns which he later saw in a different light. One experience crystallized the change in his perspective, though he did not reflect upon it until much later:

> In those days we had never heard of passing up a chance to
> kill a wolf. In a second we were pumping lead into the pack.
> . . . [W]e reached the old wolf in time to watch a fierce green
> fire dying in her eyes. I realized then, and have known ever
> since, that there was something new to me in those eyes —
> something known only to her and to the mountain. I was
> young then, and full of trigger-itch; I thought that because

fewer wolves meant more deer, that no wolves would mean hunters' paradise. But after seeing the green fire die, I sensed that neither the wolf nor the mountain agreed with such a view. (Leopold, 1966, p. 138)

A Sand County Almanac provided the contextual nest for Leopold's most fertile ideas, including the "land ethic," the "land community," and the ethical extension of rights to the land, in a framework of ecology, naturalistic observation, and the evolution of his own thinking about the land. The new science of ecology provided both the scientific background for his philosophical ideas and the metaphors for their expression. The study of ecology created a vocabulary to describe relations between different organisms and between biotic and abiotic elements. Concepts of interconnectedness, the web of life, the great chain of being, community, ecosystem, biome, and niche all grew out of the ecological scientists' perceptions that life is a holistic system with functioning parts. Leopold likened species to organs funtioning within a body, or to parts of a motor (Nash, 1989).

In contrast to that of his European predecessors, Leopold's philosophy went beyond humanitarian moralistic attitudes toward other species to an acceptance of humankind's place in the "land community," a superorganism of functioning parts. He wrote: "The land ethic simply enlarges the boundaries of the community to include soils, waters, plants, and animals, or collectively: the land" (Leopold, 1966, p. 239). In accepting its place in the larger community, humankind does not so much grant rights to other species as recognize its own *lack* of a right to destroy other species because of the greater right of the land community to exist as a healthy, functioning whole. "In short, a land ethic changes the role of *Homo sapiens* from conqueror of the land community to plain member and citizen of it" (Leopold, 1966, p. 240). Leopold's philosophy reflects values similar to those of Native American communities, including the Mohawks of the Adirondacks, which went unrecognized as the predecessors of his own.

Recognition of the land community entails respect for its other citizens. Yet for Leopold, the loss of an individual animal's life was not the moral disaster it was for the animal rights advocates, unless it was wasted. But the destruction of a species or the degradation of an ecosystem was a disaster on a level beyond human moral concerns; it disrupted the healthful balance of the land. Giving guidance to those who were trying to manage the delicate relationship between humans and the land, Leopold said, in one of his most quoted statements: "A thing is right when it tends to preserve the integrity, stability, and beauty of the biotic community. It is wrong when it tends otherwise" (Leopold, 1966, p. 262).

❧ In the sunrise hour, white trilliums gleam against green shadows at the base of a cluster of pines. The lake stretches away smooth as glass. A loon cries — an ululation that echoes around the lake. A white-throated sparrow sings "Oh sweet Canada, Canada, Canada," and the day begins. Water is the lifeblood of the Adirondacks. Its rivers and streams are the veins and arteries of a region, the lakes like organs where essential life-giving functions take place. But now, in some high lakes, acidification has rendered the waters fishless. In lower lakes surrounded by vacation homes, algae growth is rampant, choking once-clear waters. The impacts of human development on the Adirondacks are nowhere more obvious than in the state of its waters. Protection of waters in the Adirondacks parallel concerns on a national level.

❧ At the same time Leopold was writing, both in the Adirondacks and nationally the active campaign to preserve the wilderness was racing forward against the equally active campaign to harvest natural resources, from timber and water to oil and minerals. Harnessing water power preoccupied much of the developers' and the preservationists' energy alike. Hetch Hetchy Valley in California spurred Muir on to the greatest fight of his life; and it was lost, as the valley was flooded to provide water and hydroelectric power to San Francisco. John Muir died before the actual flooding took place.

Yet the preservationists realized the power of wild waterways and their surrounding scenery to galvanize public sympathy. In 1913, the same year that the Hetch Hetchy Dam was approved, voters in New York passed an amendment authorizing the use of up to 3 percent of Adirondack Forest Preserve land for reservoirs (Graham, 1978). The "Black River War," which resulted when Watertown tried to get a series of dams and reservoirs installed on the tributaries of the Black River, stirred the ire of a generation of Adirondack preservationists; the Echo Park Dam proposed for Dinosaur National Monument did the same on a national scale.

❧ The top of Mount Algonquin is fiercely cold. The wind chills hikers quickly. Yet this wet, cold, mountainous landscape draws many. The leaders of the preservation movement in the early to middle years of this century, besides Leopold, included Robert Marshall, Sigurd Olson, Howard Zahniser, and David Brower, and in the Adirondacks, John Apperson, Paul Schaefer, and others. Most spent time hiking the Adirondacks. Bob Marshall, zealous outdoorsman and outspoken defender of the wilderness, led the public movement for wilderness preservation in the early 1900s, both at the national level and in the Adirondacks. Bob Marshall's father, Louis Marshall, successfully defended Article 7, section 7, at the 1915 New York State Constitutional Convention. Bob spent his childhood summers at the family camp on Lower Saranac Lake; with a guide and his brother George, he climbed all forty-six peaks higher than four thousand feet in the Adirondacks.

After receiving his master's degree in forestry from Harvard, he developed his own philosophy of the value of wilderness, based in part on Freudian concepts of the need to break away from repressive civilization. Marshall valued the mental and physical well-being that he found in the mountains, as well as the challenge of adventure, and the peace, solitude, and freedom that the wilderness offered. He argued that the wilderness afforded "perhaps the best opportunity for . . . pure esthetic rapture." When asked how much wilderness was needed, he replied, "How many Brahms' symphonies do we need?" (Nash, 1982, p. 203).

In 1932, while taking a lunchtime break atop Mount Marcy, in the midst of a feat of climbing fourteen peaks in one day, Marshall met Paul Schaefer, an associate of John Apperson's in protecting the Adirondack wilderness. Schaefer enlisted Marshall's help in the pressing issues facing the Adirondacks: preservation versus the proposed construction of fire roads and cabins for tourists. Marshall, distressed about what had been happening in the East while he had been working in the West and in Alaska, reportedly told Schaefer, "We simply have to band together — all of us who love the wilderness. We must fight together — wherever and whenever wilderness is attacked" (Schaefer, 1989, p. 178). Three years later Marshall, Leopold, and others formed the Wilderness Society. Bob Marshall himself died suddenly at the age of thirty-eight. But his name and his hiking feats are still well known among Adirondack preservationists fifty years later as they seek to establish a new Bob Marshall Wilderness Area in the western Adirondacks. It is nicknamed simply "The Bob."

Paul Schaefer became the next leader in the Adirondack preservation movement, taking over from his mentor John Apperson. Schaefer fought against several proposed dams and reservoirs over a period of about forty years (Schaefer, 1989). One was the Black River Regulating District, authorized by the 1915 Machold Storage Law to enlarge the Stillwater Reservoir on the Beaver River. The enlargement flooded three thousand acres of the Forest Preserve but generated little protest, presumably because preservationists assumed that the 3 percent restriction under the 1913 amendment would be invoked against any further expansion.

After successfully fighting the proposed Higley Mountain Dam, also under the Black River Regulating District, Schaefer and others, including most of the preservation and sporting groups associated with the Adirondacks, banded together to fight the larger Panther Mountain Dam, which the governor supported. Eventually these groups took the fight to the state legislature, and in a referendum the people of New York voted overwhelmingly against an amendment that would have allowed a dam.

A new public valuation of wilderness for the sake of human spiritual and physical renewal was emerging. Yet challenges to the meaning and interpretation of the "forever wild" clause persisted throughout the 1940s, 1950s, and 1960s. Many preservationists believed that the strength of their cause lay in the ambiguous wording of the clause, and the fact that not every possible use was spelled out in detail (Graham, 1978). The ambiguity left much of the interpretation open to the strong sentiments of the preservationists. Challenges during these years included opposition to a titanium mine at Tahawus and its accompanying rail line, authorized during the Second World War; the controversy over cleaning up the huge tinderbox of dead trees created by the "Big Blowdown" of 1950; and the continuing debate over how to accommodate the increasing numbers of tourists.

During this period the Park's boundaries expanded to include, in 1972, just under 6 million acres, and the Forest Preserve itself expanded to 2,425,000 acres (Graham, 1978). Changes in the interpretation of the clause thus affected more wild forest land, and more small towns and hamlets within the Park, than ever before. The relation between the human and the wild became more complex and more publicly defined as groups with competing values hurried to define the Park's possible uses.

The National Emergency Act passed by the wartime government had pushed through construction of the titanium mine, despite its devastation of Lake Sanford, pollution from tailings, and diversion of the Hudson River (Graham, 1978). In 1959 the federal government expedited a plan for the Northway, a superhighway from Albany to Montreal, through the eastern part of the Adirondacks. Preservationists and conservationists compromised on the cleanup of the Blowdown; some, but not all, of the dead timber was cut and cleared, while the Adirondack Mountain Club monitored some of the salvage work (Brown, 1985).

❧ At the national level the preservation movement had taken on a new shape and was again redefining the human/nature relationship. The dream of Bob Marshall and others for a national wilderness plan was realized in 1964 as the National Wilderness Preservation Act. Howard Zahniser, president of the Wilderness Society, petitioned for the plan during the 1950s, and drafted the act, which was passed into law shortly after his death. Much of the writing was done at his cabin in the Adirondacks. Throughout his life Zahniser argued that the preservation of wilderness was not contrary to human civilization but a necessary part of any healthy culture, providing opportunities for the renewal of humanity's contact with the earth, from which all its cultures originated (Nash, 1982).

A businessman, intellectual, and outdoorsman, Zahniser, a friend of Paul Schaefer's, had early on bought a cabin in the Adirondacks. His family spent summer vacations there and went on hiking trips with the Schaefer family. Amazed by the size of the Forest Preserve, he quickly became its advocate. At the same time, he was fighting many wilderness preservation battles at the national level, including the proposed Echo Park Dam at Dinosaur National Monument.

Ranchers, lumbermen, miners, and many bureaucrats in the Forest Service bitterly opposed the wilderness bill, believing that it "locked up" valuable land in defiance of the multiple-use doctrine (Graham, 1978). The preservationists argued that multiple use did not mean that *all* land must be open to *all* uses, and that, indeed, some uses were incompatible. While many preservationists were disappointed with the compromises that had to be reached before the Wilderness Act could be signed into law, all recognized its significance for the remaining wilderness areas in the United States. Nine million acres were included in the act, with the provision that more was to be added over a ten-year review period. More important, for the first time a definition of wilderness was put forth as part of a federal law (Nash, 1982).

❧ During the 1960s the public's awareness of environmental issues was also increasing, shifting from an interest in preserving space for outdoor recreation, as well as aesthetic appreciation and spiritual values, to a concern for the health of the planet itself. Several events contributed to the public's understanding of our relation to the planet and our ability to foul and destroy our own environment; these included nuclear testing and the publication of Rachel Carson's *Silent Spring* in 1962.

In New York these changes in public thinking may have aided in the passage of the Adirondack Park Agency bill in 1971, when Governor Nelson Rockefeller was also implementing an austerity budget (Graham, 1978). Laurance Rockefeller, the governor's brother, had proposed the creation of an Adirondack National Park, an idea that was not well received by either the conservationists or the preservationists. It is worth noting that the Rockefeller family's estates in the Adirondacks total thousands of acres, making them among the largest private landowners in the Adirondack Park. After accepting the Conservation Department's report opposing the national park concept, the governor appointed a thirteen-member Temporary Study Commission on the Future of the Adirondacks to look into alternatives (E. Brown, 1985). Harold Hochschild, retired industry leader and founder of the Adirondack Museum, chaired the commission in its final year.

The commission published its report in December 1970. The first of 181 recommendations suggested the creation of an independent bipartisan Adirondack Park Agency with power over the use of private and public land in the park. Congressmen from upstate voiced their contituents' complaint that an agency and its regulations would lock up resources. But the bill passed, and the APA became effective September 1, 1971. The APA was to be run by a board of eleven commissioners, eight appointed by the governor, five of whom were to be legal residents, plus the commissioners of commerce and environmental conservation and the secretary of state. Governor Rockefeller appointed Richard W. Lawrance, Jr., a dedicated member of the Temporary Study Commission, as the chair, and Peter S. Paine, Jr., a New York City lawyer and another hardworking commissioner, as a member. Paine served on the board through the early 1990s.

Charges that the APA was an elitist agency favoring decisions that promoted the park as a "playground for the rich" came immediately from the local citizens. William Doolittle, editor of the *Adirondack Daily Enterprise*, the only daily newspaper in the Adirondacks, took a position critical of the APA almost from the start. But the anger that the citizens felt over what local government officials termed the loss of "home rule" crescendoed slowly (Graham, 1978).

During its first year the APA completed its mandated State Land Master Plan, which, after extensive surveying, divided state lands into eight categories. In the 1,034,935 acres deemed wilderness (areas over 10,000 acres in size without noticeable human intrusions), human traces including roads, summer camps, fire towers, ranger cabins, telephone lines, and truck trails were scheduled for eventual removal (E. Brown, 1985). The plan met with general approval, although the wilderness regulations later caused an uproar in particular cases. The governor accepted the plan in July 1972.

But the local furor reached fortissimo when the APA unveiled its Private Land Use and Development Plan in March 1973. In response to perceived and real threats to the "open space character of the park," including a proposed ten thousand–home development, complete with access roads, golf courses, and dams on the Grass River in an area with no zoning regulations (Graham, 1978), the plan divided private lands into six categories according to their ability to withstand use. "Hamlets" included the growth and service centers of the park, communities ranging from a few hundred to ten thousand residents. "Moderate Intensity Use" included land suitable for relatively intense development, usually near hamlets, and primarily residential in character. "Low Intensity Use" and "Rural Use" included areas intended for progressively lower levels of development. "Resource Management" lands were the most strictly limited; they included "those lands where the need to protect, manage and enhance forest, agricultural, recreational and open space resources is of paramount importance because of overriding natural resource and public considerations." "Industrial Use" included areas where "existing land uses are predominantly of an industrial or mineral extraction nature, or are identified by local and state officials as having potential for new industrial development" (APA Act).

In addition, the APA would have jurisdiction and regulatory authority over all development projects, both "Class A" (those having a regional impact or impact on a sensitive ecosystem such as a wetland) and "Class B" (those affecting only a local area, at least until the town government produced zoning regulations of its own, approved by the APA for Class B projects). Projects to be regulated included everything from opening a mom-and-pop business out of a home or building a garage or boathouse to the development of large subdivisions.

Legislators noted the outrage of the north country residents and public officials, and voted to delay the effective date of the bill for one year (E. Brown, 1985). The governor vetoed the delay, fearful that it would create a rush of development that would damage the Park forever. Compromises were made on shoreline restrictions, and on the creation of a Local Government Review Board to act as adviser and watchdog for the APA; the state also promised to freeze the levels of payments on state lands in lieu of taxes to local governments (E. Brown, 1985; Graham, 1978). The bill took effect August 1, 1973.

The conflict over land use in the Adirondacks quickly escalated into propaganda, insults, and violence. Developers, realtors, and lawyers sided with local citizens who objected to regulations that were often both stringent and ambiguous as well as to the lengthy project review process and the perceived elitism of the APA commissioners. Preservationists, including outside interest groups such as National Audubon Society and the Sierra Club, local groups including the Adirondack Mountain Club, the Adirondack Council, and the Association for the Protection of the Adirondacks, many second-home owners, and others supported the APA and the Private Land Use and Development Plan. Many others fell in between, accepting the need for some regulation but seeing the APA as too arbitrary, too divorced from the reality of local needs, and, at least in its early years, too harsh with small landowners.

Many conservationists, including some foresters and employees of the State Department of Environmental Conservation, felt that the "forever wild" concept was a mistake, or was acceptable only for a limited amount of land. As the state planned for the steady acquisition of more forestlands, which would automatically become part of the Forest Preserve and fall under the "forever wild" clause, many of those involved in the harvesting of natural resources felt that these resources were being "locked up," diminishing the economic resource base of the towns inside the park boundaries.

Anthony D'Elia, eventually chosen to head the Local Government Review Board, was an industrial designer and teacher who bought the rundown Loon Lake resort, where five presidents had stayed, with hopes of developing its 3,500 acres into 850 homesites and 2,100 acres of communal property. A member of the Sierra Club for ten years, he welcomed the APA at first. But after preparing two master plans and impact studies for the APA, at a personal cost of well over $100,000, he was eventually forced into bankruptcy. Turning completely against the agency, he helped to organize, along with Will Doolittle (then editor of the *Adirondack Daily Enterprise*) and Ruth Newberry, the League for Adirondack Citizens' Rights. In his book *The Adirondack Rebellion*, D'Elia describes the "civil rebellion" of the mid-1970s which adapted its symbols and slogans from the American Revolution (D'Elia, 1979).

D'Elia and many others felt that the APA was denying local control over land use planning and, worse, really represented an attempt to gain for the state through regulation the land it could not acquire through purchase. Thus, the establishment of the APA was a violation, in their eyes, of the "due process" clause of the Fourteenth Amendment. Many believed that the regulations restricting development on their land constituted a taking without compensation, and as such violated the Fifth Amendment, which states: "Nor shall private property be taken for public use, without just compensation."

❧ In the early years of the 1990s the takings issue spread from state to state as rural landowners and others contested government regulations limiting their use of their own lands without compensation.

Perhaps even more distressing, and certainly more of a biting insult to local people in the Adirondacks, was their lack of representation on the APA Board of Commissioners, who decided which projects would pass and which would not. Although the governor was supposed to have appointed five legal residents to the committee, many of his choices were not perceived by locals to be representative residents. The difference between a legal resident, who might have been living in the Adirondacks for as little as a year, and a person indigenous to the area, who had experienced the hardships of living in the region and shared at least some of the values, beliefs, and attitudes toward land use management expressed by other long-term residents, can be considerable.

Many longtime residents label themselves "Adirondackers," and, consistent with the notion of a cohesive culture, term new residents newcomers or outsiders. Some local people suggested that the APA staff and resident commissioners might gradually become Adirondackers, accepted in the community, as the state's game wardens had been several decades earlier (D'Elia, 1979). But many Adirondackers keenly felt that their own voices had been ignored, their knowledge of the area rejected, and their ability to make intelligent decisions slighted.

And so the battle has continued, with preservationists both inside and outside the park feeling that the issue is that of defining proper protection for a fragile and beautiful land and the biodiversity represented in its ecosystems, and the local people feeling that, regardless of their own concerns for the land they live on, the issues are those of civil rights, regulation without representation, and class oppression. The protests were submerged during the 1980s, but reemerged in 1989 and 1990, when the Governor's Commission on the Adirondacks in the Twenty-First Century released its recommendations.

Criticizing the APA, conservation writer Frank Graham wrote in 1978: "Land-use regulation at present remains less the supervision of a well-ordered, long-range plan, than the coming to grips each day with a new crisis" (Graham, 1978, p. 274). Several of the current commissioners voiced the same concern to me in interviews in 1990. Yet, as the largest area of private land managed under a land use commission, the Adirondacks are under close scrutiny from planners, developers, and preservationists all over the country. The region's management could represent, for the areas where human and wild communities interlock, either a blueprint for the future or a model of a public relations disaster.

The Last Twenty Years: From Earth First! to Wise Use

Across America, songbirds were dying, and eagles could not sit on their eggs. Mothers in parts of Michigan were counseled not to breast-feed their babies because of high levels of PCB's discovered in breast milk. Mohawks on a reservation near the Adirondacks, including at least eighty families dependent on subsistence fishing, were told by the New York State Health Department that eating even a few fish a year could threaten their health, and mothers there were also counseled not to breast-feed. Oil spills were destroying coastal fisheries, killing fish and wildlife, and leaving ugly black slicks on the beaches. By the late 1970s, the disruption of the most fundamental processes of reproduction and subsistence, combined with urban alienation from the natural environment, as well as disenchantment with government policies and private transnational corporations perceived to be responsible for despoiling the earth, were creating a widespread public social and environmental movement.

The gurus included David Brower, poets Wendell Berry and Gary Snyder, and activists Paul Watson and Dave Foreman. Brower, Watson, and Foreman all began with mainstream environmental groups, the Sierra Club, Greenpeace (which became increasingly mainstream in the 1980s), and the Wilderness Society, respectively. These groups emphasized the traditional goals of the older environmental movement, such as increasing opportunities for wilderness recreation, solitude, and aesthetic appreciation, bolstered by concerns for maintaining biodiversity and the overall health of the environment in the face of human-created disasters such as oil spills, toxic waste, acid rain, and global warming.

As suburbs and roadways multiplied, these groups campaigned for stepped-up state and federal acquisition of wilderness areas, as well as wilderness classification of some existing public lands. Wilderness preservation issues spawned lobbies in Congress, legal battles in the courts, hundreds of publications devoted to environmental issues, and action groups across the country. Greenpeace began as a radical environmental group staging attention-grabbing protests against nuclear testing in their ship the *Rainbow Warrior.* The group gradually widened its focus to encompass whaling, the slaughter of seals, the fate of endangered species, and threatened ecosystems everywhere, through peaceful protests and passive resistance. It now has an international following numbering in the millions, justifying its inclusion as mainstream, its radical tactics receiving the approval of a significant public audience. Yet Brower, Watson, Foreman, and others were dissatisfied with the mainstream environmental groups' willingness to compromise and the limits on what they were able to accomplish.

A more radical environmental movement, rejecting the model of reformist environmental groups, has evolved since the late 1970s. Beginning as small underground action groups, this movement, including Earth First! and Paul Watson's Sea Shepherds, now generates both support and hostility in the general public (Nash, 1989). Both the more mainstream environmental groups and the Earth First! and Sea Shepherd movements have many members who adhere to the philosophy of deep ecology; for Earth First! and Sea Shepherds it is a founding tenet. First mentioned by a Norwegian philosopher, Nazi resister, and mountaineer, Arne Naess, in a 1972 lecture, deep ecology found a ready audience in the United States. Since Aldo Leopold, no publicly known philosopher had taken the extension of natural rights to such extremes in its implications. The legal system had been advancing along the frontier of the idea, through Christopher Stone's 1971 essay "Should Trees have Standing?" Stone rushed the proofs to Supreme Court Justice William O. Douglas on the eve of *Sierra Club v. Morton,* a case involving the development of the Mineral King Valley in the Sierras. Douglas cited the essay on the first page of his dissenting opinion, which "implied that many other forms of life, including ecosystems, had rights that people ought to respect . . . but humans, as the most articulate of these life-forms, must . . . 'speak for the entire ecological community' " (Nash, 1989, p. 131).

The extension of rights to the "ecological community," which many proponents defended by using the metaphor of the abolitionists' education of their peers to the evils of slavery, required that humans recognize their place as "plain member and citizen" of the community. Deep ecology took

76 the final step. No longer was the human role one of stewardship, for "stewardship" implied superiority to the ecological community and the right to manage it, however carefully, to serve human needs.

Two related perspectives have also emerged in the last two decades: the Gaia theory and bioregionalism. British atmospheric chemist James Lovelock proposed the Gaia idea in 1972. He later summarized the concept in his book *The Ages of Gaia:* "The atmosphere, the oceans, the climate, and the crust of the Earth are regulated at a state comfortable for life because of the behavior of living organisms. . . . Homeostasis is maintained by active feedback processes operated automatically and unconsciously by the biota" (Lovelock, 1988, p. 19). This hypothesis led to the theory that the earth is a giant living, breathing organism which self-regulates on a global scale. Lovelock borrowed the name the ancient Greeks had used for the nurturing earth goddess to illustrate his point that the earth as superorganism has a right to exist, building on the health of its individual parts. Polluting a river is like damaging an artery of the earth. Lovelock argues that his theory provides a basis for biocentric activism. But at the same time Gaia is not perceived to be static but is constantly evolving *as a whole* to self-regulate compatibly with changing conditions (Lovelock, 1988).

Bioregionalism, as Kirkpatrick Sale defines it in his book *Dwellers in the Land*, begins with a spiritual appreciation for the implications of the Gaia theory. Returning to the sense of awe, wonder, and humility that ancient cultures all over the world showed toward the nurturing earth goddess — whether called Gaia, Nammu, Cybele, Astarte, Ashtoreth, Athar, Isis, or other names — Sale argues, modern humans are recovering this ancient understanding through a combination of an increasingly global perspective, the insights of science, and public information such as the pictures of the earth taken from the moon. The paradigm outlined by Sale focuses on the bioregion, defined as a "life-territory, a place defined by its life forms, its topography and its biota, rather than by human dictates." He believes that people should become intimately acquainted with the land they live on, understand the local ecosystems and the cultures based on them, and learn their lore. The bioregion can then be developed according to its potential and its carrying capacity. Whether living in the Pacific Northwest rain forest or in the Adirondacks, people should try to live within the ecosystem's limits (Sale, 1985, p. 43).

Deep ecology, the Gaia theory, and bioregionalism have spawned a range of ecophilosophers and activists who use these basic intuitions and principles to structure their own response to the environmental destruction they see around them. Their activism involves tactics from simplifying their material possessions to live more gently on the earth, writing essays in academic journals or underground newspapers, and filing lawsuits to public education, protests, passive resistance, and even "ecotage" — destroying or damaging equipment used in the exploitation of natural resources.

The tactic of "monkeywrenching," as illustrated in Edward Abbey's 1975 novel *The Monkey Wrench Gang,* complete with an environmental messiah, has been adopted by Earth First!, although divisions exist within the movement over the dangerous practice of tree-spiking and other forms of sabotage. One incident resulting in a near-fatal injury to a sawmill operator has caused many in the movement to consider as unethical any practices potentially dangerous to humans. They also claim that damaging property involves a higher ethics than that conceived in law; the ethical extension implicit in biocentrism makes property claims invalid, the activists believe, if the destruction of nature is involved. The movement thus claims to use tactics that are not amoral or immoral but on a higher moral plane than contemporary property law. Activists often cite the example of the abolitionists and the illegal Underground Railroad, whereby individuals helped in the release of other people's legal "property."

Max Oelschlager in *The Idea of Wilderness* contrasts deep ecology and biocentrism with mainstream preservationism: "From an ecocentric or biocentric point of view, preservationism remains anthropocentric, since human interests are the ultimate arbiters of value" (Oelschlager, 1991, p. 292). Jim Cheney criticizes the radical environmental movement as neo-Stoic, analogous to the Stoic philosophers' advocacy of a retreat to city-states when the larger civilization was collapsing (Cheney, 1990). Others have criticized the deep ecology movement as overly concerned with wilderness preservation as opposed to global environmental issues, and as insensitive to the needs of Third World countries and the poor and disenfranchised in industrialised countries (Guha, 1989).

A large body of critical difference from yet solidarity with the deep ecology movement has arisen from the perspective of ecofeminism. Ynestra King, Charlene Spretnak, and other ecofeminists argue that deep ecologists focus on anthrocentrism versus biocentrism, when they should be focusing on *andro*centrism, the patriarchal system that created the culture/nature dualism that in their view has resulted in the oppression of nature as well as women, people of color, and indigenous cultures. Many deep ecologists claim to use feminist perspectives to focus on the need to nurture and care for the earth; yet most deep ecology writers are male, and use metaphors that explicitly and vividly underline their conception of the earth as female: mother, sister, wife, daughter (King, 1990; Spretnak, 1990).

Dave Foreman, one of the founders of Earth First!, writes in his autobiography, *Confessions of an Eco-Warrior,* "Ever since the Earth goddesses of ancient Greece were supplanted by the macho Olympians, repression of women and Earth has gone hand in hand with imperial organization" (Foreman, 1991, p. 21). Ecofeminists agree (Diamond and Orenstein, 1990), yet align themselves *with* the earth rather than as (male) humans separate from the earth and thus in a relationship of duality with it. Expressions such as "virgin forests" and "rape of the earth" emphasize the femaleness of the earth metaphors as well as the maleness of what human actors, men or women, inflict upon the earth. Self-proclaimed "eco-warriors" believe that their job is to *protect* the earth. Often this means, to environmental groups from the Sierra Club to Earth First!, closing the wilderness off from human impact.

Thus, while embracing organicism, biocentrism, and the notion of humans as a part of the ecological community, paradoxically many of the most radical (male) environmentalists are maintaining a Cartesian/Newtonian duality, though romanticized, at the level of language and metaphor. Metaphors are often windows on the subconscious (Lakoff and Johnson, 1980); it may be fair to ask whether the biocentrists and environmental activists have really changed that much from the early Judaeo-Christian tradition outlined at the beginning of this chapter, which emphasized *man's* dominant role over the earth, its flora and fauna, and the role of the earth as an object to be managed and exploited for its resources.

Gifford Pinchot put these values into practice as scientific forestry; greedier corporations and industrialists plundered nature's resources with less self-control. The environmentalists responded as chivalrous men seeking to protect a female earth. As in the tradition of romanticism, the alternative forms of the male/female and human/nature relationship encompass the extremes of the other defiled and reviled or worshipped and protected. In either situation, the relationship focuses on qualities of superiority and inferiority and its inverse.

Carolyn Merchant explores the underlying analogy between women and the earth in *The Death of Nature: Women, Ecology, and the Scientific Revolution* (1983). From preliterate societies in ancient times to postmodern society, the earth has been designated as female, the fountainhead of fecundity, nurture, and sustenance. As later urban civilizations developed and drew farther and farther away from the natural world, the analogy developed:

civilization is to nature as man is to woman. When scientists moved from the concept of organicism to the concept of mechanism, there was no longer any particular reason to respect and revere either nature or women. Their mysterious life-giving force was completely explicated; it was just a mechanism that could be taken apart and exploited, a resource to use and to be harnessed to man's civilizing works.

Nature, like femaleness, was seen as disordered, wild, out of control, physically reproductive, and ultimately inferior; culture, like maleness, was seen as ordered, civilized, controlled, mentally productive, and ultimately superior (Merchant, 1983). While deep ecologists have denied charges of Cartesian duality in their thinking about nature, their definition of wilderness as a place without the influence of "man" reveals a deeply entrenched form of the nature/culture dichotomy. Men are separate from the femaleness of nature, and function as its protectors and defenders. At the same time that they adhere to the idea of humans as part of the land community, the deep ecologists see the most natural communities, wilderness areas, as those where humans are not present, or at least leave no traces.

In contrast, the ecofeminists believe that relations of complementarity rather than superiority and inferiority between culture and nature, the human and nonhuman, male and female, are desirable (Oelschlager, 1991). Some ecofeminists have criticized biocentrism for remaining androcentric in extending male rights to the nonhuman other: "Biocentrism . . . fails to include moral categories that arise from a feminine experience of self and world. The experience of relatedness reported by many women gives rise to a morality of caring for the concrete needs of those with whom one is related" (Michael Zimmerman, quoted in Oelschlager, 1991, p. 312). Whether or not one accepts the tenets of ecofeminism, the model of a human/nature relationship based on mutuality and interdependence provides a useful alternative to models of exploitation on the one hand and romantic worship and protection on the other.

🐚 In a 1990 "Forum" in *Harper's*, Michael Pollan, the executive editor of the magazine, Daniel Botkin, professor of biology and environmental studies, Dave Foreman, cofounder of Earth First!, James Lovelock, Frederick Turner, Founders Professor of Arts and Humanities at the University of Texas, and Robert D. Yaro, senior vice president of the Regional Plan Association in New York City, discussed the theme "Beyond the wilderness": whether wilderness must be kept intact or "managed" to retain its wildness; and whether humans should be a part of that ecosystem.

Pollan writes in the introduction: "The ongoing public conversation about the environment is grounded in the ancient dichotomy of man versus nature. . . . [Some] say that we must radically change the conversation and begin to talk not of man *versus* nature but of man *and* nature" (Pollan, 1990, p. 39). He gives the example of Tabernacle Pines in Connecticut, a grove of ancient trees destroyed in a hurricane. The virgin grove contained trees more than 150 feet tall, but was isolated from ecologically similar stands. What should be done? he asks. Should the Nature Conservancy clear and replant it, or leave it alone?

Foreman counsels against clearing and replanting, arguing that after trees fall, they provide as much or more service to the life around them as they did when they were standing. He says, "Nature is not a pretty, manicured place maintained for human beings. It is a dynamic continuum, often a violent one."

Lovelock points out that since the grove was isolated, it would have been a kind of garden anyway. But had the land been surrounded by other forested areas, he would have agreed with Foreman. Turner disagrees, arguing that human intervention is also natural. It would be a violation of nature to leave the people out. "Humankind is what nature has been trying for, all these millennia," he says.

Botkin would let the area grow back through the same stages of succession that the pilgrims observed: "This means gardening the forest and weeding out the exotics." Yaro argues that the landscape of Connecticut is as artificial as Central Park in New York City — a human creation. He would leave Tabernacle Pines alone so that people could learn about the natural processes that shape their landscape. With such radically different perspectives on the role of humanity in the human/nature relationship, the participants eventually come to an impasse. Foreman argues: "Our environmental problems originate in the hubris of imagining ourselves as the central nervous system or the brain of nature. We are not the brain, we are a cancer on nature." Turner replies: "The nervous system is a glorious cancer that has evolved and I stand with it. I am that cancer." Foreman answers: "And I am the antibody" (Pollan, 1990, pp. 38–48).

Pollan continues the discussion in his 1991 book, *Second Nature,* where he argues that we must "garden" nature to retain its naturalness, because "chance and contingency are everywhere in nature" (Pollan, 1991, p. 184). Nature is historical, turning on luck, rather than stable, logical, and ahistorical. Ecosystems themselves are more of a hypothesis than a reality; their boundaries are poorly understood, he says. Our own role as members of nature is complicated because — by chance — we gained the power to reason. We are "second nature." Pollan contends that "nature" is dead: "The old idea may have taught us how to worship nature but it didn't tell us how to live with her. It told us more than we needed to know about virginity and rape, and almost nothing about marriage" (Pollan, 1991, p. 189). He argues for taking up man's natural role as gardener, weeding and managing the earth to protect its most positive natural aspects. In essence, Pollan is saying that the anthropocentric *is* biocentric; yet he often seems to be missing the point of what preservationists from Muir to Brower have seen as the primary value of wilderness: its wildness.

Bill McKibben, writing from the Adirondacks, discusses the issue in *The End of Nature* (1989) with none of Pollan's optimism. He sees the end of nature as an actuality, not just a metaphoric shift. Humans have created environmental problems to such an extent that no place on earth is without them. Human management of nature — through wilderness parks, genetic "banks," and biotechnology — has effectively ended the naturalness of nature. The deepest tragedy for him lies in the philosophical sea change from a world in which humans could look to something more powerful and more mysterious than themselves to one in which humans are the only standard. The notion of being caretakers of a managed world, "custodians" of all life, depresses him deeply. He argues that only by keeping humans apart from nature can we see nature return to independent functioning.

The dichotomies between the human and the natural, and between a human/nature relationship based on dominion and one based on protective worship and aesthetic appreciation, are in fact deepened by the wilderness preservation focus of the radical environmental movement and the mainstream environmental movement. Women, through their roles as mothers and family caretakers, and through traditional subsistence practices, can offer a different perspective on the human/nature relationship, a perspective that opens a window on the relationships of indigenous people to the land.

Women's relations with nature have often developed from a very specific kind of experience with nature and wilderness. In rural areas, according to pioneer journals and accounts by twentieth-century farm women, contact with the natural world could be as mundane as picking berries side by side with bears and birds. Women have washed clothes and babies in creeks, gathered herbs and greens to feed and heal their families, plants for dyes, firewood. They have constituted an edge species foraging the clearings and the new growth that springs up after a clear-cut or a fire. Conquering mountains was largely out of the question; the babies and children they were taking care of could not walk that far, and chores could not wait.

Other women were painting and writing about the environment — not always in the large scale of the sublime but on the canvas of the close-at-hand, as depicted in Mary Austin's and Annie Dillard's work. What emerges from women's understanding of nature is a sense of intimacy, an interrelatedness that has in fact moved women toward mutuality. The old Papago woman in Gary Nabhan's *Gathering the Desert* (1985) collects wild devil's claw for baskets and plants the seeds of the varieties she favors, but lets them grow up wild. Ginseng is more potent in its wild form; harvesters in Appalachia have traditionally left the best wild roots to regenerate. Among the Dogon of West Africa, women toss the seeds of the baobab on the dump heap and transplant the emerging sapling to the wild. Perhaps what is needed is not Pollan's gardening metaphor, in which man is a second nature "gardening" first nature to restore a human conception of naturalness, but instead the coexistence model of women's and indigenous peoples' traditional intimacy and interdependence with nature.

In this light, "wilderness" is a male-defined concept of the unviolated female earth, a notion necessary in a world based on a relationship of domination and extraction. In a world in which violation plays no part of the definition of the human/nature relationship, the kind of protection that excludes humans would play no part either.

❧ Preservation is necessary to maintain the biological diversity and stability of the earth, as society exists now, yet as a concept it denies the fundamental interrelatedness of the human/nature relationship and blocks subsistence use by poor, indigenous, and local peoples. Resource-based jobs are necessarily affected. When preservation fails to address socioeconomic inequality exacerbated by putting some of the available land base off-limits, it becomes a force in class, race, and gender oppression.

Ramachandra Guha criticizes the American deep ecology and radical environmental movements for disregarding the concerns of Third World peoples. She charges that the implementation of a wilderness agenda is causing serious deprivation. In comparing the American movement to the German Greens and environmental movements in India, she points out the American preoccupation with wilderness preservation. The Greens, by contrast, challenge industrial society to accept environmental limits to economic growth and argue that such growth in the West has historically rested on the economic and ecological exploitation of the Third World. India's environmental movements involve grassroots resistance to nonsustainable demands placed on the land base by urban centers and industry. Guha outlines two features that distinguish the Indian movements from their Western counterparts: "First, for the sections of society most critically affected by environmental degradation — poor and landless peasants, women, and tribals — it is a question of sheer survival, not of enhancing the quality of life. Second, and as a consequence, the environmental solutions they articulate deeply involve questions of equity as well as economic and political redistribution" (Guha, 1989, p. 81).

"Locking up" some land as a means of wilderness preservation may be necessary so that some large corporations do not commit further atrocities. But it must be combined with a positive value for human beings. By caring for people at the individual level, we respect our integrity as a moral species. It is thus not acceptable, as some deep ecologists propose, to refuse to help famine victims in Africa, or to ignore the needs of local Adirondackers in order to "protect" more acres of their homeland. When the bipolar human/ nature relationship of domination or protection approaches either extreme, resulting in the destruction of wildlands on the one hand or "locking up" the land and its resources from human contact on the other, it is the people who are in the positions of most direct intimacy and daily interdependence with the wild who suffer most.

Because the preservation movement in the United States has failed to address issues of political and socioeconomic inequity, its escalation of activity has loosed a backlash across rural America. As the environmental movement has grown and expanded to include the radical groups Earth First! and the Sea Shepherds, they have moved preservation issues to the level of campaign and litigation, and even, in the case of the radical groups, sabotage and violent confrontation.

Elements of the public, including many rural people dependent on natural resources, people with natural resource–based jobs, and companies involved in resource extraction have organized around resource use and related economic concerns. Many rural people think that their way of life, their very ability to continue to live in rural areas, is threatened (Lee, 1994). The Wise Use movement claims to speak for these divergent groups.

The movement is based on a wide-ranging interpretation of Gifford Pinchot's classic phrase "wise use of natural resources," which played a prominent part in the foundation of conservationism. Extractive and recreational industries including Exxon, Homestakes Mining, the Motorcycle

Industry Council, Chevron USA, Kawasaki, Yamaha, and even the Reverend Sun Myung Moon's Unification Church have backed and helped fund the Wise Use Movement, which the Oregon Natural Resource Council in its newsletters calls "an industry-funded 'grass roots' movement."

The Wise Use perspective, while not accepted by all movement affiliates, adds a powerful freedom of interpretation to the human side of the human/nature relationship. Adirondack home rule advocates have affiliated themselves with the Wise Use movement through membership in the Alliance for America, a national coalition of 125 related groups and the local Solidarity Alliance (Pendley, 1994). Others hesitate to join the alliance but support its efforts. Paradoxically, the Wise Use movement, which seems to many rural people to be supportive of their local natural resource–based economies, is being backed and encouraged by some of the industries that perpetuate destruction of the environment. This destruction ultimately results in the loss of jobs locally, as is happening in the forests of the Pacific Northwest, and in increased economic disparity. In Brazil and elsewhere, preservation efforts include basic usufruct and extractive rights for local or indigenous populations. But so far in the United States, preservation has meant keeping the people, and their needs, out.

In addition, the polarization of the environmental and natural resource debates between extremes willing to escalate the conflict to violent confrontation has led to a further breakdown in communication between the different worldviews. Many who may not agree completely with the tenets of Wise Use or Earth First! have allied themselves with one of these movements in the absence of other possibilities for making their own distinct voices heard.

Charles Cushman, a Wise Use leader and head of the National Inholders Association, describes the conflicts between the environmental and Wise Use movements: "It's a holy war between fundamentally different religions. . . . The preservationists are worshipping trees and animals and sacrificing people" (Donnelly, 1993, p. 15).

Religious perspectives play a greater role than the literature on land use conflict and the human/nature relationship has generally acknowledged. Many Christians and people of other traditional faiths feel that environmental extremists have reverted to a pagan earth worship that minimizes the moral responsibility of human beings toward one another. The "lifeboat" ethics of some radical environmentalists who proposed not to help people suffering under extreme poverty in the countries of the South both ignored the North's collusion in their suffering and contributed to this perception of radical environmentalists as misanthropic. Christians and many other traditionalists in communities rooted in the land believe in biblical and other oral and written texts' mandates for good stewardship of the earth. Yet, while only a small portion of the traditional religious groups have allowed the Wise Use Movement to speak for them, the Wise Use Movement has appropriated Christian theology, often out of context, as a moral expression of its agenda.

Interpretation of biblical stewardship ranges from dominion theology to a deep spiritual bond with the earth. The Amish believe that they should give proper toil, nourishment, and rest to the soil. The soil has a spiritual significance to them, and human stewardship over it is continuous, ending in a day of reckoning when humans will be called to give an account to God (Hostetler, 1993, p. 114). Amish farms now have some of the richest soils in America. And again, in a misunderstanding that only serves to demonstrate the ever-widening rift between the specialized scientific community and the public, people in some communities believe that all scientists who speak of evolution do so out of a mechanistic understanding of nature that denies the existence of God. Yet in many of these communities, farmers operate their daily business with a comprehension of nature as an organic whole (including natural selection) that would have pleased Aldo Leopold. Such apparently deep value differences prohibit all but the most superficial of conversations unless both sides are committed to exploring their differences and mutual interests, taking time and patience to understand one another. Although I am not able to treat this subject adequately in this book, it would greatly behoove natural scientists to rethink the way they present information to the public if they wish to collaborate in any meaningful joint management efforts.

The recognition not only of nature's right to exist but also of human intimacy and interconnectedness with the earth could restructure our view of the human/nature relationship into one in which social equity and ecological health coexist. For instruction in interdependence, it helps to look to the land use patterns of indigenous peoples and local people living close to the forests, including Adirondackers — especially those who live and work in daily intimacy with wildlands.

Woods and Woodspeople

Introduction

IN THE CONFLICT OVER LAND USE IN THE
Adirondack Park, various groups of people negotiate for representation of their views, and struggle to control at least some of the decisions. The government bureaus — the Adirondack Park Agency, which
manages private lands within the park, and the Department of Environmental Conservation, which manages the public forest lands — ultimately control the decision making. But their decisions are influenced by the groups
both inside and outside the park that are lobbying for different land use
management strategies. Some favor protective, preservation-oriented mea-
sures. Others favor conservation with some extraction. Still others lobby
for greater freedom to develop the area. Many others promote special interests. A clamor of voices arises in the press, in letters to the editor, in
publications, in public meetings, and in other forums. Yet the voices of one
group go virtually unheard, a group that is scattered and without the money
or the access to information technology to participate in aggressive lobbying. Paradoxically, this is the group of people that spends the most time
in the woods, and knows local places intimately, through the seasons and
through generations. Their silence in the controversy over Adirondack land

use constitutes one of the greatest losses of this kind of interest group politics; the indigenous knowledge of the land and the forests which members of this group possess, and their connection to both land and local communities, put them in a unique position of understanding what kinds of management could work best. I interviewed members of this group in the hope that others might then recognize their potential role as mediators in the conflict — mediators who could show how people can live *with* the forest because this is what they do.

It is as difficult to categorize and label the group of people I interviewed as it is to impose boundaries on running water. They are not statistically definable or describable through generalizations, since all of them make individual and deeply personal bargains with the woods. They are not "forest products" people, because their contracts with the forests reach deeper than that. They are not simply harvesters of natural resources, because they also manage, manipulate, and change the natural environment at times. Nor can they be defined as those who make a living from the woods, because that category includes myriads of tourist industry workers and others who may rarely set foot in a forest.

Instead, I would call them woodspeople, as they call themselves. They include those whose lives and livelihoods immerse them in the forest — the guides, trappers, hunters, fishermen, loggers, maple syrup producers, boat builders, craftspeople, and others who are the repositories of their communities' indigenous knowledge of the woods. Many have multiple occupations based on this knowledge and experience. The local people know who they are and value them for what they know, believing that somehow these woodspeople represent the distilled qualities of what is most "Adirondack" in Adirondack culture.

It is easy enough to find such people. I asked local residents with whom I had established some level of trust who the people are who know the woods. Most of these woodspeople were named by several sources; their identity as bearers of knowledge about the woods is firmly established. Yet they are a heterogeneous group — men and women, old and young, natives and a few who moved here years ago. But by and large they are not the professors, professionals, specialists, and others who read a great deal about the woods. Instead they spend time, loads of it, in the woods. Their knowledge thus differs qualitatively from that of the scientist.

Indigenous knowledge has been defined as the "accumulated knowledge and traditional skills and technology" of a people, culture, or subculture

(Brokensha, Warren, and Werner, 1980, p. 1). The woodspeople are recognized specialists in indigenous knowledge about the forest. It is their job to retain, refine, and expand this knowledge and convey it to the next generation of Adirondackers. Indigenous knowledge may not translate smoothly into the observations of "objective" science; yet it is based on many accurate observations of ecological systems. Interaction between indigenous knowledge systems and scientific systems can benefit both, because each has different strengths and weaknesses (Awa, 1989; DeWalt, 1994). Whether or not the indigenous observations of the Adirondacks fit exactly with the observations of scientists, recognition of this knowledge should include an understanding of its validity as a *system* that operates within the worldview of a particular culture or group.

In the indigenous knowledge of maple sugaring, logging, trapping, crafting, and so on, the overriding paradigm is "Whatever works." Yet there is a tacit understanding about the positive role of humans in the human/ nature relationship which allows holders of indigenous knowledge to explore interactions between humans and nature, as well as the essence of nature itself.

Although it does not use fixed paradigms and strict scientific methods, indigenous knowledge in the Adirondacks and elsewhere is based on careful and exact observation. Its hypothesis testing is driven by both practical needs (Hunn, 1982) and intellectual curiosity (C. Brown, 1985). It uses intuition-guided experimentation which is stochastic in nature and rooted in a concept of knowledge based on *relationships* rather than isolated specialization. It is fundamentally ecological as much as taxonomic. Whether the pear thrip will destroy a maple stand is the key question to which knowledge of the pear thrip life cycle contributes.

It is the relationships which matter in a practical sense and also in a spiritual sense. Mythologies tend to be about ongoing relationships, between Rabbit and Coyote, for example, rather than about the distinctions between Coyote and a red wolf. It is not the gypsy moth itself that is important to understand, but rather why and when and how it eats the trees, and which trees it will eat. It is not Coyote alone that is "good to think" but rather the relationship of Coyote and Rabbit, and of Coyote the trickster to the efforts of humans to make sense of their world.

Few anthropologists would want to deny the intellectual curiosity and creative abilities of indigenous people by assigning to their thinking purely utilitarian goals. Yet when social scientists measure their knowledge by skill in classification, they miss the point. Western academic science, with enough money to pay for specialists to study one species or subspecies and dissect it genetically, will clearly score higher in the differentiation of species. Scientists may also make classifications based on goals and objectives that differ from those of local people (Awa, 1989). For example, even while adopting modern agricultural inputs, Andean potato farmers maintain high levels of genetic diversity in their potato crops as a matter of choice for cultural reasons; consumption preferences and patterns play a key role (Brush, 1992). Mende farmers in West Africa emphasize imagination and inventiveness in agricultural transformation; experimentation with different varieties is intellectually stimulating as well as potentially rewarding economically. The farmers are interested in varieties developed by scientists, often experimenting out of curiosity or even "for fun," but they choose what to plant from the spectrum of indigenous and scientific varieties according to their own rationales (Richards, 1989).

Biology and ecology have to do with relationships that go beyond individual taxonomies. Whereas taxonomy itself describes relationships in a genealogical, evolutionary sense, these relations tend to offer tunnel views and fragments. Biological scientists themselves will tell you that while they study bears, for instance, they also notice the red squirrels and nuthatches; while they study trout and their relations with their predators and prey, the scientists also notice the crayfish scuttling on the bottom, the pickerelweed, blue in the swampy edge of the lake, and the clouds of trillium growing in the acid soil under the pines. These observations are not so different from those of an expert local fisherman or guide. Yet these "irrelevant" details rarely make it into the scientific reports.

The indigenous knowledge bearer or woodsperson is naturalistic in attitude and holistic in thought. Relationships make sense in the larger whole. Understanding an ecosystem allows one to interpret smaller facts within it. Fine details such as the timing of spring turnover in a lake, which brings trout to the surface, make sense in a wider trend of warming. An increase in cancers in animals, as hunters, trappers, and fishermen observe, or the reduction in the number of migratory songbirds makes sense as part of a process. When trapper Nellie Staves says about her ability to find animals, "I know where to look," she means that she understands animals in context — in their relations to geologic formations, plant communities, other animals, and their own life cycle and daily habits. The different strands of her knowledge of relationships coalesce into a pattern; she sees the animal where it ought to be.

Maple producers hypothesize about which trees will produce more sap or sweeter sap (Tucker and Tucker, 1989). Their experimentation is directed by the exigencies of practical conservatism as well as scientific conservatism. If an experiment is not working, they may quickly change tack and try a different direction. It is doubtful that a producer would risk the whole crop on a single hypothesis.

In some ways, biological scientists and woodspeople function remarkably alike in the forest: both make observations, though the scientists' are more often written down; both construct experiments, though the scientists' are more strictly defined; both base their experiments on experience, intuition, and questions that are both practically and intellectually motivated, though in each case different motives are emphasized to the outside world; both become increasingly aware of the connections that bind the elements of the natural world together. Many times information is shared between them.

But the end products differ. For the biological scientist, the results of an experiment must be measured, quantified, interpreted, and reported. Science generally requires a narrow focus. "Irrelevant" data, such as nuthatches in a report on bear hibernation, are dropped from professional journals, remaining only in the back of the scientist's mind, where they may shape the intuition that guides other experiments. For the woodsperson, the results of experiments are also measured and quantified, but interpretation and reporting take the form of economic success: Did he or she trap enough of the animals whose pelts currently bring a high price? Did the maple syrup sell, and did market value bring in enough to cover costs? Did the guide take the fishermen to the right spots often enough? The information the woodsperson gathers accumulates in his or her mind; and as anecdotal exchanges and the basis for teaching the next generation of woodspeople, this information becomes part of the pool of indigenous knowledge available to the culture.

Unfortunately, this knowledge is often devalued or seen as illegitimate in scientific circles. Agricultural researcher Robert Chambers, who works with farmers in international participatory research, writes: "Modern scientific knowledge is centralized and associated with the machinery of state; and those who are its bearers believe in its superiority. Indigenous technical knowledge, in contrast, is scattered and associated with low-prestige rural life; even those who are its bearers may believe it to be inferior. It is difficult for some scientists to accept that they have anything to learn from rural people, or to recognize that there is a parallel system of knowledge to their own which is complementary, usually valid and in some respects superior" (Chambers, 1987, p. 33).

But the point is not only how much, or what, any group knows about the wildland around its community, but rather the way of thinking, the view of the forest that focuses that knowledge, sharpens it to the point of a decision about the interaction between the people and the wildland. These values and the knowledge, both scientific and indigenous, that is available in a community are what shape the human/nature relationship.

❧ The following three chapters present three different kinds of indigenous knowledge of the forest: loggers' knowledge; the knowledge of crafters and hunters, trappers and gatherers; and tree farmers' knowledge.

Loggers, in addition to their technical knowledge of machinery, must know how to harvest large quantities of a single species which will conform as closely as possible to uniform standards set by the mills or the landowners. They must have a shrewd understanding at the stand level as well as of individual trees because they deal in both quality and quantity.

Craftspeople, trappers, guides, and gatherers, in contrast, look for uniqueness, not uniformity. They must make decisions that reward them with specific individuals — plants, animals, unusual formations in a tree. They value uniqueness in nature rather than conformity, for it is the unusual that brings the high price of appreciation.

Tree farmers and maple syrup producers are the group most likely to change the natural landscape at a complex qualitative level. While logging in the Adirondacks generally leaves the small clear-cuts or selectively cut sites to reseed themselves, tree farmers decide which species should predominate, how many of each, and where they should be in relation to one another. The tree farmers are involved in subtly redrawing the blueprint of the natural forest with a human hand; their knowledge is architectural as well as technical and ecological.

All of these kinds of indigenous knowledge could be included in the planning for the Adirondack Park. Anthropologist Billie DeWalt highlights the strengths and weaknesses of both indigenous knowledge and scientific knowledge, and their potential for working together. He believes the contextualized, holistic understanding characteristic of indigenous knowledge systems can combine well with the more in-depth specializations of scientists (DeWalt, 1994). Unfortunately this synergism of effort is possible only in an environment in which indigenous knowledge, and the indigenous knowledge holder, are acknowledged and respected. Up to now, woodspeople and their knowledge of the Adirondack forests have largely been ignored by the planners, who have chosen in each instance to rely on outside experts for scientific support of their decisions. The chapters in this section represent an attempt to highlight some of this useful knowledge. In them I argue for the inclusion of the woodspeople as active participants in decision making about land use in the Adirondack Park of the future.

4

The Woods and the People: Tupper Lake Loggers

I N LATE OCTOBER, THE FIRE COLORS OF THE sugar maples, birch, and aspen have vanished, buried in a slick mass on the forest floor. The leaf peekers, mainly East Coast residents who drive through the Adirondacks to view the fall foliage, have gone too. The tourists, brightly dressed apparitions on the main streets of the hamlets, will not be back until the snow cover is deep enough for skiing. The souvenir T-shirts have retreated to the back racks of the stores; only the locals remain, amid the bare structure of the community.

In the forests the bare gray branches stretch in angular gestures among the shadowy greens of white and red pine, hemlock, balsam, spruce, and pale green cedar. The beech branches cling to bleached gold leaves. All the forest seems subdued, darkened; the skies are often heavy with rain. But then there are the larches, known locally as tamaracks. The larches flare upward through the gloom, like candles on the blue altars of the mountains, solitary immolations warming the chill November air. They grow in micro-climates of moisture, beside bogs, springs, and tiny brooks, in little vales of wetland by turtlehead and ladyslipper, wherever they can reach sunlight through the spreading crowns of maple and ascendant pines. Although the larch can grow taller on the drier uplands, it cannot tolerate the shade of competing conifers; it outcompetes the other conifers in wetter soils by its ability to withstand permanent immersion of its roots. The larch is an anomaly, the only conifer whose needles change color. The delicate spray foliage turns gold and falls, usually in November, leaving knobby twigs and tiny, smooth-scaled cones. Its timber has been used for telegraph poles and railway sleepers, but now, as useful timber or aesthetic resource, the larch, like the local population, has largely been forgotten.

When one talks about either wilderness, wildlands, or natural resources in the Adirondacks, one is talking primarily about forests. From an eagle's-eye view the forests spread in every direction, great heaving mounds of mottled green like trout in the fall, stippled with lakes and villages. Public State Forest Preserve lands and private forests lie adjacent to each other throughout the park, though the difference is not always evident from the air. Widely divergent ecotypes intermingle in the lowlands and slopes of the Adirondacks: paper birch and fire cherry in fire and disturbance sites;

Photo 4. Logging truck. Photo D. Kuklok.

maple, beech, gleaming yellow birch hardwoods, and hemlock on fertile soils up to 2,500 feet above sea level; mixed forests on less fertile glacial outwash, including red spruce, balsam fir, hemlock, red maple, black cherry, yellow birch, and sometimes white pine, which can be identified from a distance by its great height; and wet or semiflooded forests with swamp dwellers — red maple, black ash, balsam fir, black spruce and occasionally Northern white cedar. Above 2,500 feet, in the boreal zone, cold moist conifer forests cover the slopes with red spruce and balsam fir; on the highest peaks these dwindle to stunted, wind-twisted krummholz, and bare rock with pockets of lichens and tiny leathery alpine flowers.

But these forests are vulnerable to a complex mixture of natural and man-made conditions that threaten their health. Recently, patches of reddish-brown dying spruce have begun to appear, higher up the mountainsides, weakened by acid rain and then damaged by disease or insect blight (Ketchledge, 1990; Mello, 1987). The sugar maples also appear to be vulnerable to acid rain, and that in turn may make them more vulnerable to pear thrips, a devastating pest on the rise in the Northeast which has maple syrup producers worried. The giant white pines, harvested farther south for the masts of the English navy centuries ago, have long been susceptible to white pine blister rust; hence the gooseberry eradication campaigns of a few decades ago to wipe out blister rust's intermediate hosts.

Changes in land management bring out the peculiar vulnerabilities of particular areas. Logging or development in wetlands may change the area permanently because of altered runoff patterns and decreased absorption. In other places, trees succumb to erosion, windthrow, or fires. Human influence, through high cutting rates, clearing for development, or development pressures on adjacent land including roadways, runoff, changes in water flow patterns, and increased human traffic, change the nature of the wild forestlands and may threaten particular species or ecosystems. Fire control, practiced strictly here because of the proximity of human inhabitants, suppresses natural disruptive forces that complete many ecological cycles. Yet the human/forest relationship is not directed solely toward destructiveness. Other patterns exist which permit the coexistence of human communities and forest communities.

People who depend on forest resources, whether extractive or aesthetic, must work to ensure the sustainability of the forests, and therefore of their livelihoods. The Adirondacks have a long history of cultural adaptations that use the forest as a source of food, wood, and livelihood. Along with this reliance on the forests for material resources, people developed cultural symbols, rituals, mythmaking, and indigenous knowledge that depend on the forest as a matrix. The relationship between the human community and the forest is complex. It involves much more than simple proximity. A relationship exists in which there are mutual effects, mutual benefits and drawbacks — in the language of ecology, parasitism, mutualism, and symbiosis. Some people, such as developers, are dependent on forest resources, yet their daily life is lived apart from the forests. Others are directly dependent on and directly involved with the forest. The chapters in this section are about the latter.

❧ Like the larch, the local people survived the wet and the cold and the deep snow. They included the Mohawks, French-Canadian loggers, New England farmers trekking west who stopped at the mountains, and a random scattering of European immigrants who came as laborers or itinerant tinkers and traders. They built hamlets in the valleys, by lakeshores and waterways, but even in the twentieth century, transportation and communication between the hamlets was often difficult. Communities grew up more isolated from one another and from the metropolises only a few hundred miles to the south than did similar rural communities in less rugged terrain, where roads and railroads linked populations more easily. Independence was a necessity where families could be snowed in for days each winter; being able to depend on neighbors for help developed as a social security network.

Since the arrival of the Northway and increasing numbers of tourists, a gloss of easy urbanity shines in the shop windows of the larger hamlets. But under the surface at least some of the old conditions and cultural adaptations still hold. In 1990 a winter storm knocked down power lines in Tupper Lake, and the residents went without telephones or electricity for several days. This hamlet of seven thousand did not boast its own doctor at the time. The residents took care of those who got sick during the blackout, transporting them to doctors twenty miles away. By contrast, locals comment that newcomers "don't even stop when they pass someone broken down by the side of the road."

The major sources of employment have changed, too. Although the distribution of the hamlets still roughly follows the valleys and waterways, now factors such as tourism, the Olympics, and prisons, in addition to logging, mining interests, sanatoriums, and health spas, determine population densities.

A constellation of villages spreads across the park. The Tri-Lakes—

Tupper, Saranac, and Lake Placid — glitter across the northern half of the park like the stars in Orion's belt. Small hamlets — Bloomingdale, Franklin, Vermontville, Wilmington, Keene, and Keene Valley — cluster about them. Long Lake, Blue Mountain Lake, and Indian Lake lie to the south, along the line of Orion's dagger; Newcomb falls to the east of these hamlets, at Orion's unmarked solar plexus, at the center of the Adirondacks. These hamlets formed my research base. To the north, Potsdam, Malone, and the Chateaugay–Ellenburg area outline the head and shoulders of Orion, just outside the park. To the south, at Orion's knee, Ticonderoga with its paper mill, Warrensburg, and Lake George gleam with all the brightness of political maneuvering, development, and old family money.

Of the Tri-lakes hamlets, Lake Placid, the smallest, is most famous for hosting the 1932 and 1980 Winter Olympics, and draws the largest tourist crowds. Saranac Lake, the largest, at around ten thousand residents, used to provide the health benefits of balsam-laden air to tuberculosis patients who came to Dr. Trudeau's sanatorium and nearby cure cottages; now hundreds of wealthy families have second homes or "camps" on Upper, Middle, and Lower Saranac Lakes. Home to the park's only daily paper, the North Country Community College, and the yearly Winter Carnival with its enormous blue ice palace, the hamlet serves as the hub for the business community of the northern half of the park. It was recently named New York's best small town.

But it is Tupper Lake, the most depressed economically of the three towns, that I end up visiting most often. Here I find woodspeople, those whose lives are intertwined economically and physically with the forest, whose daily space is the forest itself. Loggers, foresters, sawyers, tree farmers, craftspeople, guides, trappers, hunters, and fishermen all struggle to derive a living from the woods. Started as a logging and sawmill town in the early 1800s, Tupper has steadily lost its wood products industries, including the Oval Wood Dish Company, which now manufactures plasticware, manufacturers of bowling pins and wooden spoons, Draper Corporation, U.S. Bobbin and Shuttle Company, the Tupper Lake Veneer factory, which closed in 1990, and half a dozen sawmills.

Driving in on the main highway that runs west through Lake Placid and Saranac, I pass through a swath of windstruck forest — state land. Trees lie crisscrossed like a giant's game of pick-up sticks. But no one picks up the sticks in "forever wild." Many Tupper residents, the stock of logging and woods products families, lament the "waste" that the recent blowdown represents to them. "It's a mess. The state should go in and clean it up," I hear often. At the crest of a hill, the Thibodeaus' trim green and white motel is being readied for the tourist season. Mémé Thibodeau, in her eighties, talked to me at length about the old days one afternoon; her best advice to me turned out to be her suggestion that I visit her younger sister Rita. Visiting Rita quickly became a regular part of my trips to Tupper.

One winter day, as on many others, I drive down into town, past the huge buildings of Sunmount Developmental Center, snow-white ramparts in the midst of immaculate green lawns now covered with the grimy half-melted snow of late winter. An institution for the developmentally disabled, it has replaced sawmills and wood products industries as the primary employer in town. Well-kept houses line both sides of the street. I pass a small store and find the dead-end street where Rita lives.

The old black car is parked in the yard, the sign for her permanent porch sale hangs in the window. A cook in logging camps for nearly thirty years, she still works a twelve-hour day. She presses a jar of homemade gingersnaps into my hands. "I've been saving these for you," she says. Rita's house always smells of fresh laundry, the sharp dry heat of ironing, and

Photo 5a. Rita Chiasson, lumber camp cook for nearly thirty years.

soups, stews, pies, bread, or cookies. At seventy-six, she begins work at four in the morning, rising to bake for regular customers. Her French-Canadian meat pies are renowned in the town. She also takes in laundry. This morning Rita is busy ironing a rainbow-colored pile of golfing pants. "Sit down! sit down!" she orders; she reminds me of a wood thrush with her high voice and quick movements. She asks me what I have been doing since she saw me last; she still speaks with a lilting French-Canadian accent. Born in the Gaspé Peninsula of Quebec, one of ten brothers and sisters, she came to Tupper with her sister while still in her teens. Her husband was from a family of twenty-two children, all boys. Together they cooked

Photo 5b. Rita Chiasson at home in 1994. Photo D. Kuklok

at logging camps until he disappeared one day, leaving her with five children. She continued to cook, living in the camps through the winter. While
they were small, her children stayed with her, helping in the kitchen, peeling
vegetables. When they were older, sometimes they boarded at a neighbor's
during the week; later they managed by themselves at home while Rita
worked, and worried about them.

While she irons, Rita tells me stories about her days in the logging
camps — stories about bears, the loggers, accidents in the woods, the many
faults of choreboys. When I ask her about conditions in the forests now,
compared to her time in the woods, she remarks on the difference in logging
operations. "They got all that big machinery now. Those skidders, they tear
up the little trees."

She also fills me in on town gossip, carefully editing it for my ears, I am
sure, and tells me which people I should talk to. Most of the old-time
jobbers she worked for are gone, but she mentions the names of a few, as
well as loggers and forest managers who are in the area, some still working.
In return I bring her a little news of these old friends, also carefully edited,
but I wish I had more to offer her for her generous friendship. In the end I
get the Adirondack Center Museum in Elizabethtown to invite her to their
harvest festival to tell some of her stories. She is an instant hit.

Leaving Rita's, I have other people to contact, people I have never met
but have heard of through various connections. I stop at the local Stewart's,
where the roads to Long Lake and Lower Tupper meet. The garish orange
roof of the convenience store seems out of place, overmodern in an old-time
town. But the local residents have adopted it. They stop in for gas, the
paper, meet over a cup of coffee to hear the latest talk. I know I can always
get accurate directions here. This morning I stop in to get directions to a
logger's house in Lower Tupper. It turns out that his brother-in-law is
standing in the parking lot. He asks me what I'm going to talk about with
Pete. I explain briefly. "Oh, yeah," he says, "you already interviewed my
cousin," and gives me the directions cheerfully.

❧ Logging represents the most visible impact of the relationship between
the human and forest communities. Logging began in the eighteenth century, when the French and British harvested marine timbers (White, 1985;
p. 22), and later as settlers cleared their land. Early mills used nearby
timber; when it ran out, workmen built roads to bring more logs to the mill.
In 1813 the Fox brothers, who had rafted logs down the Hudson to mills
in Glens Falls, tried floating single logs on the Schroon River branch

(White, 1985). It worked, and the practice spread. Timber deep in the woods and far from the sawmills could be logged, cut into thirteen-foot lengths, pulled by oxen over iced roads, and pushed into the river in times of spring flood. The dangerous river drives spawned many tales both true and elaborated. River drivers had to be quick-witted and nimble and in excellent physical condition to control the huge rolling logs with cant hook and pike, survive the plunges into icy water and the occasional log jam. When a log got stuck, hundreds of other logs could pile perilously high. Releasing the "key" log was extremely dangerous; as soon as it was free, the other logs would shoot forward (Tyler, 1969).

In the mid 1800s French Canadians migrated to the Adirondacks and proved to be some of the most skilled lumber workers (White, 1985). Jobs as teamsters, log drivers, or cutters provided seasonal work for the French Canadians and some of the earlier settlers. The camps where loggers stayed, isolated in the woods for weeks and months at a time, working long, hard hours, sleeping in bunkhouses, and reputedly eating enormous amounts of food (up to a dozen eggs apiece for breakfast, according to Rita, as well as pancakes, bacon, and potatoes), created an aspect of Adirondack culture that remains important today. The rituals, skills, and traditions of the early logging days are passed on now in the "Woodsman's Days," celebrated every year in Tupper Lake. But the ideals of physical strength and stamina, courage, skill, knowledge of the woods, resourcefulness, independence, and hard work are still part of the culture of Adirondack logging towns.

Throughout the nineteenth century, Adirondack white pine continued to be shipped to Europe, and sledded or floated down the Hudson to be used in American seaboard towns (White, 1985, p. 23). Logging crews cut hemlock, stripped the bark for use in the tanning process, and left the logs to rot in the woods. In the second half of the century, red spruce was heavily logged, both for lumber and, later, for pulp and paper mills. While lumbering could use only logs of at least eight to twelve inches in diameter, the pulp industry could use the fibers of any log; by the end of the nineteenth century, the destruction of the forests was so obvious that inhabitants of New York City feared a diminution of their water supply from the Hudson River, whose headwaters are at Lake Tear of the Clouds, nine hundred feet below the peak of Mount Marcy. The Forest Preserve was established, and in 1894 the "forever wild" amendment was added to the state constitution to protect the preserve from cutting.

Logging has continued throughout the twentieth century, although operations now take place only on private landholdings. Major companies, including International Paper, Champion, and Finch, Pruyn, own large holdings in the Adirondacks, and have cutting operations on their own and other private lands. In addition, many smaller companies and independent loggers operate on private lands such as the large holdings belonging to wealthy estate owners, including the Rockefellers, the Whitneys, and the Litchfields. Small landowners hire loggers to clear land for development, or to harvest a stand at maturity.

While logging has remained an important component of the Adirondack culture and communities, a 1990 report found that the future of the logging and wood products industries is seriously threatened by lower construction demands, increased mechanization, and, more significantly, limits on the available stumpage, and the movement of raw products from the Adirondacks to outside the region for finishing. Without the entry of more secondary woods products industries into the Adirondacks, the report predicted a slump that would have serious effects on local economies and on the sociocultural well-being of families dependent on logging and other woods products industries (Ratner, 1990).

Interviews with loggers and company foresters bore out these findings. Many loggers and foresters told me that the market was tight in 1990–91; some of them were driving logs to mills in Canada. Several secondary woods products industries, including the Tupper Lake Veneer factory, had already closed. More recently, Champion International announced that it was assessing its ownership of nearly 145,000 acres of Adirondack Park lands, about 95,000 of which Champion considers "nonstrategic"; the cost of owning this land has become burdensome. To the south, Lyons Falls Pulp and Paper placed 20,000 acres of northern forest land on the market, 5,000 acres of which are in the park, because of financial troubles.

For most loggers, logging is much more than a job. It is a demanding and rewarding way of life which surrounds the logger with an occupational community and culture (Carroll and Lee, 1990). Carroll and Lee documented occupational community and identity for loggers in the Pacific Northwest; many of their findings resonate with findings in the Adirondacks, although the circumstances are somewhat different. Members of an occupational community, they write, "tend to look to each other as a primary reference group" (Carroll and Lee, 1990, p. 142), and the individual member looks to other members in developing and defining his or her identity or sense of self (Blumer, 1969). Carroll and Lee found that the "logger identity" included independence, pride in skill in facing danger, and a sense of being in a unique category of workers (Carroll and Lee, 1990, p.

147). The set of interrelated values and shared meanings among the loggers touched on several themes, including three that predominate in the Adirondacks as well: loggers view themselves as rugged individualists; good loggers have common sense and a "can-do" attitude that results in creative problem solving to get the logs to the mill; and, very important to understanding the loggers' multiple roles in the land use conflict, most prefer a rural way of life and express strong dislike for cities (Carroll and Lee, 1990, p. 148).

In the Adirondacks, logging as a profession is often passed from father to son, in some families going back several generations. Many loggers I interviewed expressed the belief that "greenhorns" who came from a city or had no logging experience in their family would never really make it in a logging career. "I was out there in the woods with my dad, learning the woods since I was a little boy," said one logger I interviewed, echoing many others. Rita described how one of her sons was driving most of the heavy machinery at the camp where she was the cook by the time he was eight years old. All three of her sons worked in the woods. By the time they are in their teens, many children in logging families act as a regular part of the team. "Learning the woods" represents a long period in the logger's life when he spends a great deal of time walking and working in the forest, usually in the company of older, more experienced loggers and jobbers who show him the ropes — the qualities of different species, which trees to cut, how heavily to cut in different situations, how and where to build skid roads, and so on. This long apprenticeship happens naturally in a family.

❧ I get to Pete's house a few minutes early. Truck tires have churned up the driveway so much that inches of mud cake my boots by the time I get to the porch, which is under construction and missing the stairs. His wife answers the door and shows me into a small, neat living room with dark wood paneling, where I take off my boots. A baby sleeps in a cradle. We sit on high stools at a counter in the kitchen so that we won't wake the baby. Pete comes in; he shakes my hand and grins under his heavy black beard. His brother, who works with him, should be here soon, he says. I explain about the tape recorder and the use of a pseudonym for him. After he gets a cup of coffee and pulls a stool over, I turn the recorder on and ask him about the history of his logging work.

He and his brother began their careers working in the woods with their father, who is a forester. Later they both went for six months to a vocational school in Maine which taught all the aspects of logging, surveying, and use of equipment. They came back to Tupper Lake, and decided after a few years to start their own business. "When we started, we bought one skidder. I was cutting and he was skidding. So we worked like that for other jobbers for a couple years, then we bought a loader and would buy other stumpage, and we were working for ourselves. Bought a little firewood truck, hauled firewood, and then the logs to Tupper Lake Veneer here, and we did that, just him and I, about five or six years. In 1987 we bought a newer loader and bought a second skidder, and then we started hiring crews, and got OWD [Oval Wood Dish] stumpage from my father-in-law — he's the forester of that — and then we started cutting stumpage on that."

They have picked up different markets for both lumber and pulp while struggling to maintain their equipment. "There's more money if you do the whole job yourself . . . more headaches, too!" Pete shakes his head and laughs. His wife hurries to pick up the baby, who has started to fuss.

"We both work together — he does the slashing and loading and I do the marking of timber, road building. We usually do a diameter limit on the trees. I walk and check where we go and lay the roads out. We go fourteen inches and up on all the hard maple, ash, cherry, soft maple. And then the beech . . . I would say, we go eight inches and up on it — just because mainly it's dying [from disease]. And the same with hemlock and spruce. We end up cutting a lot of hardwood. A lot of our pulp goes to Finch, Pruyn in Glens Falls. Cavanaugh's trucks for us, up from Tupper. . . . Then we've got ash and cherry — we send that out of town. Ash goes to Frankfort. Cherry goes to Booneville to Ethan Allen. The beech and the soft maple we did send here to Tupper Lake Veneer. They're closed now," he adds with a rueful chuckle.

When I ask him about marking, he says that in most of the areas, he and his brother show the loggers what the limits are, and the loggers go out and cut. "You check them every other day or so, and if they are going a little too small, you tell them. . . . Certain areas near roads, we may go in and mark it just to make sure they don't cut it so heavy. . . . Keep it like a buffer zone, for the public mostly. Keep it so it looks halfway decent, so they don't get such a bad impression." He explains that most of the landowners try to leave a buffer zone of uncut stands near roads. We talk about the aesthetic and ecological results of logging, and what the land looks like after selective cutting. "We had one area where . . . we went through and selectively cut it and had some nice stuff coming up, and we got that windstorm, and it looks bad now. . . . When you look at it, it looks like it was cut hard. But it wasn't; it was all blown over."

Landowners determine much of what gets cut. In some places that Pete logs, the landowners already have the area marked, so that they have established what they want it to look like after the timber has been taken out. "Where they don't mark, you try to please them and make it look as good as you can, so it gives other people the impression that you can log without destroying everything. In some areas, you get way back in, you do tear it up, just because you end up running into something ledgy, rocky, or the weather gets muddy."

When the job is already marked, Pete is not always satisfied. Sometimes too many junk trees (trees that should be culled) are marked and too few good ones. "They're leaving too much of the good stuff, but by the time you go back again, that good stuff is . . . overmature then. Sometimes they overcorrect what they are trying to do." He feels that this practice is probably due to the foresters' education.

Regeneration should not be a problem. "Even within five years after you've been in, the skid trails are filled in and the grass starts growing and the trees start coming up. Certain areas, if they are managed right, within let's say five or ten years, you could keep coming back and going through it again." I ask if other jobbers have the same standards. He nods and says that over the years, throughout the forestry system, it became conventional wisdom that if loggers limit themselves to trees fourteen to fifteen inches in diameter, they could come back and cut the same area again within ten years. In some areas jobbers will leave trees of even bigger diameter.

But now, says Pete, "a lot of places are almost clear-cutting their land . . . and selling it to the state." The Department of Environmental Conservation, under pressure from environmental groups, has actively sought to buy many of the larger private parcels; the agency's willingness to pay a fixed amount for the land, whether or not there is still standing timber on it, has encouraged many owners to move from selective cutting practices to clear-cuts on land that they plan to sell to the state. Pete has learned this from talking with the logging crews working on these parcels, who tell him that they are having to cut more heavily than they should. "The owners are getting rid of [the timber], that's the way they want. You're working on their land, and if they say, 'We want this cut,' if you don't cut it, somebody else will. Around here, if that's where you're working, you got to keep working."

Pete's brother Brian arrives and listens to the conversation while he takes off a heavy plaid wool shirt and stamps his boots to loosen the mud and snow. He looks younger than Pete, clean shaven, and leaner.

Pete thinks the biggest factors limiting their business are the market and the weather. A lot of the mills are cutting back, he says, lowering prices and inventorying their paper to bring onto the market later. "If you can't get rid of your product, that works on how many people you are going to hire. If you can keep all your employees working, usually in the winter you can get rid of everything [all the wood you can cut]. This winter you're up and down. They put you on a ticket system. If you are capable of producing maybe twenty loads a week, and they give you ten tickets, that's all you can do. That cuts down your production and your employee help, too."

Brian describes the small sawmill that the brothers have been setting up with the intention of doing enough milling to keep the logging going. Eventually they hope to sell lumber to local contractors. Yet Brian and Pete prefer not to expand their business much beyond its current size. "If you get too big, then you can't control or keep track of what you have," Brian says. In addition, they try to work closely with the mills and talk to other jobbers to keep informed about current market trends.

Right now they both feel that they are producing less than they could, owing to market restrictions and the weather. It has been an unusually warm winter. The logging roads, which have to be frozen hard to support the weight of the trucks, took a long time to freeze this year, and now the freeze is already breaking up. The crews will be off in two months, but Pete and Brian will still have payments to make on their machinery.

Discussion shifts to less tangible topics: land use values and reactions to the Adirondack Park Agency. Pete and Brian don't think that conflict is inevitable between logging, wildlife, and recreational values, but when I bring up the APA, Brian shakes his head impatiently and argues for its abolition. When I ask about specific dealings with the APA, he says they have not had much to do with the agency, except for applying for permits to cross creeks; as far as that goes, the APA has been very cooperative. Yet Pete and Brian share the perception that the APA supports an attitude that logging in general is wrong. Brian slaps his hand on the counter. "Logging provides a lot of employment. It's a way of life around here."

Aesthetics is a more sensitive topic. Loggers often feel that they are perceived as low-skilled laborers with little aesthetic sensibility. When I speak with preservationists, those perceptions of loggers are often exactly the ones presented to me. Yet in talking with both loggers and preservationists, I come to see that it is not so much a matter of one group valuing aesthetics in the woods and another group valuing only production and economics but rather two different aesthetic views of the woods. Many preservationists prefer old growth. Loggers and other woods workers, who very often can identify many of the diseases and pests associated with an aging forest, sometimes, though not always, prefer younger forests. When I ask Pete and Brian what kind of woods they like to look at, they say they like second growth. "It's a prettier sight to see," says Brian. "It's a healthier forest." Pete agrees. "End up going hunting, most of the time you're in there looking at the wood . . . the size and the species."

❧ Hugo Jumel runs one of the largest logging operations in Tupper Lake. He logged with his father in New Brunswick until the age of eighteen, when he moved to Tupper Lake. Now he hires loggers both locally and from Canada. As a boy he logged with a horse; now he owns skidders, loaders, tractor-trailers, a low-boy, pickups, and a D-6. He has crews logging in Litchfield Park and other private parks, and also buys land to log and resell, or buys the stumpage. He logs hardwoods and softwoods to sell to Deferiet, Finch, Pruyn, and Gibeault in Canada. In the summer he is able to log birch and cherry, which he has sold to Ethan Allen, the furniture company in Vermont. Usually a forester marks the trees to be cut, some in four-foot and some in eight-foot lengths. Jumel builds the skid roads and freezes and grades them. Logging in warmer weather generally takes place where roads are blacktopped; otherwise the trucks become mired in the soft mud.

Jumel probably will not increase the size of his operation because of the amount of personal responsibility. Besides, logging is just not as good a business as it used to be. His wife remembers when the mills would take everything the loggers offered. Now they've had to cut back on what they'll buy, or the loggers need a "slip," a contract for a certain number of logs. But Jumel is proud of his job and is training his twelve-year-old son in the logging business. The boy already drives all the equipment. Logging just runs in the family.

❧ Just south of Tupper Lake I connect with a logging operation in progress on a large private estate. The jobber says he can give me an interview if I can get out to the logging site. I park where the road turns to ridged, frozen mud and hitch a ride with one of the loggers returning with an empty truck. The truck is enormous. It rattles down the steep curves, giving views of forested mountains, and a wilderness lake, but Jack, fairly large himself, handles the gears delicately. We discuss the logging operation, and he tells me about his job. He does everything — drives the trucks, cuts logs, builds roads. He works in a construction business with his father in the summer. His eyes brighten when we see two deer in a fragment of uncut Nature Conservancy land. The trees are noticeably larger here, close to fourteen inches in diameter breast height (dbh). Jack says the logging operation is cutting trees eight to ten inches and up. If he had it all to do over, Jack thinks he'd be a schoolteacher — teach shop or something. Get paid well and have summers off. Wouldn't he miss all this? I ask. "Oh, yeah," he says, and points out another view of the midnight blue lake. "That's the best lake for lake trout in this whole area." In another few minutes we come down a short steep hill into the middle of the logging operation. Machinery and logs crowd the clearing. Six or seven men move quickly among them.

Rugged and big-boned, with heavy straw-blond stubble on his jaw, the jobber has the raw, reddened skin of someone who spends most of his time facing into a cold, wet wind. He is standing beside a loaded truck with its engine running. "Can you ask your questions while we drive?"

"Sure," I shout over the noise of the engine, and scramble into the other side of the cab, which is nearly four feet off the ground. Jim tries the hill with the skidder hauling us. He has to unload some logs before we can wind up the hill behind the skidder. He sits beside me in the huge truck, fighting with the gearshift and the clutch to get the truck up the hill. The truck shudders to a stop halfway up. Jim leans out the window and calls for a machine with a winch to get us up the long winding hill.

"That's the worst, right there," he says, after a long moment hauling. "See that curve? The sun warms that part of the hill above it and the water runs off, turns to ice."

Jim's business deals in both hardwood and softwood — maple and occasionally cherry for furniture, beech, pine for lumber, spruce and hemlock for pulp. He likes to do shelterwood cuts when he can. The main constraints on his business are the market, the standing wood quality, and labor. The market and wood quality alternate as the most restrictive condition, depending on the year. Working conditions and labor always run a close second. He tries to keep the same workers a long time. It is hard to get skilled loggers, he says. This crew is from Tupper Lake. His brother is working with three more men on another private estate. That estate is almost clear-cutting the land, he says, frowning. It was high-graded, taking off the best wood, and leaving the "junk," not so long ago. He doesn't like to log the way that estate wants. "Just go in and cut everything, tear up the land. They say, 'Just make the most money.'"

But here, where he is working now, he likes it much better. The men are trusted to cut; the trees are not marked. Jim knows what the owner wants, and his loggers know what he wants. Sometimes he has to get on their case — they'll leave a log that is difficult to get to. They are cutting everything mature, over a certain diameter. "These guys don't know dbh or anything like that — they know what to look for, that's all."

"They can eye it?" I ask. He nods.

Sometimes his father marks the trees. His father is a forester; he went to Paul Smith's College. So did Jim and his brother, but the brother, who is in the logging business with Jim, didn't graduate, going into military service instead. Jim's father wanted him to get a four-year degree, but Jim didn't want anything more to do with school. He learned a lot at Paul Smith's, mostly about books, but he doesn't use his education on the job. All this — he takes his hand off the steering wheel and sweeps it across the wooded expanse visible through the windshield — he learned, especially the forestry aspect, from his father. He has been with his father in the woods since he was a little kid. He was marking trees himself before he was out of high school. He worked as a foreman for another jobber for two years, then decided it was better to work on his own . . . same money, fewer headaches with other people. He learned a lot growing up in the business. His father was a logger as well as a forester, and Jim learns from daily experience now. He learns what makes good logs, what to look for, and what marks are bad, by cutting, which is usually what he does now. He cuts, grades, and sorts the logs into different truckloads going different places according to what each mill will take — four-foot pulp logs or eight-foot hardwood logs.

This year the market is real tight, Jim says. Loggers have to have slips, and some mills are getting choosy about what they will take. He talks about the need for a wood producers' group to negotiate with the mill owners, who, when dealing with individual loggers or producers, can drive a harder bargain. But a wood producers' group is tough to organize, he says, because the producers are all individuals and independent. He sighs. "So independent," he says.

I ask what, in the whole chain of his operation, start to finish, is his weakest link. "The trucks," he answers. "They're not made for these kinds of conditions." Adirondack mountains, and Adirondack winters, he means. "They wear out fast, they're expensive, always breaking down." He once tried to let outside truckers do the hauling, but they were unreliable. Jim would watch the wood stacking sky-high, and the trucker would not be there. So now he trucks his own, up to a hundred miles — to Canada, some to Finch, Pruyn in Glens Falls, and some to Deferiet.

He criticizes state forest management practices. He likes healthy woods, and thinks the state's "forever wild" lands are often not healthy. "Look at all the blowdowns between Saranac Lake and Tupper Lake," he says. Big landowners now often hire state foresters to mark their trees; he has cut where they have marked the trees, and thinks they make a lot of mistakes. "Either they mark too much, or too little. Seen them mark balsam wrong several times. And I've seen them mark nest trees. I think that's a big mistake. I don't ever cut nest trees." I ask what nests he looks for, and he says hawks, owls, and other big birds. He opposes the APA for the most part, and thinks that the Governor's Commission report is worthless. Adirondackers know how to manage on their own. There will always be a few who are greedy and overdevelop. He guesses a couple of bad ones like that are what got the APA started.

We are driving now, rumbling and lurching through a recent shelterwood cut. The remaining trees are slenderer, the woods more open. But it still looks like part of a forest. I ask about the quality of the woods coming up after a cut here. Jim believes that the quality is much better, and the trees grow straighter. Diversity is a different question. Often now there is too much beech, a lot of hardwood. Especially after a clear-cut, the loggers eventually see a lot of hardwood.

When I ask, Jim says he enjoys being out in the woods. Couldn't work indoors. He likes to see the animals. I ask what kind of woods he likes best. "White pine. Doesn't everyone? Best logs. Also hemlock. I guess I like softwoods the best."

"What about just to walk through, if you know you are not going to cut them?"

"You know," he says, "I can't walk through a woods without seeing it as timber."

❧ Not all loggers see the woods the same way. A generation gap exists between those who logged more than thirty years ago and those who began logging more recently; those thirty years represent a generation of trees, as well as a generation of logging families.

Pierre LeBrun, soft-spoken and white-haired, moved to Tupper Lake from New Brunswick. Huge-boned, well over six feet, with hands that could girdle a tree twenty-eight inches around, even in his seventies he retains an aura of Paul Bunyan's grandeur. In fact, he won the Woodsman of the Year award at the first Tupper Lake Woodsman's Days, years ago. His voice is gentle, rich with the French accent and expressions he heard as a child. He looks out the window of the house in Lower Tupper where he lives alone, reminiscing about his logging days, back to the time of horses and crosscut saws. He stayed in logging camps where Rita cooked at times. She was a good cook, he says, closing his thumb and finger in a circle of perfection, "Comme ça!" She cooked her French-Canadian meat pies as part of the loggers' huge meals. At town festivals, meat pies and traditional fish dishes used to draw loggers, who would come by train and on snowshoes, but those festivals occur only in Canada now. Pierre still eats meat pies when he can get them, and speaks French with old friends, but the presence of French-Canadian culture in the town is no longer so obvious.

He spent all his life working in the woods, and loved being there. "In the woods is rough, but is good for yourself, for your health, the fresh air. . . . I feel good. When you go in the woods, you change, you are not the same. It is so beautiful — the birds, the deer, the porcupine." He went hunting only once. He tells me the story, shaping the outline of the deer with his huge hands, his eyes large with empathy. "I look at the deer, I couldn't shoot."

He misses the big trees now. Now there are none, compared to when he began to log, not too many places where you can see big trees. "The old trees, you got to go on the state. Or sometimes along the road they leave twenty to fifty feet — all the rest is cut, unless you go on the state land." He is upset by what he sees happening in the western United States. "The way they cut, in no time there won't be no wood left."

❧ I visit the home of Jacques Brossard, a retired jobber who also bought wood for Finch, Pruyn. He reminisces about Pierre LeBrun, who used to work for him. "What a good logger!" he says. At one time Jacques had up to thirty-two men and ten pairs of horses in the woods. He never did any clear-cuts. "What good is it to cut a tree like this?" he says, pointing out the window at a sapling. "Wait twenty years and come back and cut it." He underlines the severity of the cutting now. "I see lots of log trucks go by here, and the softwood is awful small." When I ask him if he sees any big wood now, he says, "I can take you in the woods and show you where it is *all* big woods — like that!" He leans forward, spreading his arms to show the size. His granddaughter stops her pirouetting around the table to look, and I wonder if she has ever seen any tree that big.

"Where is that?"

"Oh — on the state land."

Yet he believes the state should not buy land, or even own what it does. He thinks that locking up the timber on state land is largely to blame for the severity of the cutting on the remaining forests, and that with proper management, opening state land to logging could result in healthier forests, bigger trees left standing throughout the region, and a more stable economy.

Before I leave he proudly shows me a grove of forty-year-old trees that he planted in his yard. Cherry, white pine, some maples: he sees them every time he goes out the door.

🍂 Ben Frederick is equally concerned about cutting rates, although more from the perspective of looking at what comes up after the cut. He started in construction and switched to logging. In 1952 he had two teams of horses and started to buy his own stumpage. Eventually he converted to machinery and bought larger and larger tracts of stumpage. He harvested hardwoods, many times in virgin timber stands, cutting trees fourteen to fifteen inches dbh. The largest trees he cut might measure thirty-five to thirty-eight inches dbh; the average ranged from the high twenties to thirty inches. He cut more hard maple than anything else; beech wasn't marketable in those days, and toward the last years when beech came back into the market, the beech bark disease had arrived. In the early 1960s he got into the pulp business. At that time the loggers still had to hand-peel the wood. In 1965 he had fifty-three men on the payroll, and they peeled five thousand cords. Before he retired, he worked as an adviser on private lands until they were bought by International Paper. Even then he spent all his days in the woods with the loggers. Now he lives in Tupper Lake, in a house that overlooks the fields his father used to farm. It is filled with the ticking of antique clocks, the chimes interrupting the silence of a home where everything is in place.

Although he does not have a degree, he looks at the ecological relationships in the woods with the shrewd eye of a forester. He has heard that loggers now are cutting hardwoods for pulp down to about six inches dbh. This bothers him. "Because they are denuding the forest so severely, this is letting all the sunlight in, and this releases all the undergrowth. . . . The second growth is coming up so quick now, you can hardly walk through. A year or two after we left an operation you could see a lot of nice big trees. But today you don't see this anymore. All you see is a lot of small trees coming up." He shakes his head and leans back, pulling at his suspenders. "I really do wonder what will become of it."

I ask him if he enjoyed being in the woods. "Oh, sure. I still enjoy the woods." He has an eighty-acre parcel which he bought in the 1960s to cut. "But it is such a pretty piece of land, I hate to log it, really. It's mostly cherry, a few real big pines on it." Mainly he enjoys walking on it. "Take my grandson out, walk the property lines, keep them clean and painted, talk to the neighbors."

❦ The knowledge that these loggers and jobbers and others like them have of the woods is real, but often goes unacknowledged. Outside their occupational community, loggers are often perceived as uneducated, low-skilled "timber beasts" whose sole motive is to cut as much wood as possible and get out. What is missing from the picture are the loggers' own conflicts of interest: their knowledge of sustainable logging practices coupled with their ability to critique the kinds of operations that owners are demanding, on the one hand; and on the other hand, the need for dependable, sustaining work in an unstable economy. Loggers see themselves as skilled workers, knowledgeable in the highly complex context of the forest.

Theirs is primarily indigenous knowledge based on experience and passed on through families in the logging community, rather than academic knowledge, although jobbers sometimes find college courses useful in increasing their awareness of different options. The indigenous knowledge of the forest and logging operations shares several features with other indigenous knowledge systems. These include daily experiential contact with the forest, a long apprenticeship begun in childhood, a tradition of this work and knowledge in the family, exchange of knowledge in discussions in the community, and the long-term perspective of elders in the community.

The daily experiential contact provides the basis for an intense understanding of the details of tree physiology, forest ecology, and the machinery necessary for ecologically and economically sustainable operations. Observation, combined with opportunities to do different kinds of operations, and "see what happens," permits loggers to learn how to develop a relationship with the forest that is interactive and ecologically viable rather than destructive. In addition, maintaining daily contact with one another updates the loggers on the always changing conditions in the forest, whether owing to disease, human interference, wildlife, vegetation shifts, or weather. Knowing how to repair machinery, and understanding which machinery does the least damage to the forest floor and to trees left standing, is highly valued and important. Outside the forest context, jobbers must continually update their knowledge about the market, stumpage availability and quality, landowners' needs, labor, equipment, health and safety requirements, insurance, and transportation.

The long apprenticeship begun in childhood ensures that the logger acquires a good grounding in the complexity of logging requirements in different ecotypes and under different conditions. Practicing with different equipment, as well as gaining experience by working different jobs in the operation, helps the apprentice logger acquire the necessary versatility to be a part of a team. Problem solving emerged as an important skill in many of the interviews I conducted. Learning how to get along well with other crew members and the jobber is equally important for the apprentice's future ability to hold a job and contribute to a productive team. Logging is also physically demanding, and starting young gives the logger an advantage in terms of health and fitness. In the Adirondacks, winter temperatures may drop to thirty below, and strong winds, ice, and deep snow create rigorous and sometimes hazardous working conditions. Because of the heavy equipment, uncertainty factors in felling, and stringent weather conditions, logging presents many health and safety hazards. Most loggers I talked to have lost a friend or relative in a logging accident. Exposure to the skills, necessary knowledge, and physical demands of the job under the tutelage of an older family member with whom the apprentice has a deep emotional and kinship bond may help prevent accidents.

The tradition of this work and knowledge in the family provides loggers and jobbers with two critical foundations for successful operations. First, logging families value their work. Pride in the skills and knowledge it takes to be part of a successful logging operation sustains loggers on emotional, social, and cognitive levels, especially since monetary rewards are relatively low for their skill levels and for the long hours they are expected to put in under difficult conditions. Second, constant immersion in the terminology, discussions, and experiences of logging helps loggers develop expertise early. It also encourages consistency in their worldview, as the logging community creates its own concept of human relationships with the forest through language patterns and group norms.

These cultural norms become tradition when they are passed on from older to younger men in the family — grandfather to father to son, or uncle to nephew. As with any tradition, this cohesion is a strength in typical teamwork situations, including problem solving on a practical level. The cohesion can become a liability, however, when norms outside the community change faster or in different directions from norms within the community. Atypical work situations, or the dissolving of traditional work expectations, as is happening in many logging communities in the Pacific Northwest, demand problem solving of a different nature. Wider diversity of experience, language patterns, and behavior can offer more solutions to choose from in a cultural crisis.

Another feature of indigenous knowledge systems present in logging communities helps to sustain traditional norms, and may also help the community respond effectively to change. Elders in the community, such as Pierre LeBrun, Jaques Brossard, and Ben Frederick, provide both continuity and perspective. As keepers of traditional standards in logging practices, from dbh limits to appropriate cuts, elders in the community help maintain loggers' sense of identity and goals, as well as giving the community a knowledge of its history and continuity. At the same time, paradoxically, these elders who seem to represent the most static traditions and norms are actually the community members who have experienced the most change in their lifetime. Their ability to compare different working conditions and forest conditions over time may actually provide the logging community with some of the wide diversity of forest experience that will help in finding solutions to current changes.

The indigenous knowledge system of the logging community in the Adirondacks permits extensive observation of the forest and experimentation with different interactions between humans and the forest. It gives the loggers an opportunity to develop cultural norms that define these interactions in the context of a long-term relationship. Most logging families in the Adirondacks have lived in the same area for several generations and plan to stay longer. Harvest sustainability, the ability to come back and log the same area several years later and get a harvest of similar quality, occupies much of their thinking about different cuts and diameter limits. Ecological sustainability, the ability to maintain the biodiversity and quality of flora and fauna as well as soil, water, and air conditions, is a requirement that lies just below the surface, as loggers take all the opportunities they have to observe the ecology of the forest and to note changes. Their aesthetic concerns touch all aspects of the forest, although different members of the logging community may value different aspects. Aesthetic and ecological interests may not be articulated as frequently as practical ones; but when asked, loggers and jobbers offer concrete examples of their awareness.

Unfortunately, although indigenous knowledge ought to lead naturally to decision making, this rarely happens in the Adirondacks because the decision makers come from outside the community that possesses the indigenous knowledge. The timber companies can choose to log off a parcel, sell it, and buy another parcel elsewhere; private owners with large holdings can clear-cut a parcel of land that they plan to sell to the state or to developers, and increase their profits when they move to another region. But the local loggers who work for them, and who possess the knowledge, remain. These men and their families, more than anyone else, have the urgent need for forest management that is sustainable in all ways. They know the forests intimately, yet they are without a voice in the decisions.

5

Crafters, Trappers, Gatherers, and Guides

SKEINS OF WOOL THE COLOR OF RASP-berries, of pumpkins, and of maize — the subdued colors of fire on a rainy day — hang from a rack behind the weaver. Her blue eyes bend a clear gaze on the emerging cloth stretched over the floor loom as she throws the shuttle back and forth; her feet on the pedals raise and lower the threads of the warp, as she creates the weft from the wool of Adirondack sheep and her own ingenuity. I am amazed to think of this elderly woman hiking through the forests to collect the plant materials for her dyes. Rock tripe, a leafy lichen, gives the raspberry hues; goldenrod, marigold, and tansy give yellows; yellow birchbark and butternut hulls give brown and tan. Swamp alder and other barks and leaves add variations. "Dyeing with natural substances, I always have a new color, a new shade," she says. A shawl woven from these dyed wools carries memories of the forest in its hues.

Crafters, trappers, gatherers, and guides differ qualitatively from loggers and tree farmers in their relationship to the woods. Each approaches the woods searching for uniqueness: trappers must find the runs of individual animals; guides value the unusual wildlife sighting, special fishing hole, or extraordinary aesthetic experience for their clients; and the crafters look for raw natural materials that will lend a special character to each piece they craft.

Crafters

Intimate with the smell, touch, and textures of the forest — spruce roots, balsam boughs, birch bark, shelf fungus, or gnarled misshapen pieces of trees, the character of the tree's aging through natural forces imprinted as clearly as an individual handprint — crafters tend to pay attention to the ecological history that causes individuals of a species to differentiate. The crafters are collectors, roaming the woods, often solitary, learning where to find the particular bits of the woods they need, and how to take what they need in such a way as to leave enough for next year, and the year after. Because they are often looking for unique features existing in nature rather than trying to fit nature to human norms, crafters value the crooked wood, the patterns of disease, and the quirkiness of natural forms. Barry Gregson,

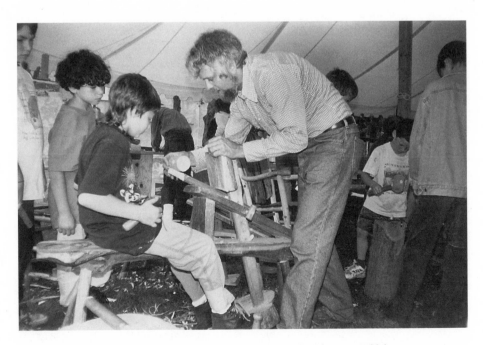

Photo 6. Barry Gregson, Adirondack furniture maker, Schroon Lake. Photo D. Kuklok

122   a furniture builder, finds burls and gnarled branches in the woods for his craft. While loggers and tree farmers usually seek to find regularity or impose it on nature, the crafters reap benefits from individuation; craft buyers value uniqueness rather than conformity.

BOATBUILDERS

The canoe slips through the blue-green water of Raquette Pond, the early morning sun pouring like honey over the wooden gunwales, the bare cedar-strip interior, the pale ash seats. The only sounds are the soughing of the pines on the shore, the soft thump of the paddles against the sides of the boat, and the faint plash as the paddle, dipped and pulled back, leaves the water and swings forward, a veil of droplets flying off the end. Fishing poles propped in the bow, bare feet against warm cedar — there is nothing that gives a feeling of serenity more than spending a day on quiet waters in a wooden boat. This particular boat, an Old Towne model with narrow prow and sponsons which has not been made for fifty years, belonged to a guide who used to take his famous clients fishing in it. He sold

Photo 7. The Vincents in two of the Adirondack chairs they make in Jay. Photo D. Kuklok

it to a friend, who rehabilitated it, refinished the wood, gave it a coat of forest green paint, and sold it to me at a friend's price.

Those who favor wooden boats often look down on motorboats as noisy, smelly, and unaesthetic, a lazy person's version of water travel, though useful when one wants to get anywhere in a hurry. Synthetic boats — aluminum, ABS plastic, or fiberglass — may be lighter to portage, but they lack the aesthetic appeal of the wood, the handcrafted lines rather than factory-pressed outline of each boat, and the connection, through the wood itself, to the surrounding forest. People coming to the Adirondacks for the first time may have to learn to appreciate wooden boats. Those who live here or who have visited for any length of time have the chance to feel the lure of the shining wood and the silence it permits.

Wooden boats, unless one makes them or buys them from a good friend, are not cheap. The guide boat, the classic wooden boat of the Adirondacks, slightly shallower and wider than a canoe, and made to be rowed by a single person while another person fishes or just enjoys the scenery, costs around seven thousand dollars new. In the Lucknows' boathouse on Lake Placid, the guide boat hangs above an old wooden Chris Craft motorboat. The Lucknows live half the year in one of the many "camps," elaborate mansions often featuring the Adirondack great camp architecture, a mix of log cabin rusticity and Swiss chalet charm, which line the shores of Lake Placid. Their two-story boathouse, large enough to house comfortably a family of four, with its fleet of watercraft, including fiberglass canoes and a new speedboat as well as the wooden boats, is typical of many of the larger camps on Adirondack lakes from Tupper to Blue Mountain to Lake George.

Carl Hathaway's boat shop in Saranac sells one or two new guide boats a year. When Carl retired in 1991, a young boatbuilder who had worked for Carl for five years bought the shop. He uses all local wood for the boats: white pine, which he saws with his own portable band saw, cherry for the seats and gunwales, and maple for the oars. He digs his own spruce roots for the curved ribs and stems. Most of his business, however, comes from the restoration and repair of wooden boats, for which he charges twenty dollars an hour, plus materials. He buys the wood for repairs locally as well. Two part-time workers help with restoration; a single boat can require a hundred hours of work. Easily.

Over in a nearby hamlet, a slim wooden canoe hangs outside the barn that serves as workshop for another boatbuilder, Mark, and his full-time assistant. The interior stretches to high rafters; at floor level piles of lumber, sawdust, and half-finished boats fill the space. Mark has a degree that would permit him to work for some of the state agencies, but he prefers boatbuilding and being his own boss. He too depends on local materials, except for white cedar, the traditional material for guide boats and wooden canoes, and the one thing that he still needs from outside the Park. He explains: "So much land in the Adirondacks [is] locked up, and everything else gets logged too frequently. It takes cedar a long time to grow, and to get . . . big enough and clear enough it takes a hundred and fifty years." As far as he is concerned, it is already impossible to get the wide plank cedar in the Adirondacks. He can still find it in Michigan, though.

John, a boatbuilder and guide in another hamlet, still manages to find cedar locally, but it is difficult. He has a deep commitment to using the traditional materials. A native Adirondacker from a well-known local family, he describes how he became a boatbuilder: "I always liked the history, read the history, and wanted to do something that fit in with the Adirondacks. . . . After three years of college I took a year off, and in that year I found boatbuilding." In the end he had to go to Maine to locate a course in boatbuilding; the few local wooden boat builders had mostly given up on hiring and training young people because they always left to find work elsewhere after a couple of years. Several years after he returned from Maine, the local community college finally began offering a similar course.

John's family, mostly Irish with some French, had no boatbuilders before John. There were guides, and uncles on his mother's side who were involved with carpentry through work at the great camps. His family did impart to him his woodsman's skills and his love of the woods during frequent camping trips. John tells me proudly that his family went cross-country skiing in the remote places of the High Peaks before it became a tourist fad. One year they were the only people the Colden Lake ranger saw from one end of the winter to the other; now Colden gets visitors all year.

When he first started the business, with his partner and his cousin, they guided trips as well as building boats. They used mainly guide boats to take people around the lakes on week-long trips. Different inns provided lodging —"just like in the old days." In the first three years it seemed as though they got all the people who had always dreamed of doing a guide boat trip, and then business tapered off. It was hard to sell guide boat trips outside the region because people did not know what a guide boat was. And part of the problem was the uneven quality of the available inns; some were excellent, others not up to standard. His cousin moved on, and John and his partner provided weekend trips and outfitting services, including their renowned trip food, with homemade rolls, breads, and cookies. Now they run a retail store, and John builds boats and does restoration and repairs. The repairs are the mainstay — guide boats, canoes, small sailboats, and once in a while a bigger Chris Craft. When I visited, he was working on a twenty-five-foot war canoe from Long Lake, once used in tavern-sponsored races and now going to a private camp on Tupper.

John uses all local materials. For the guide boats he goes out and digs the spruce roots. He may buy cedar or pine for the hull and seats from a local mill, but most often he goes up to a logging site and buys the trees right from the logger. He has them trucked in or he trailers them to a lot, where he hires a portable band saw mill, which he pays for by the day, getting the wood sawn just the way he wants it. He talks with the loggers, and if any of them are working in a spruce stand, he will go along and get the roots. When he finds what he wants, he buys the whole spruce tree, because the logger must cut as close to the ground as he can since he is paid according to how big the butt of the log is. To get the rootstock, John needs to cut three or four feet above the ground. Sometimes he picks up spruce from road-building areas. But you have to be careful, he says. Unless the ground is wet or muddy, when heavy machinery pushes a tree over, the roots may be stressed, and then they won't be any good. It seems that the time-consuming work of digging the roots is the only thing that could create a shortage of materials. This year he built one boat, and that cleaned him out. He has enough rootstock left to repair boats for two years, but not to build a new boat. Occasionally he finds other sources. "I found an old guy that has some," John says, "and he's had them for twenty years. And there's a guy that cuts them commercially, but they're tamarack roots, not spruce, so I could obtain some that way if I get an order in for another boat. It's hard work; you got to be active all the time, and you always got to be looking for boat lumber." He knows some local boatbuilders who bought some cedar that was not indigenous to the area, just to experiment with different wood. John will be watching the results with interest.

Although he subscribes to several boatbuilding magazines, John's main source of information seems to be other boatbuilders. He still has his contacts where he went to school. A couple of the older boat shop owners are always welcoming and willing to talk. He knows many other boatbuilders, in New Hampshire and Vermont as well, who are building small canoes and rowboats. He smiles, thinking of them, and it is clear that they are friends as well as compatriots in a rare and difficult business. "We're always calling each other up all winter long and trading ideas and discussing techniques."

When I ask about the constraints he feels in his business, and whether he hopes to expand, he pauses for a moment. When he answers, it becomes clear that profit is not the primary issue for him. Instead, it is pride in his work, and the good fit of the work, and the lifestyle it demands in the Adirondacks. "Now, for me to build this guide boat, it's more a labor of love than it is a profit-making venture. I can go out and do carpentry work and make fifteen to twenty dollars an hour, but if I stay in my shop and build a guide boat maybe I make five bucks. Do you log your time that you spend walking in the woods looking for a spruce tree? Digging the root? And it seasons its first three years before you use it. You drive to all these logging sites, mark trees, buy cedar and pine, put it away for two years. All that time is not counted. You get your order, go in your shop, and cut everything out. That's when you start counting your time — when you've got your materials all ready. . . . You are never going to get rich at it."

Thinking of the next step for his business, John says he is at the point where he could hire someone to work full-time on boat repairs, since he has more repair jobs than he can handle. But to hire someone, he would have to create room for him to work. That means additional shop space. If he were to make that commitment, it would mean another five or ten years to pay off the cost of building an addition. Right now he has a skilled part-time worker who paints boats for him and can use the shop space when John is not using it. Until he found this helper, his main problem was hiring skilled people. "I would train them and after two years the prison would steal them. A young kid is not going to work for me even for ten dollars an hour if he can make thirty thousand a year as a prison guard. That's depleted [the skilled labor]. You've got to find a person with a certain character — that's like me, does the work because they like it. You can't blame these kids. I mean, they get married, and they start a family and want security. I'm thirty-four years old, and I still don't have a family yet. I don't know if we can afford it."

Wooden boat building demands highly skilled, highly specialized wood-workers with a devotion to the trade that surpasses economic need. In addition to carpentry skills, the boatbuilder must know the different kinds of wood and the variations in usable quality of the cedar and the roots of the spruce. As a historic emblem of Adirondack culture, depending on both the use of indigenous materials and the knowledge and skilled labor that translate the materials into the highly finished product, the wooden boat cannot be surpassed. It is both pure symbol of a possible relationship with the wilderness and concrete product of that relationship. Yet under the economic constraints of the need for cultures to reproduce themselves through families as well as artifacts, the craft of boatbuilding using indigenous wood and indigenous skills is foundering.

The Adirondack North Country Association (ANCA) serves as a regional private-sector catalyst, working with small businesses to create jobs and advance the quality of life within the region. More than 75 percent of ANCA's funding comes from the state, yet in 1992 its state funding was cut drastically from the year before. Despite this loss, ANCA continues to work with other organizations to improve the lot of small businesses, especially those directly related to Adirondack natural resources, through crafts or tourism. If ANCA could enable boatbuilders to provide salary and security competitive with the prisons and the lure of urban jobs, the skilled workers might stay. A program to support apprentice boatbuilders by offering training in business skills necessary for the transition to independent boatbuilding, along with low-interest business loans and professional advertising, such as ANCA has done with its Lake Placid Crafts Center, might do much to encourage the longevity of wooden boat building in the Adirondacks and its viability as a career for Adirondackers, including those like John. Wooden boat building uses the natural resources of the forest, with the maximum of value added within the Adirondacks (Ratner and Ide, 1985). The boats themselves contribute to appreciation of the forest, and help return to people the opportunity for a relationship with nature within the quiet spaces of sky, water, and trees, at the oared boat's slow pace.

BALSAM CRAFTERS

Balsam fir blankets the mountainsides at the middle elevations. With its smooth, gray-brown bark sliced with resin blisters, the pointed crown of Christmas trees, and shiny dark green needles with two narrow white stripes on the underside, the balsam is easy to recognize. The sure test comes by crushing a handful of the needles; the scent is so pungent that one is jolted back into Christmas past with startling immediacy. Tree farmers in the Northeast grow balsam for Christmas trees; crafters cut the boughs of forest-grown balsam for wreaths and use the needles to stuff aromatic pillows.

Mary Duryea has been working with balsam for ten years. She is originally from Long Island but came to the Adirondacks to attend Paul

Smith's College, where she earned a forestry degree and met her husband. They decided to stay. Her interest in balsam products began when she was a student at Paul Smith's. Her physical education teacher, a local woman whose family has lived in the Adirondacks for generations, took the class on a hike one day and taught them to make balsam pillows as a way to appreciate the forest around them, and to take home something that was unique about the Adirondacks. Mary experimented for several years with this traditional Adirondack use for balsam needles. She worked with friends and neighbors selling pillows at craft fairs and local stores. Not long ago she began working with four local women at the Asplin Tree Farm, which grows balsam fir for sale as Christmas trees. The women's creativity and success in making new pillow designs is evident everywhere in the work-room: in addition to traditional pillows of every size, there are needlepoint pillows, stuffed loons and golden Christmas geese, and aromatic ornaments. Asplin Farm has recently listed their products in the Smithsonian catalogue. In the workroom where we are talking, the floor is littered with heaps of needles, scraps of cloth and thread; the tables are covered with partly finished pillows; sewing machines whir and hum. Outside the windows the field of dense, dark green balsam trees stretches away to the edge of vision, their pungency as valued as gold.

Dropping by a friend's house, I find her standing in the unheated basement, surrounded by heaps of balsam boughs which she is clipping into different lengths to weave into wire wreath frames. She works very fast, even while carrying on a conversation; within minutes she finishes one and is halfway through another. Ida Moquin is small, tough, and muscular from cutting and stacking wood and working with her husband to build their home. The strength helps with the strenuous task of cutting and hauling balsam boughs out of the woods; her determination sees her through the wreath making and the business end of the process. She must compete with other wreath makers each year submitting sealed bids for the town of Lake Placid's holiday decorations.

Ida and her husband Chris grew up in the Adirondacks, and showed an Adirondack sensitivity in helping us many times to adjust to life in the North Country. Friends to us from the first summer we spent in the Adirondacks, Ida and her husband took us fishing, shared their favorite camping spot, fed us venison, gave us potatoes and Christmas presents and advice about our car, and in general made sure we survived. When we came up for the winter, Ida stopped by to visit the day we moved into an old, unfurnished apartment. She sat in one of the children's chairs we were using in the kitchen until we could find more furniture and contemplated our bare living room in silence. That night she and her husband showed up with a truckload of furniture, including a table and chairs, beds, armchairs, extra silverware and glasses and table mats. They wouldn't listen to any thanks. Later both of them helped me establish contacts with guides and old-timers in the area. We still have the balsam pillows she made for us one Christmas; they emit a faint lingering fragrance, a memory of the powerful smell of fresh-cut balsam, and a token of unique friendship.

Trappers

Trappers worked the Adirondack forests before most other people even arrived. Trapping requires skill, stamina, attention to detail, and some level of indifference to snow and bitter cold. The Department of Environmental Conservation sets the seasons for the different furbearers, including mink, beaver, otter, and others. The best trapping takes place in the winter months, when the animals' coats are at their thickest. The DEC also educates and licenses trappers, monitors the harvest and trade in furs, and encourages the development of techniques and devices that provide for the most humane treatment possible for the animals (DEC, 1989).

Craig Rondeau is a burly man in his fifties with heavy, dark eyebrows and an expression of patient kindness, despite all the questions I ask. He was born and raised here, on a farm in one of the hamlets. "At one time we had our own cows and other animals. . . . The only thing we had to go to the store to get was flour and coffee and sugar." The hamlet has encroached on the farm since then. Now Rondeau pieces a living together, using his diverse skills in different areas. He is widely known as a trapper, wreath maker, and honey farmer. He also raises hounds and turkeys and has a few chickens and a garden. He sells hand-tied wreaths for part of his income in the winter. The family starts working on the wreaths around Thanksgiving, but collects the cones for them earlier in the fall. When I arrive to interview him, I find him in the barn, repairing an old truck for a friend, while a rooster crows incessantly. He is also a caretaker for a large camp and, what fewer people know, works for the postal service for a steady income.

Craig was about eight years old when he started trapping. An older neighbor taught him. "You learned, sometimes the easy way, sometimes the hard way. . . . When I first started trapping alone, he'd come and set a trap right next to mine, just to show you that you've got to cover everything. You don't leave anything out." He continued to learn from other trappers and from neighbors. "Mostly it's experience," he says. "Once you start, somebody can tell you how to do something, or what you do here or there, but if you don't experience it for yourself, you're not going to learn anything. It doesn't stick."

When he was sixteen, Craig began working for a fur farm nearby. They sold mink and fox furs, but also kept wild animals for show. He worked there for eighteen years, until the farm closed. He tells me a few anecdotes about the wildlife, about chasing a bear with a shovel, and trying to live-trap an escaped badger for two weeks; it kept digging tunnels. Now he traps on his own.

I ask if he uses more than the furs. He says that he doesn't usually eat the animals he traps, but once in a while he gets a meal out of them. "I have eaten beaver before; it's good meat, nice red meat," he says, then adds, shaking his head, perhaps at the thought of those who have, "I haven't eaten muskrat yet." When he is after food, he hunts to get it. Venison helps keep the grocery bill down in the winter. But he doesn't hunt for sport. "I don't believe in shooting something I'm not going to eat or use the whole thing. That just doesn't make any sense to me."

His friend comes back for his truck, and they begin talking about collecting pinecones for wreaths. The best way is to find the piles a squirrel has made and take some of those. His friend says, betraying the sense of shared existence that he and Craig seem to have with wildlife, "We leave part of the pile, just take a little from each pile, you know, so the little buggers won't starve."

Stan Montgomery is fourth-generation Adirondack. His ancestry is a combination of French, Indian, Norwegian, and Welsh, he claims. He grew up trapping and fishing. When I ask him how he gained his knowledge, whether from watching others or instruction, he says, "By doing." He is also a maple syrup producer, tapping trees on the lands where he works as a caretaker. His favorite journals, *Fish and Game* and *The Maple Digest,* give him tips and things to think about. Stan runs one thousand to fourteen hundred taps with his brother in their sugaring operation. Between the sugaring, the trapping, and the caretaking, he spends a fair amount of time in the woods in winter.

He feels a certain frustration with the misconceptions that tourists seem to have about the woods, and the amount of knowledge and preparedness necessary for spending time there. "The woods, the mountains are very unforgiving. There's a number of times bones have been found, human bones, some of them just off the trail." A heavy, muscular man, he sits with big shoulders hunched, cramped in the little kitchen chair I have offered him. He folds his hands in front of him—raw hands, reddened from plunging through the snow again and again to set his traplines. "Mother Nature is a bitch," he says softly.

He talks about his sugaring operation, the pluses and minuses of maple production, and the decisions he has to make. He taps trees on several pieces of land he does not own, and exchanges some syrup for the privilege. He notices, like other maple producers I have interviewed, a difference in sweetness between individual trees. Trees that grow alone, with spreading branches, and trees along the road may produce sap with a sugar content of 3 or 4 percent—up to twice what one finds in forest trees. The most difficult—and dangerous—part of the operation comes when Stan and his brother have to make decisions about crossing the ice on a large lake to get to an island where he taps several hundred maples. The same weather that is good for sap flow also encourages the thawing of the ice. Every year he wonders if they will fall through. The freezing water does not allow much leeway for survival.

He applies the same careful attention to detail to his trapping. He traps on some of the islands, on some private land, and on State Forest Preserve land. He traps most of the legal furbearers, and checks his traplines regularly, tramping through the deep snow on snowshoes. He must look for animal runs and likely places to set traps; otter traps must be set under the ice in the frozen lakes. His experience serves him well; each year he sells furs for an additional source of income.

Spending so much time in the woods, he notices changing conditions. He is upset by the amount of disease and decay he sees on Forest Preserve land, particularly among beech, the mast trees that wildlife depend on, and the spruce trees. The spruce are dead or dying everywhere he looks, he says. Insects and fungus are attacking the mature beech, which threatens the food sources for many wildlife species. In addition, he feels that the conditions of decay and large numbers of dead trees make many areas ripe for wildfires. His own land, like that of many Adirondackers, lies adjacent to state land; he worries that a fire started in a tinderbox of dry fuel on state land might spread to his land.

The trapper's life can be grueling when it is a full-time occupation. But many Adirondackers pursue trapping part-time, to bring in additional income by practicing a skill their fathers and grandfathers, and sometimes grandmothers, taught them. Nellie Staves, who shares her views in Chapter 7, is such a grandmother. She now teaches trapper training courses in

Franklin County, training the trappers of the next generation. While members of People for the Ethical Treatment of Animals (PETA) in the Adirondacks and elsewhere challenge the practice of trapping each year, trapping is unlikely to disappear from the Adirondacks for a long time.

Gatherers

Golden pears gleam in jars along the table, setting a counterpoint to the deeper brown-gold of the wood paneling. A huge potful of jars bubbles on the stove. The woman who is canning sits on a high stool, her white hair curling in the steam like sea foam. Her limbs tremble ever so slightly; she tucks her hand against her side to still the palsy. Talking takes extra effort. Her husband, a logger, carpenter, and woodsman still muscled and tan, holds restless hands halfway up from his side as if to guide conversation her way; as he helps with the canning, he praises her with looks and words. She bore him a dozen children, and lived with him through lean times, gathering cones for the seed company for extra cash.

"It was enjoyable work — you got outside in the fresh air — but it was *hard* work. Those sacks were heavy," she says. She would take her daughter, her daughter's baby, and her own youngest child of the same age, and collect the cones of cedar, pine, spruce, the small red bunchberries, and high-priced wintergreen.

Oftentimes they found piles the squirrels had made. Leaving some encouraged the squirrels to build up the piles again. "They forgot where they put them, sometimes. I used to feel bad until we found some old piles they had left the year before." The family could go back to the piles to collect from the squirrels' fresh heapings. Saturdays, she and neighbors who collected would stand in line at the Herbst Seed Company, to be paid by the bushel or the pound, depending on how much they had collected.

"It was good money," she says. "One morning —" and her husband nods his head, remembering the day, "it was 1974, I think — we made a hundred dollars. Just in one morning."

"You each made a thousand collecting seed one year," her husband adds. He smiles at her and waits for her to say more, his hands restless again.

She learned the trees from a book he gave her, and trips to the library. She also picked berries — wild blueberries, blackberries, highbush cranberries — and made jams and jellies, and learned about herbs. She speaks softly, remembering. Her husband's laugh leaps out; he tilts back his head, hair streaked with gray. His cheekbones and steeply curved nose remind me of a Mohawk, maybe a French-Canadian. He was part of the Alpine division in Italy in World War II, recruited from the Adirondacks for his skiing ability.

When I ask him questions, he answers, but then looks to her. He is waiting for bear season to open. He keeps a hunting camp, a tent set up on state land during hunting season. He takes his children, grandchildren, and even one great-grandchild with him into the forest.

Guides

Guides have worked in the Adirondacks almost as long as trappers. Some of the earliest guides were trappers. Writer Harvey L. Dunham describes them: "Originally trappers, they settled in the forest on State lands or lands of the Lumber companies. As squatters they built the cabins and lived off the country. They hunted and fished; they trapped and picked spruce gum and made maple sugar, trading the furs and these other products at settlements for supplies" (Dunham, 1952, unpaginated).

Wealthy sportsmen discovered their camps and cabins in the woods, and asked the trappers to take them hunting and fishing. By the mid-1800s, guiding wealthy "sports" became a frequent occupation for many year-round Adirondackers. Hunting and fishing parties came up from New York and other large cities, and hired guides to take them where the sport would be good. Each guide worked in his own part of the Adirondacks. The guide had many duties, including rowing and carrying the guide boat and providing stories for entertainment. A guide "had to know where to find the best camping spots, how to pitch a tent or build a temporary shelter of bark, to make balsam beds, set the fire, and keep smudges going day and night. He knew how to cook trout, venison, and flapjacks and how to supply them. He knew how to skin, not pluck, a partridge. In addition, he had to carry the pack basket of supplies, sometimes a load of sixty pounds" (White, 1987, p. 157).

Several guides during this period took famous people, including presidents, into the mountains; some of these guides became legends whose history has survived into the present. Old Mountain Phelps, French Louie, John Cheney, and Native American Mitchell Sabattis became known as much for their unique characters and storytelling as for their skills in the woods. Historian Alfred L. Donaldson writes of Sabattis: "His knowledge of woodcraft amounted to animal instinct. In the woods he saw and heard and reasoned with a refinement that was uncanny. The stories of the big game he killed, of his coolness and resourcefulness in danger and dilemma, would fill a volume" (Donaldson, 1921, 2:83).

Mart Moody and his brothers worked in the Saranac Lake area. He guided famous historians and the governor, and was the favorite guide of Chester A. Arthur and Grover Cleveland. He was one of the guides at Emerson's Philosophers' Camp, and guided many other people important in the history of the Adirondacks (Donaldson, 1921).

In the last decades of the nineteenth century, the larger hotels employed "house guides." But they were not as well versed in the woods as the older guides, and eventually the trade of guiding began to lose some of its former status. Many guides became caretakers, and continued to guide for the owners, and the children of the owners, whose property they maintained.

Guides operating in the Adirondacks now range from older guides who still rely on one or two wealthy patrons to provide steady employment and benefits, to young guides who take new people each trip. Almost all still specialize in a particular area; guides also specialize in rock climbing, canoe trips, hiking, winter trips, white-water rafting, and hunting and fishing. The DEC has continued the licensing program started early in the century, but has added a test and a two hundred dollar fee. Some of the older guides feel that this is ridiculous. The New York State Outdoor Guide Association is a professional organization that provides conferences, training, and support for guides of all kinds.

Bill Frayne, whom I interviewed several times, regularly guided eminent judges, including a Supreme Court Justice. He learned his trade from his father. His equipment consisted of an old canoe, a small boat with an Evinrude motor, his own hand-tied flies, and a fair number of fishing poles. A couple in their early thirties who moved to the Adirondacks several years ago lead rock-climbing weekends and mountaineering trips for a constantly shifting clientele. Their equipment consists of expensive climbing and camping gear of all kinds. Most of their knowledge they brought with them when they arrived. Between these two extremes there lies a wide range of experience and approaches among Adirondack guides.

Another guide I interviewed works in the prisons part-time to bring in a steady income. He would prefer to guide full-time, but is still building up his clientele. He is still in his twenties, well over six feet tall, and his arms show the thick muscles of a canoe paddler. He grew up in the Adirondacks and always dreamed of guiding. An old trapper got him started, telling him endless stories of the woods. Now he learns, he says, about half of what he knows from experience and observation, the other half from books. His goals for a trip include explaining local natural history, teaching environmental ethics, and using outdoor adventures as a way to build personal development and teamwork among his clients. Before I leave his house, I ask him how he feels about the woods. He throws his arms wide, leaning back. "The forests are my cathedral!" he almost shouts. There is no doubt that his view is different from Stan Montgomery's.

I first meet Chuck, the executive director of the New York State Outdoor Guide Association, on a portage trail — a "carry," in Adirondack terminology. It is in the middle of a chain of small, clear lakes which represent some of the best wild water in the Adirondacks. He is under a canoe, striding in one direction, and I am under another canoe, going in the other direction. From under a canoe one sees mainly the needle-covered trail, but I catch a glimpse of a man big enough to be on a professional football team. On the return trip across the portage trail we cross paths again, and I see that he is probably in his thirties, with thick strawberry blond hair, and faint lines of concentration on his forehead. His clients and an assistant guide walk behind him, shouldering their packs. His own is enormous.

The next time we meet it is at his outfitting store in town, where he has agreed to an interview. We end up sitting on the back steps watching his small children play in the yard, while he tells me cheerfully about the trials, and the pleasures, of running his own guiding business. He tells me what many of the other guides have told me about their concerns to promote ethical behavior in the wilderness, their worries over deteriorating conditions in the wild, and their support for wilderness areas in the Adirondacks. Many of the guides support the creation of the Bob Marshall or Oswegatchie Great Wilderness in the western half of the Adirondack Park. The idea of this proposed six hundred square mile wilderness appeals not only to their sense of promoting places for their guiding but also to their desire to protect the wildlands they love. Love and reverence are the operative words for the guides. Most of the guides I interview talk about their love for the forests, and their feelings of awe and renewal when they are in the wilderness. Chuck echoes the younger guide's feelings of reverence; he says that nature is a church for him, a source of joy and awe.

Yet many of the guides I interview, especially the ones who have grown up in the Adirondacks, even though they approve the creation of more wilderness, express reservations about the Governor's Commission on the Adirondacks and its recommendations. They think that the makeup of the commission does not include real Adirondackers, and the methods of the commission do not facilitate participation. The guides also object privately to the lack of real knowledge of the woods on the part of the commissioners, most of whom are city dwellers who only vacation in the Adirondacks. I sense a real frustration on the part of the guides that they — the holders of much knowledge and experience of the woods — have not been asked to join in the discussion.

The guides have much to offer. They have a unique view of the forest, and a unique view of their own relationship to nature. Like other woodspeople, they are reservoirs of indigenous knowledge about the woods, and they represent to many Adirondackers what is most characteristic of their culture. At the same time, they go beyond the ordinary boundaries of the cultural transmission of knowledge from one generation to the next, because it is their job to interpret and transmit knowledge of the local environment, and how to behave in an ethical relationship with it, to those who come from outside the local culture. In their views on wilderness and their special position as interpreters, teachers, and role models of human relationships with nature, they come closest of all the woodspeople to appreciating the ideals of the preservationists. It is especially poignant, as well as indicative of the extent to which participation has been considered a non-issue, that they have not been included in the decision-making in Adirondack land use planning.

6

Tree Farmers and Maple Syrup Producers: Architects of the Forest

TREE FARMING IS THE ART OF MANAGING
trees to produce a desired end: sawlogs, maple syrup, firewood,
Christmas trees, or other products. Logging has the most visible
immediate impact on the forest. Craftspeople, trappers, guides, and gatherers harvest the unique from the forest without changing its overall pattern;
but tree farming causes a change from the natural to the human design.
Tree farmers are the quintessential tinkerers, altering nature's blueprint for
the forest to meet their own ends. This tinkering ranges from human dominion over trees as a crop, a close cousin to agricultural crop farming, such as
takes place on large commercial Christmas tree plantations, to the minor
tinkering that a farmer does in a sugarbush, removing a tree here and there
to release a desirable maple, or putting in a road to the top of a hill.

At Asplin Tree Farm in Bloomingdale, for instance, strict rows of even-
aged balsam march across the fields, scarcely resembling a forest. But some
birds find food and shelter there. A few miles east of Asplin, the Browns'
farm represents a middle ground; they have mapped the natural stands in
their pioneer tree farm and say that they intend to work with what is there.
Carl Brown has logged some of the softwoods for lumber for the house he

and his wife are building, and has cut firewood. Together they have planted future groves of white pine and cedar. Abbey Brown shows me the blueprint they are working from: in addition to the natural stands, patches of crosshatching and neat X's show hypothetical stands of species that the Browns think will fit in well ecologically and will have some practical use for them. When I ask about a patch of silver maple, Abbey says shyly that they are there because they are her favorite trees.

The Browns, who both work for the DEC, moved to the Adirondacks from other, more urban places. They are working with the DEC's tree farm program, which helps them plan for the best productivity levels consistent with their forest base. As a certified pioneer tree farm, they qualify for a special tax break so long as they follow the DEC-approved plan. Both have biology backgrounds and experience in the woods. The plan promises to preserve the original mix of species while enhancing productivity for human needs. It suggests a new and hopeful version of conservation, one that includes human beings as a part of the natural world. But the Browns and their plans are still young. Their small children gambol around us in the barn loft they are using as living quarters while they build their house. The future may still change. I wonder what else their children will need from the forest.

Maple Syrup Producers

Maple sugaring probably represents the oldest form of tree farming on the continent. Native Americans made maple syrup and sugar and used it to sweeten their foods before the Europeans arrived; they introduced it to the pioneers (Erichsen-Brown, 1979, pp. 79–83). James Smith, a captive of the Huron in Ohio, recorded the Hurons' sugaring techniques: "In this month (February) we began to make sugar. . . . On the sugar-tree they cut a notch, sloping down. . . . They drove a long chip, in order to carry the water out from the tree, and under this they set their vessel, to receive it (being without brass kettles for boiling they froze the water in shallow elm baskets and threw away the ice every morning, until syrup remained)" (Erichsen-Brown, 1979, p. 81).

Now maple syrup operations range from large businesses which alter natural sugar maple stands through thinning, planting, and road building, to small family operations, often dairy farms, which use a few trees to make enough syrup for the family and a few sales. The sugarbush and the traditions of sugaring are often passed on from one generation to the next.

Because of its long history as a family occupation and the wide range of management practices, maple syrup production offers a close view of how indigenous knowledge of tree farming works.

It is late February. The sky radiates a brilliant blue, suffused with early spring warmth. The heavy snow of last week weights the branches of the balsams and hemlocks and the tamarack by the brook, but the sounds of soft drips and rivulets signal the beginning of change. Suddenly, a loaf of snow slides from a balsam tree, releasing a branch which springs upward to dry in the sunlight. Tonight the temperature will drop below freezing again. Tomorrow it will rise above freezing, creating positive pressure within the maples. In the sugarbush, the hardwood stand composed mostly of sugar maples which stretches over the hillside, the sap is ready to harvest. The sap that the maple syrup producers collect is flowing through the xylem cells, the woody tissue of the tree, carrying carbohydrates and nutrients necessary for flowering and the initiation of spring growth.

The producers are ready for the beginning of the sap season. Bundles of black tubing, lined up together like four long fingers, traverse the spaces

Photo 8. Lewis Staats, extension specialist and researcher, Uihlein sugar maple research station, Lake Placid. Photo D. Kuklok

between the mature maples at head height. Each tree has up to three taps, from which sap flows directly into the tubing; these run downhill alongside the newly graded dirt road down to the sap house. Suction created by vacuum pumps like those used in milking machines enhances the harvest. At the top of the slope are sap dump units, which use a vacuum chamber to separate the sap from the vacuum, and from there it flows by gravity down the hill. In the sap house the sap pours out of the pipeline into corrugated metal tanks like small swimming pools, where it sits like a chilly bath, crystal clear.

In the research station across the road, Lewis Staats, New York State's extension specialist for maple syrup production, paces beside the boiling pans. Lines of anxiety crease his forehead; he expects this sap run to continue well into the night, and almost all the storage tanks in the sap house are already full. Chris Moquin, his right-hand man, has been boiling down the sap in the pans for hours, but the vapor-compression evaporator, which removes 85 percent of the water in the process of sap to syrup, has had an equipment component failure. Lewis has called Steve Dorsey, who designed the unit, but he won't be there for a few more hours.

Meanwhile, the pans fill, and the sap in them turns a deep golden brown. The men dip some out to test; after testing, they stir it into their coffee. Clouds of aromatic steam drift upward from the pans; taking a deep breath is like inhaling ambrosia. Yet Lewis and Chris, hurrying from pan to pan, seem not to notice. Later, when barrels are filled with finished syrup from the pans, and the sap has stopped flowing for a few days, Chris will can the syrup in plastic containers labeled light, medium, or dark amber, according to the level of translucency, which determines the grade. The syrup is sold to Cornell alumni and shipped to the Cornell University dairy store. The price hovers around thirty-four dollars a gallon — liquid gold — but Lewis has to be careful not to undersell neighboring producers who are clients in the extension business.

Down the road, at the vast Pfennig farm, Mr. Pfennig's old sugarhouse stands empty and cold. Tom Dodd, who worked for Mr. Pfennig as a caretaker and hunting guide, also did the sugaring. He took us there to see the old sugaring equipment one cold morning after a snowstorm.

White drifts bury the farm. Silence covers the house and the outbuildings like a quilt. One worker, far away on the other side of a building, is clearing the drifts from a driveway; the rest of the huge acreage is still, stretching in an unbroken field to a postcard view of the snow-shouldered mountains. The sugarhouse stands at the edge of the sugarbush; the door creaks, stiff with disuse, and our boots echo on the floor as we stamp to shake off the snow. Inside, neat stacks of buckets and drawers of spiles line the boiling room. A little kitchen table and chairs stand to one side. Kerosene lamps hang from the walls.

Tom stands tall and lean, his eyes red-rimmed and watery from the cold, reminiscing about his work at the farm. He used to arrive before dawn to get the pans going, so that by the time Mr. and Mrs. Pfennig came up after breakfast, they could begin sugaring. They sugared with buckets, using horses on the steep hillsides and tractors on the level ground. They kept two wood-fired stoves going until the sugarhouse was hot. The stoves are still there.

Tom learned to sugar as a child, the youngest of thirteen in a farm family in Chateaugay. Back then, he said, the neighbors all helped one another with whatever needed to be done, whether cutting wood or sugaring. "We had good neighbors then," he says. The Dodds sugared as a family, Tom's mother boiling the great pots of sap in the kitchen until the wallpaper peeled from the steam. As a boy he worked early and hard, driving a horse and cart fourteen miles to deliver milk before school each day. Sugaring was hard work, but it was pleasurable, too. Sugaring is still largely a family affair.

❧ Loggers, guides, hunters, trappers, fishermen, craftspeople, and gatherers all harvest from the woods. They learn the interrelationships of the land through experience and the accumulated wisdom of the community passed on from the older woodspeople. All have an impact on the forest and manipulate certain aspects of it; but none of them attempts to change the face of the landscape or to replace the natural architecture with a human-directed architecture.

The tree farmers, by contrast, take the amorphous, shifting body of local knowledge about the woods, from which the others can fish out bits of information about ecological relationships a piece at a time, and use the whole body of it as a science to transform nature. They become architects, imposing a blueprint ordered by human values on the natural order of the woods. Yet tree farmers, more than corn or wheat farmers, have to work within living ecosystems whose properties are largely unknown to them. The business of discovering these properties through observation, experimentation, and intuition, and then applying that knowledge to decision-making processes to alter the natural character of the woods illuminates qualities of indigenous knowledge.

Scientific knowledge, gleaned from journals or extension agents, applies. But tree farmers must constantly reinvent it because, unlike modern cornfields, each sugarbush has great variation in its slopes, streams, soils, exposures, microclimates, wildlife — a natural history that has been building for generations. And unlike fields of genetically identical corn plants, each tree is a different individual. Many different species may populate a parcel. Among these, those of the same species have differences in genetic makeup, age, growth patterns, histories of disease — difficulties revealed in the burls on a trunk, a gnarled limb, a lightning scar, an owl's nest, a trunk bent like an old man from a heavy snow.

Indigenous knowledge, applied to decision making, has to work from a database of apparent randomness and chaos. It has to discover the natural patterns of reaction to spring temperatures that activate sap flow in a stand of individuals. It is the variation itself which must be figured.

Maple syrup operations, by virtue of the fact that they need forty-year-old trees to start with and rely on the rhythms of temperature and spring sap flow, are probably the most sensitively attuned to the intricacies of ecosystem function of all tree farms. The successful maple syrup producer has to be able to work with random information, to shift position constantly. It is like playing a board game without access to the rules, and without even the certainty that the rules are consistent from day to day or year to year. The weather is as chancy as a roll of the dice.

The flip side of knowing the woods and the weather in sugaring is knowing one's own labor, materials, and financial constraints, and being able to extend these boundaries creatively, sometimes through invented technologies. Since the weather contributes a large component of the success or failure of a particular year, owing to the number of freeze-thaw days, and the ability of the producer to predict when they will occur, maple syrup production ends up being something of a gamble. There is at times a fine line between making money and losing money at sugaring.

With a tree physiologist doing research on sugar maples, I developed a survey questionnaire for New York State maple producers at three yearly extension service tours of maple farms. The survey was designed as a qualitative assessment of the farmers' application of their knowledge to decision-making processes. We received seventy-five usable responses. Operations ranged from 500 taps or fewer to huge 10,000-tap operations where the latest vacuum-pumped tubing, oil-fired, and vapor compression units are used to transform sap (2 to 4 percent sucrose) into syrup (67 to 68 percent sucrose). It was clear from the responses that the maple farmers, using experimentation and observation, generated working hypotheses about the ecology of the woods and sugar maple ecology that guided their decisions about the choice of site and of which particular trees to tap.

We asked the New York maple syrup producers, "Are there any signs you look for in a sugar maple tree which tell you whether it will produce a high-sugar sap?" Fifty percent stated that they looked for a large crown, and 33 percent looked for healthy, vigorous growth. In addition, three respondents said that they looked for trees with many limbs, and two believed that stressed trees might produce a high-sugar sap. When asked what signs they looked for to tell whether a tree will produce a large quantity of sap, 53 percent said that they looked for large crowns, 19 percent looked for healthy, vigorous growth, 5 percent looked for a moist site, and 4 percent mentioned many limbs. The maple producers rely on the advice of other producers and older generations, as well as their own intuitions, observations, and experimentation.

Charles Dent, a retired state trooper whose family goes back three generations in the Adirondacks, remembered the time of wooden buckets: "When you used buckets, there were trees that you got to know that ran sweeter sap — or more often you noticed one that ran more." Now he looks for expediency first. "If it's a large maple, and it's alive, then I put a hole in it."

Another question we asked was, "Are there any signs which tell you what area will make a good sugarbush?" While some people mentioned accessibility for tapping, the majority gave answers related to the ecology of the woods. The largest number of responses were concerned with the orientation of the slope. Most respondents thought southeastern slopes offered the best sugarbush areas; a few mentioned south and southwestern orientations as well, though one person said that a south or southeastern slope should not be chosen because, although the run starts earlier, it also ends earlier.

Soil fertility was important for 25 percent of the maple farmers. Some said that loamy soils were good; others preferred heavy soils. Some used groundcover types as indicators of soil fertility.

Weather conditions, and deciding when to start tapping, are always a gamble, but there too, maple producers and others use their intuition and their knowledge of the different variables that make up the weather to try to predict its shifting patterns. Talk among producers about the weather and news of who has started sugaring travels fast in the mountains.

Individual interviews with both directed questions and informal discussion revealed a deep complexity in the maple producers' indigenous knowledge of the woods. Whether or not the university scientists had figured out the nature of current trends with any certainty, maple producers had to make decisions about their operations based on their best judgments of the situation. They worried about the pear thrips, already infesting maple stands in Vermont, and whether acid rain would weaken maples and destroy syrup production.

Each maple producer must decide the wisest course of action for his or her own operation, including the tricky question of when to start each spring. Maple producers rely on the extension specialist, Lewis Staats, and his commonsense evaluation of the findings of academic research scientists, as well as the latest technology for production. In addition, they use their knowledge and observation of the ecology of their woods, and the shared wisdom of the community of maple producers.

Observation, though based in a conception of natural history passed on from one generation to the next, is an intensely personal interaction. "I don't know if it's from acid rain or what — a lot of the big spruce trees are dying, black spruce on McCutcheon's property, hundreds already on West Lake. Can't look up on the side of Saddle [Mountain] without seeing dead spruce," said one producer, remarking on deteriorating forest health. Decisions are based on an accumulation of observations, sorted and shifted in the observer's mind according to the importance and bearing of each detail. Logic must follow inductive lines, since no one can observe all the trees or see all the interconnections in the woods.

In the end, each maple producer creates a pattern in his or her mind that connects the patches of knowledge about the forest in a meaningful way and makes decision making possible. Another producer might see a different picture. But generally there is a shared sense, which grows through conversations and meetings between producers, of what is happening in the woods and of wise courses of action, given different conditions. Those who depart from these agreed-upon paths generate gossip, speculation, and close attention to their results. If something works, others are likely to try it. But maple production depends on more than indigenous knowledge of natural history and ecology. The indigenous knowledge itself has to go a step further, and involve the practical aspects of technical interactions with the woods, and the eventual modification of the woods.

Deciding which trees to tap has changed as equipment use has changed. When they used buckets, maple farmers could readily tell which trees were producing more sap or sweeter sap. With the advent of tubing, the distinctions in production between individual trees are not obvious. Nevertheless, farmers are still aware of the factors they have traditionally used to predict which trees will be better producers. Distinctions at the stand level still determine choices.

Ross Putnam and his cousins Rod and David all run sugaring operations. Ross has lived in the Adirondacks all his life. He was born in Lake Placid; his father was Pennsylvania Dutch, his mother French and English and Native American. He first tapped maples around his house when he was ten years old. He always wanted to make syrup but did not have the land to do it. Now, as a caretaker, he taps trees on the owner's land. He has 1,700 taps that all run right into the sugarhouse. Ross thinks that trees with a big crown do best; he taps any tree that is eleven inches in diameter or over. He tests with hydrometers. In the open areas he has found some maples with a sugar content as high as 4 to 5 percent. He learns something every year, he says. This year he has learned to dislike squirrels: they caused a lot of damage to his tubing. There seemed to be more squirrels than usual this year, perhaps because it was a good seed year.

Ross spends his free time in the woods. He used to hunt until he started sugaring, but he mainly hunted just to be in the woods. "I always liked the woods, even when we were small," he says. His boys used to go hunting with him all the time; he taught them all he could about survival — the quickest way to build a fire when it's wet, and the different kinds of trees. "Usually anything in the woods I notice, but I don't know a lot of names. The bark on the yellow birch — you can eat it. It tastes just like wintergreen."

Ross now owns seventy-five acres, but he doesn't have enough hard maple on his property to sugar it. He goes there to hike and cut his own firewood; and he picks berries and gets burls from the trees, mostly yellow birch, for his son, who makes vases out of them.

His sons help him with the sugaring. The owners of the land never participate in the sugaring. They take the best of the syrup as their share, to give away as Christmas presents, in a non-cash, non-taxable exchange that seems startlingly close to feudal relations of medieval times. Apparently it is a fairly common practice. It seems not to bother Ross at all.

His cousin Rod's father used to be a guide and caretaker at Ausable Lake. Rod's parents owned a farm where they raised chickens, cattle, hogs, and turkeys, and were "pretty self-sufficient." Rod sugared growing up, but didn't do it seriously until he started as an adult, when he had free time from his job in law enforcement. His information comes as much from talking to other producers and extension specialist Lewis Staats as from experience. He regularly reads the *Maple Digest.*

David Putnam first started sugaring because the sap season coincides with a slow time for building contractors, his work the rest of the year. His father sugared nearby and now helps David, along with David's ten-year-old son, while his wife and daughter do the canning. David runs between 1,700 and 2,800 taps and generally ends up with more syrup than he can sell locally. He hopes to find more markets soon, perhaps through mail order. The most difficult thing about maple production for David and his wife, Donna, is the uncertainty of the labor demand, always dependent on the weather and the number of freeze-thaw days. In 1989 they started boiling on March 27 and worked sixteen-hour days straight through April 17. He rents a sugarbush, where he has 2,000 taps, and on his own land he puts in up to 800 additional taps. He owns about ten acres of sugar maples. But sugaring is always fraught with challenges. Last week, he tells me, a batch froze. When these kinds of problems arise, he turns to other producers for advice.

Economics and ownership of the land determine many choices. Susan Whitehead figures her family farm has a maple stand going up a mountainside that could support about 8,000 taps, an enormous operation. But she needs someone knowledgeable to start and run the operation. After her husband died suddenly several years ago, Susan had to take over operation of the farm as well as their successful bed and breakfast. Now her daughter and son-in-law live with her with their baby, but with outside jobs as well, no one has time to start a large maple operation. Others are constrained by competing occupations, cash flow considerations, or labor shortage during the intensive sugaring period.

Some producers find ways to tip the balance of uncertain profits from sugaring in their favor. Keene Valley cuts between some of the steepest mountains in the Adirondacks. Driving to Keene Valley past rocky cliffs, deep cold lakes, and dark forests, one feels transported to one of the Grimms' fairy tales. One waits for the beast to step out of the woods or a castle to appear on a ridge. High Valley Farm, a white house with green trim and a sign hanging out front, stands as a reminder of pioneer farms a century ago. The smooth wood floors, the iron stove and wood table where Stephan Jones plants his big elbows, underline the strength and comfort of human habitations. Stephan is a man of the outdoors, big-boned and soft-voiced, wearing a plaid wool jacket and wool cap, his heavy boots ready by the door. He and his wife have about 500 taps on rented land, a comparatively small operation. They tap using buckets and horses, capitalizing on the nostalgia it invokes to give wagon rides to tourists during the sap season. He also works as a caretaker and guide, and does some carpentry work on the side. His relationship with the woods is actively exploitive yet respectful; he relishes his role as a woodsman.

Woods ecology, labor, and economics all constrain maple production. The most successful producers are those who reinvent the art in some way, bricoleurs of maple technology, who turn a constraint into a catalyst for invention. Their decisions alter the woods: trees are cut down or planted, roads are put in, sap removed. Their knowledge becomes part of an active managing relationship with their environment; yet at the same time the forest maintains its mysterious ecology, its functioning a collection of seemingly random events from which the maple producer must intuit or discover experimentally the information that will allow for economically viable production.

Woodspeople and Indigenous Knowledge

For the holder of indigenous knowledge, the process of seeking knowledge offers few clear answers. The variables are often nebulous, and prior knowledge is as hazy and indeterminate as the future. It is a process of following smudged tracks, a broken twig, a crushed leaf, or a bewildering crossing of the paths of deer and dogs and bears, not knowing what the outcome will be. The knowledge often arises not from the final result, the venison or the pan of syrup which provided the impetus for this zigzagging research, but from the observations gleaned from various viewpoints along the way, and from the trails that went astray.

Anthropologist Billie DeWalt argues that knowledge systems based on Western scientific traditions could be interacting productively with indigenous knowledge systems. But rather than presenting either Western science or indigenous knowledge systems idealistically, DeWalt considers the strengths and weaknesses of each. He argues that Western science enables us to know extraordinary amounts about very limited areas of knowledge. Scientists understand basic principles by which things work and have an effective means — through the scientific method — of approaching problems. This knowledge may be readily transferable across time, space, and social setting. But science's tendency toward reductionism leads to ignorance of the wider context: "Complex systems and those characterized by myriad interactions are likely to be ignored" (DeWalt, 1994, p. 124).

Indigenous knowledge, by contrast, is malleable; it can shift to fit the continually changing circumstances that define a particular locality. People who are holders of such knowledge may know a great deal about the local environment, and may have a deep awareness of interconnections between plants, animals, and soils. They become good at fashioning solutions to the problems of fitting human activities to local ecological conditions.

Indigenous knowledge deals with randomness and unknowns. Whereas science searches out patterns and poses mainly those questions to which it predicts it can find a discrete answer, indigenous knowledge operates in the realm of uncertainty. In the language of recent theories of chaos, woodspeople must look for the order underneath the randomness, the aperiodic systems which almost repeat themselves but not quite. Averages and generalizations are of little use if the hunter cannot predict where on a specific mountainside the deer will be and what it will do in that afternoon's snowstorm and westerly winds.

Often there is failure. Experience, which is the accumulated balance of failures and successes, cannot be supplanted by any amount of reading or other kinds of learning. The Athapaskans differentiate in their language between primary, experiential learning and secondary learning from sources other than personal experience. Researcher Scott Rushforth states that they value the former above the latter, and so, in the Adirondacks, do the local people value the knowledge of those with primary learning over the knowledge acquired secondhand. Rushforth knows that the Athapascans value primary learning because they rely on those with primary learning for decision making (Rushforth, 1992). Woodspeople in the Adirondacks are also referred to as knowledgeable about the forest and are respected as repositories of knowledge gained through experience.

The potential for interaction between local woodspeople and scientists seems high. The example of Orie Loucks' work in Appalachia with woodspeople there shows that this process can work. The research centers in the Adirondacks, including the Uihlein station, the Atmospheric Science Research Center, and the Ecological Center in Newcomb, could provide excellent opportunities for such interaction. In addition, the scientists could meet the woodspeople on their own ground. Unfortunately, scientists are often nearly as removed from the decision-making process as the woodspeople.

In the Adirondacks, those who do make the decisions about land use — the APA bureaucrats, the DEC officials, the politicians, lawyers, and members of special interest groups — are not, for the most part, people who spend their days in the woods. Nor are they scientists. Their knowledge, sophisticated as it may be, is largely secondary, highlighted with intense, brief experiences in the wilderness. The attitude of bureaucracy, which requires a level of abstraction and categorization relevant to legal systems and regulation, often seems to be that the indigenous knowledge available in the community is irrelevant or not usable. This view of indigenous knowledge severely limits local people's active voice in decision making. Why are those with primary knowledge so frequently ignored in the decision-making process? For an answer, one has to look beyond indigenous knowledge itself, to the interactions between communities with different worldviews about the forest, to the ongoing conflict process, and to the role of power in a democratic system.

Photo 9. Bill Frayne, fishing guide, Lake Placid. Photo D. Kuklok.

Community and Conflict

Introduction

THE LIST OF LAND USE ISSUES IN THE Adirondacks spans many categories, yet the conflict over each issue derives energy from the central debate between differing worldviews, perceptions of how humans should relate to the natural environment and to one another. "Debate" is probably the wrong word for what is occurring, since a debate by definition is entered into by two willing and equal partners, and some local people would argue that this is not the case in the Adirondacks. "Argument" can imply inequalities between different parties, but it also implies a level of communication at which there is at least some give-and-take, an exchange of meanings in which the participants understand one another and accept the legitimacy of what the others say. In this case it is not clear that the different sides accept the legitimacy of the others' worldviews, or even understand the language the others are using to define the problems and suggest solutions. "Conflict" can include both of these terms, as well as terms reflecting higher levels of aggression. The word "conflict" represents a scale on which interactions can escalate or de-escalate; it reflects a process of change.

Journalistic presentations describe the escalation of conflict using war

153

154   imagery (Lakoff and Johnson, 1980): words such as "battles," "confrontation," "opposition," "targets," and so on symbolically illuminate the fixed
stances, isolation from other viewpoints, and alternating explosions of violence and standoffs typical of what is taking place in the Adirondacks. Yet
one hesitates to paint such a grim and final picture over the whole canvas
of activity on land use issues. Rather, it is a process, a progression of
both battles and bridge-building, as well as moments of hopelessness when
neither approach seems productive.

Bridge-building, actions of reaching out to other people's realities and
compromising enough to permit holders of different worldviews to see the
views of others, can accomplish peaceful solutions. Battles, too, whether
verbal, territorial, or otherwise, are not wholly destructive. They serve to
reestablish the identity of each side, which may have been compromised in
the act of bridge-building, especially in the case of the subordinate, less
powerful side. In such conflict, those who have less of a voice may be the
initiators; those who dominate the issues may protest the actions as irrational or counterproductive; and those who are voiceless to begin with may
continue to stay out of the action. The more active participants in both the
battles and the bridge-building frequently claim ownership of the voiceless
for their own side. In the Adirondacks, each side claims to represent the
majority of the local residents.

Why have the land use issues in the Adirondacks escalated to this
level? When, as in many serious conflicts, the different sides represent
substantially different worldviews, each of them is threatened by changes
in the current land use status of the Adirondacks.

"Culture" may in some cases seem too strong a word to describe the
different sides in the Adirondack land use disputes. The people involved
share American citizenship, public schools, a legal system, and a common
government. Yet their experiences of these systems is qualitatively different.
Within these bounds, subcultures define individuals within a way of life, a
way of work, and a way of seeing. These subcultures develop tangentially
to one another and can result in worldviews that conflict. When worldviews
differ substantially, getting the facts is just not enough; understanding the
differences between the worldviews and why they are what they are is
equally important.

In the interviews in Chapter 7, the speakers represent different
worldviews and competing voices in this process of battling and bridge-
building. Each one is a well-known figure in the Adirondacks who reflects
a different side of the conflict for many people inside and outside the

Adirondacks. Although their worldviews are uniquely their own, they are substantially shared by others who have had similar experiences. Yet many people concerned with local land use issues do not know the personal history and experiences that produced these individuals and their views. When people do not know the individuals behind the philosophies and values represented in the process, they may be unable to understand the worldviews that have produced these processes. In terms of culture, a particular worldview is inseparable from the individual who holds it; an individual is both a product of his or her culture and a creator of it. The biographical details in each interview allow us insights into the formation of each person's worldview.

In addition, each person interviewed has the advantage of having pursued more than one occupation; each is a "reflective practitioner" (Schon, 1983; Whyte, 1991), in the sense that he or she uses several different frameworks to reflect on the actions that he or she has taken in this process. Reflecting from another framework often changes a person's actions. Collectively, such changes can alter the course of the process.

James Frenette characterizes a balanced position on the views of local government officials; his experiences as a schoolteacher, APA commissioner, and lifelong Tupper Lake resident give him a variety of perspectives.

Nellie Staves symbolizes the views of Adirondack sportspeople; her experiences as a trapper and her ethic of citizenship in conservation issues, as well as the unusual status of being a woman trapper, and an officer and chosen representative for the Adirondack Conservation Council, add depth to her reflections.

Louis Simmons is both a newspaper editor and a local historian. Though not a spokesman for any particular group, in some ways he reflects the collective voices of the Town of Altamont and the village of Tupper Lake through his awareness of the events and personalities in land use issues over time.

John Stock speaks for both forest management expertise, as a result of his work on private and public forest holdings, and the ideas of forest economists. His experience as a local resident and past APA commissioner give him an angle on land use issues that is unique in the Adirondacks. Many local people view him as an able spokesman for their perspective on the issues.

Frank Bencze condenses the views of industry from his perspective as both a forester and a manager. As a local resident whose work and life have been affected by changes in the Adirondack forest industry, he reflects the

156   thoughts of many wood products and timber workers who have seen their
lives change.

Gary Randorf speaks for the preservationists, both within and outside
the Park, who subscribe to mainstream preservationism, typified by special
interest groups such as the Audubon Society, the Sierra Club, and the
Wilderness Society. As an artist working in natural landscape photography,
Randorf also sees the wilderness he is trying to perceive in a critical aesthetic light, and he creates images that affect the aesthetic appreciation of
others.

Finally, Dick Sage characterizes the worldview of resource-based forest
ecology and of scientific research in general. In addition, he functions as a
community leader in the small hamlet of Newcomb, whose pioneering part
in the process is discussed in Chapter 8. His views of community transcend
both ecology and the political process of resolving land use conflict. The
two extremes of deep ecology and home rule advocacy are presented in
Chapter 9.

Not all the worldviews or cultures involved in the land use conflict are
represented in Part III. Traditional Mohawk views were discussed in Chapter 2, and the diverse views of woodspeople in Chapters 4 and 5. If I have
not given more room to the preservationists in this section, it is because
their words and views have already been better documented for the public
than those of local government and forest resource workers. In Chapter 3
I discussed their general environmental philosophies and their complex
history.

🌿 Contemporary Adirondack land use issues cover many topics, including
cultural differences, class struggles, aesthetics, ecology, preservation of biological diversity, zoning, sovereignty or "home rule," usufruct rights, rights
of access, and the rights of nature. In Chapter 7 each individual describes
these issues using the terminology of the group whose worldview he or she
represents. The difference in views, and thus in language, at times prevents
the groups from talking to one another without creating misunderstandings
and stalemates. In the process, the participants tend to stereotype one
another and their arguments. In this way, the process becomes less one of
real communication, in which the different sides are able to listen to the
others and join in negotiation, and more a standoff between nonnegotiable
symbols and positions.

Defining the symbols of each worldview is a first step toward the mutual
understanding and communication necessary to building bridges between

the different groups engaged in land use conflict. This bridge-building is crucial for productive decision making in land use management — for the sake of the forest and the people who live there, as well as those who enjoy vacations there. For that reason I prefer to let the representatives of these different worldviews introduce the issues in the language that is congruent with their views, rather than imposing a generic terminology that could obliterate the sources of differences between them.

The story of the small hamlet of Newcomb, and its fight to define its own land use planning through the locally specific language of ecology rather than the imposed language of zoning is told in Chapter 8. Newcomb's planning process is nested in the realities of community and individual personalities. Its story illustrates how local voices have surfaced in the Adirondack land use controversy, and how the struggle continues between the more powerful regional planners and interest groups and the locals, who have less power but who know their community and the forest around them intimately. It also demonstrates the blending of scientific and indigenous knowledge through the work of the Adirondack Ecological Center and its cooperation with the community, a hopeful example for small rural communities everywhere — a hope that is rare in these times.

7

Reflective Practitioners

JIM FRENETTE IS A QUIETLY EXTRAORDI-
nary man. Small and compact with eyeglass frames that date back
to the 1970s, he tilts his head, eyes thoughtful, to listen to my
questions. When he answers, he speaks in concrete examples, reasoning by
anecdote and analogy rather than abstractions. Yet he never drifts from the
point. He plays down his accomplishments as elementary school teacher for
twenty-five years, Franklin County legislator for seven years, and chair
of the Intercounty Legislative Committee which created the Adirondack
Planning Commission, the center of the political maelstrom over land use
in the Adirondacks, in 1990.

Frenette embodies the values of Tupper Lake and is the epitome of the
residents' definition of good citizenship — family man, respected teacher,
sensitive and forceful politician. And yet there is an analytic awareness, a
gently ironic edge to his conversation which allows him to step away from
these roles and to see his part in the Adirondack land use struggles in a
wider context.

When then-Governor Mario Cuomo set up a commission to plan for
the future of the Adirondacks, the Governor's Commission on the Adiron-

dacks in the Twenty-First Century, his environmental advisers chose commissioners and technical advisers largely from outside the park and from
among the privileged within the park. When the commissioners presented
their report in 1990, a glossy book with 245 recommendations for land use
regulations in the park, including a map showing planned acquisitions,
many local people responded angrily. Some were openly hostile. The county
legislators, concerned about the rifts, tried to work with the state government. The Intercounty Legislative Committee, consisting of legislators from
twelve Adirondack counties, realized how important it was for local government to have a role in land use planning and regulation. The ILC created
the Adirondack Planning Commission, made up of elected representatives
of the twelve counties and planners, to define this role. Each county had a
representative on the APC. Jim Frenette was the Franklin County representative.

Governor Cuomo was excited about the group and agreed to meet with
them to negotiate over some of the controversial recommendations of the
report, which were scheduled to be presented as a package to the state
legislature. The APC met with Commissioner Jorling and Bob Bendick of
the Department of Environmental Conservation; Frank Murray, the deputy
secretary for environmental affairs; Joe Martens of the Office of Environmental Affairs; Denis Allee of the Department of Economic Development;
Bob Glennon, the executive director of the APA; and the governor. The
governor said that he was looking for the "voice of reason"; he wanted to
talk to locals, but not to the polarized segments already making themselves
heard in Albany and the Adirondacks.

Using the frameworks of democratic empowerment, education, and language, Jim Frenette analyzes the crisis over the Governor's Commission
report, and the ongoing frustration some local people feel with the intrusion
of government into what they consider their right to manage and use their
property as they see fit. From the perspective of empowerment, Frenette
looks at each situation to see how much local involvement is occurring, and
how often local people are involved in the decision making. As a spokesperson for the local population, especially Tupper Lake's, Frenette says, "We
do want to protect, we do want to preserve, and we do want a say in what
happens. We've been denied that role, of having a say, and that's been a
very contentious issue."

At another level, from an educator's framework, he sees the whole
process as one of educating each side to the needs of the others — the state
government to the needs of the local government, the environmentalists to

the needs of the conservationists, the outsiders to the needs of the locals, and vice versa. "There's got to be an educational process here. Locals have to realize there is a treasure here that has to be protected. Environmentalists have to realize they are stepping on toes."

But then he shakes his head and looks at his clasped hands. "We have to find a way to describe people other than the normal way. We talk about the environmentalists on the one side and the locals on the other. That's a form of polarization." Some administrators criticize the press for capitalizing on these polarizing terms. Frenette tries to redefine both the problems and the actors to reflect the insights he gains by looking at the problem from his various perspectives.

The major plank in the Adirondack Planning Commission's platform of objectives was to place five local people on the Adirondack Park Agency's Board of Commissioners. Although the governor appointed Adirondack residents including Anne LaBastille, an ecologist, and John Collins, a schoolteacher, many Adirondackers do not consider them to be representative of local opinions and feelings on land use issues. The Planning Commission would prefer the five members to be chosen from among elected officials, or picked in some way that would allow the majority of Adirondackers to have a voice in the choice.

The governor suggested several different areas of focus for his discussions with the Planning Commission. These included social and economic issues as well as protection of backcountry and open space, shorefront and roadsides, and access to public lands. The battle over shorefronts presents one of the most difficult issues, illustrative of many facing the Adirondacks in land use because so many people want to live in these areas, which have prime development value. Yet ecologically these are among the most sensitive areas; and aesthetically, the undeveloped edges of lakes and rivers function as a symbol of the pristine Adirondack wilderness for many people, both locals and outsiders. The state does not have enough money to buy that land, or even get easements. Frenette looks up with an almost imperceptible nod. "The governor admits, 'If we can't do it by purchase or easements, then we'll do it by regulation.' "

Frenette thinks that if the APA and environmentalists want to impose more regulations on shorefront, local governments should have a say. As the commissioners and local governments listened to one another, each side modified its positions. Yet as early as 1991, Frenette could see that there would have to be a restructuring of the Planning Commission. Half the commission was made up of planners taken away from other work, which they couldn't neglect. The APA suggested that the proactive Planning Commission replace the Local Government Review Board, the citizen watchdog group for the APA, which had long been run by what the APA considered to be extreme reactionaries. Frenette thinks that this move was a device meant to further divide the locals among themselves. In fact, it now seems that this was exactly what happened, whether the result was intentional or not, although the Planning Commission refused to take over the Review Board's role. Local groups began to accuse the Planning Commission of speaking too moderately and negotiating away citizens' rights. The issue of representation still remains unresolved. "There has to be a vehicle to allow locals to participate," Frenette says. "Back in the history, when the Park Agency was formed, I was on the town board here. We were almost totally isolated from the whole process. There were some real extremists on the Park Agency. . . . It was a steamroller. Locals were totally ignored, to the point where 99 percent of the local government became antagonistic to the agency. The lines were drawn."

Now the situation has changed, Frenette believes. Locals have come around to accepting the fact that there have to be some regulations on land use. The APA staff members have lived in the Adirondacks for years now, coping with the long winters, raising their children there. They are becoming acclimatized, and, in the process, the locals are beginning to accept them.

But the Governor's Commission jump-started the quiescent engines of conflict. Underneath the adjustments of daily living, basic values about the land remain different. Some of the commission's 245 recommendations were clearly outrageous to many locals, who pinpointed them quickly, and the environmentalists realized that they would have to be dropped or modified. These recommendations included "a one-year moratorium on subdivision, [and] changes in land use and development within 660 feet of any shoreline in all land use areas except hamlets." For resource management and rural land, "all owners would receive one SDR [structural development right] per ownership unit [all the land held by an owner in the park] as of April 1, 1990, up to 2,000 acres and one for each 2,000 thereafter." Furthermore, "a remediation goal should be set for the Park so that existing human-made objects and structures outside of hamlets are substantially invisible from travel corridors or set back 200 feet." Also, "standards to minimize visual impacts should be developed and may include standards on roof color, exterior materials and visibility against the skyline" (Commission on the Adirondacks in the twenty-first century, 1990). The APA was largely in favor of earth tones for houses, that is, browns and greens. All across the park, the proposed house color regulation was discussed in coffee shops and gas stations. It served as a symbol of the absurdity of regulations imposed by outsiders, while the building moratorium recommendation fueled real anger. Frenette says, his voice growing louder, "Do we really have local representation here? Any local who sits on the Park Agency here, who says buildings have to be earth tone, is somehow missing the heartbeat of what's going on here."

Many wondered how the Governor's Commission had come up with its recommendations. The commission had held fourteen public meetings, but only two of these were in the Adirondack Park itself, within the lands to be regulated and held under ever tighter reins. The local outcry raced unabated through the newspapers in fiery letters to the editor, in editorials, and in the gleeful reporting of minor scandals connected to the environmental community.

But the discussion is all part of the education process, which consists of people talking to one another. "I went to New York City to testify when the Planning Commission had public hearings and met a hell of a nice guy," Frenette reminisces. "We were talking about fishing and paddling. . . . Turned out to be Neil Woodworth, lawyer for the Adirondack Mountain Club. If people with different viewpoints could sit down and talk . . ."

Frenette and I both think immediately of George Davis, executive director of the Governor's Commission, and his presentation on the commission report. "It was a bad scene," Frenette sighs. Locals deeply opposed to outside regulation interrupted and heckled Davis in the Paul Smith's College auditorium while he tried ineffectually to stem the tide and talk over the crashing waves of disapproval. He was nearly forced to give up. A similar dynamic broke up a "heal the wounds" session that the Adirondack Planning Commission held, inviting environmentalists and representatives of local groups. The "extreme fringe" of locals, as Frenette calls them, came and stood in a ring around the table, disrupting the session. Finally the APC just called a halt to the proceedings. Later, the APC held a more successful meeting in Lake Placid, granting each group equal time to speak at the microphone.

Frenette sees legislation as the key to a solution. All the rest is rhetoric. He feels that this is the only way to ensure local participation in decision making. For example, in the matter of shorefront protection, the environmentalists want the state to have the right of first refusal on large landholdings; locals, including Frenette, want local involvement, including veto power. But the state, through the APA, threatens more severe regulation if its legislation is not passed. What has happened since the Governor's Commission report came out has, in fact, constituted an implicit extension of the regulations. Although none of the 245 proposed regulations has been passed in the legislature as of spring 1997, the APA commissioners are using them as guidelines in its decisions on permit issues brought before the board in its monthly meetings, according to some. Frenette has noticed the difference. "They [the APA] got talking about boathouses. . . . What I got out of it was, since we can't define boathouses, let's prohibit them. It would be much simpler if we just said no boathouses, prohibit them. And I thought, now wait a minute. You go up on St. Regis, Upper Saranac — those boathouses are a part of the landscape. They're beautiful."

There is little consistent differentiation, on the commission's side, between aesthetic and ecological concerns. Of the 245 regulations, 10 deal with aesthetic concerns only; another 20 involve a mixture of aesthetic and ecological concerns. Only six of these regulations are in a section specifically labeled "Aesthetics" and prefaced by the following statement: "Aesthetic standards — matters of taste, what is pleasant to see or hear — are difficult to agree on. . . . In harmony with the spirit of the Park, buildings should be screened and set back from roads and lakeshores and they should blend with the natural background. Eyesores [such as abandoned or junk cars and equipment] should be cleaned up, utility lines buried, scarred land restored, and roaring motors quieted." Yet the question *whose* aesthetics remains unasked in the report. To the locals, these aesthetic regulations seem among the most arbitrary and unfair. Although they do not share a value system that promotes a wilderness aesthetic, and have limited access to the urban cultural context in which such aesthetic standards have meaning, the locals are nevertheless required to submit to regulations upholding them.

For many of the environmentalists involved, from the Adirondack Council to the APA commissioners, the wilderness ethic and the wilderness aesthetic entwine so completely that it is impossible to imagine one without the other — either a healthy environment with faulty views or a beautiful view of an environment that is known to have been disturbed by humans in some way. Either condition results in incomplete, unnatural wilderness, an oxymoron that seems intolerable to the proponents of wilderness.

Frenette's house, a converted hunting camp, overlooks a quiet stretch of the Raquette River. Wide glass windows open onto a view of the water and mountains beyond. Shorefront property. From his perspective, the APA

164 makes too much fuss over shorefront aesthetics. There was an issue over
building a footpath down to the water. The APA "insisted it be diagonal, so
you couldn't look up and see it. . . . If I go in my canoe, I see a path from
here. . . . I am thinking, that's getting pretty fine — if I am going down but
at this angle, I can see it."

Increasingly Frenette sees elitism in the environmentalists' positions on
both aesthetic and ecological issues. He quotes an environmentalist who
said, "Anytime you involve the locals, you are throwing the baby out with
the bathwater, bowing down to development pressures."

He talked to George Davis about this lack of inclusion. "I said to him,
'George, don't make the mistake you made last time you came in.'" Davis
was the assistant director for natural resources of the APA at its inception.
"'You totally ignored the people. Involve the people in this thing, you've
got to deal with people.' . . . They ignored that process. If you'd asked me
several months ago, I'd have given a different answer, but I've been worn
down, and I'm coming around to believe that the people who wrote [the
Governor's Commission report] are really elitist. They honestly believe that
because they believe it, it's the absolute truth, and everyone ought to see it
the way they see it — and if you don't see it the way they see it, then you
are wrong. I hesitate saying that because I don't like to categorize people
that way, yet I almost have to believe it. . . . Just from talking to a lot of
people, and seeing the rejection of [the proposal for] the five locals on the
agency, and the reasons for rejecting them — locals don't know what they
are talking about, they can't be trusted. Guys like Harold Jerry [on the
Governor's Commission] who totally rejects the people, he looks right down
his nose at you. 'You're beneath us.' And you get that from talking to those
people. . . . There is a strong feeling on their part that they have the holy
grail."

I ask why local people's knowledge of the woods and their ability to
take part in decisions on land use is so rarely recognized. Frenette answers,
"Part of the problem is the people who possess this knowledge almost lack
the ability to articulate it." He gives the example of a talented carpenter he
knows. "This whole thing flows in the guy's mind — and he can't tell you
why. The other side seems to look and say, 'No, I know what's best, we
know what you need here,' instead of trying to sit down with the people
and work it out, which is certainly more time-consuming and difficult. It's
much easier to say, 'Here.' But at the same time that's — " and he draws his
finger like a knife across his neck. A small-town politician knows these
things. Where the regulations are concerned, "it is a little bit like guerrilla

warfare. The thought process in Tupper Lake, so help me, it's, 'To heck with them, just do it anyway, don't even ask about the laws, just go ahead and do it . . . find a way to beat it.'

"In the beginning, the zealots who came around [in the APA] and were beating on every little thing totally turned people against the APA. Local people would say, 'Hell, you can't deal with those people, let's not even try to deal with them.' That kind of changed. The zealots became less zealous, became acclimated and more adjusted and incorporated into the thinking process of the community. But now they're dragging their feet on the permit process."

People trying to work with the APA frequently complain of being frustrated. One small developer complained to Peter Paine, APA commissioner for twenty years, "You guys jerk everyone around, horribly." Local groups, pressured by the threat of eminent domain, the construction moratorium, the 2,000-acre zoning restrictions, and difficulties encountered in the permit process, have started a slow erosion of the fragile buildup of confidence in the communication process between local socioeconomic interests and the interests of environmentalists and the APA. Frenette sees the Planning Commission as effective in disarming, temporarily, some of the antagonistic groups. "I say temporarily," he emphasizes. "They are going to come back." He has been through this cycle before.

We look out the windows of his house at the birch and maple, shaking their leaves in the chill breeze, and at the lake, empty and blue as night below. The house is full of crafted wood and pictures of Canada geese and loons. "Wait! Before you go, I want to show you something," he says. He pulls out a book of photos and descriptions of hamlets in the Adirondacks. The villages are as much a part of the Adirondacks as the wilderness, he demonstrates, flipping past pages of gray weathered houses, some with gables and gingerbread, others destitute, pages of busy streets in small towns. An image appears between the pages of Frenette canoeing in the river, passing quietly under the birch trees, watching the mingling of human artifact and wild shore from his own unique perspective.

In the fall of 1992, the APC came apart at the seams. State Senator Ron Stafford, with close ties to some large landowners, refused to negotiate with the governor further on regulations for the Adirondacks, claiming that he alone represented the citizens of the Adirondacks. Dick Purdue stepped down as head of the APC amid controversy over closed sessions with the governor and accusations that he was negotiating away the rights of Adirondackers; without him, the APC collapsed. Negotiations came to a halt. Communication lapsed from exchanges of meaningful words to the language of gesture and stance: nonnegotiable symbols of different value systems. The only good that seemed to come from this state of entropy was the governor's appointment of Jim Frenette to the post of Adirondack Park Agency commissioner.

Later, local politicians attempted to recover some of the pieces, working together to form the Adirondack Association of Towns and Villages. Most of the towns and villages in the Adirondacks became members; they planned to work on Adirondack issues and to serve as a voice of the residents. By 1994, according to Jim Frenette, the association had suc-ceeded in forming a collective voice for at least the elected officials of the Adirondacks. The question remains whether their voice will be heard.

❧ Louis J. Simmons, retired editor of the weekly *Free Press,* and village and town historian, called his history of Tupper Lake *Mostly Spruce and Hemlock.* He was referring to the response given to an inquiry about the population of Tupper Lake around 1890. Both the tree population and the human population have changed since then, but the image of a town based on the forest has not; it resides in the minds and hearts of the local people.

I meet with Louis Simmons at his home, where we discuss the changing conditions in the village of Tupper Lake and the town of Altamont, local opinions about the APA, and his own views of the woods. "If we didn't have a concern for the woods, we wouldn't be here," he says earnestly. Silver-haired, his face expressive of quick changes of humor, reminiscence, anger, and reflection, he is easy to imagine as an energetic editor. Raised in Tupper Lake, he returned to work on the paper after finishing college in Syracuse. In his retirement he wrote the detailed 450-page history which, now out of print, sells for over a hundred dollars a copy.

"They've logged in this area for 150 years," Simmons tells me. "Started about 1840, and you can look around and there's still woods. Attractive and woodsy, still. The lake up here would probably be comparable with any in the woods. . . . Anybody who lives here, who makes a living here, I think they're 99 percent unanimous. They don't want to see any bad impact on the forest. But the forest business has been going on for 150 years, and it's still pretty decent country to live in. . . . In the old days they were not too particular; they logged and then left the branches and had forest fires. . . . That's a thing of the past." Forest practices changed, and state regulations were enacted to protect the forests, including the APA limit of twenty-five acres for a clear-cut, unless a special permit is obtained. Simmons believes that these changes are good. "People will go along with those sound, sensible ones," he says.

"Actually, the state might far better put a little more time on properly using their foresters' knowledge. They've got the State Forestry College. They plant trees by the thousands, and rarely thin them out. They grow so thick you can't cut them. So thick they're like grass. They're useless. If they were properly harvested, you'd have a continuing resource, which would help support the North Country and would be a lot more attractive. . . . Instead, they lock it all up and let it fall down."

Simmons thinks that the forest industry is gradually tapering off. "But it will always be an important part of the Adirondack economy. . . . Any further restriction on logging would be very detrimental to the economy of this region," he says, including in his comments the state land purchases, which drive land prices up on developable land and reduce the land available for logging.

Tupper Lake, which has lost nearly all of its mills and forest industries over the past few decades, has turned increasingly to other industries.

Photo 10. Walking through the forest. Photo D. Kuklok

"Tupper Lake tried to get the Visitor's Interpretive Center here. They'd welcome any kind of an industry. . . . They had plans for a wood chip industry here, but it was a $70 million project to get an industry that would employ forty to fifty people. It costs too much for what it would generate. . . . They had plans to convert the Oval Wood Dish plant into a wood-fueled power plant, to generate electric power." Instead it makes plastics, employing around two hundred people. Sunmount, a large facility for the developmentally disabled, is now the number one employer in town, employing between five and six hundred. Tourism, including a mountain with a ski development, brings in some money. Town and hamlet administrators are hoping to get a new state prison located here, but many local people feel ambivalent about it. Simmons feels that the town can't turn down anything that will improve the economy, but if they didn't get the prison, he wouldn't be disappointed. "If the prison comes, they will bring half their guards with them, so you're not too sure you will get more than a handful employed [from Tupper Lake]." Other losses have accompanied the downturn in the economy and the loss of the mills. "I can remember when we had nine resident physicians in town. And they all made a living," Simmons says. "Now there are none."

About the possibility of further development in Tupper Lake, Simmons expresses concern for the village and its citizens, and also a certain pride in the way Tupper Lake is today, despite the hard times it faces economically. "You can talk to woodspeople, you can talk to other people who are concerned about this country being spoiled. It is lovely country. All my life I've lived here, and I don't know anyplace else I'd rather live. It's good country and it's good people. . . . It can be spoiled, I know that." He wouldn't be unhappy if it didn't grow; the bigger towns get, the more problems they have, he says. But he'd like to see Tupper get a little more prosperous.

I ask him about his own and other Tupper Lake residents' thoughts about the APA and the Governor's Commission report, and their own sense of what needs to be done in the Adirondacks. As the editor of the town newspaper since 1932, Simmons is in touch with local sentiments as well as local events. "I know how most of them feel, believe me, I know. . . . They feel just like I do — strongly concerned. *Deeply* concerned and strongly opposing these restrictions that we have no voice in, nothing to say about, *nothing.*" He thinks that most people are not financially hurt by the APA, but are irritated and angered by the APA board's approach and that of the Governor's Commission. He mentions that he himself would have been financially hurt by the effect on forest industries had the APA been initiated when he was just starting out. "We were a small newspaper, a weekly paper, and it was a struggle getting by. In those days the loggers, the lumbering business was very, very important to *everybody* in the town." Mostly what angers people is "the high-handed way the whole thing's been handled. Sets people against them." What the people really need, he says, is "a bigger representation on any of these boards which have such an impact on our way of life."

When I ask Simmons his opinion of the current state of the woods, he replies that the state should concentrate much more on the pollution problem. "The woods are in sad shape in that respect, as everyone knows, and the lakes. They talk. They've been talking for ten years about the acid [precipitation] and nobody's doing anything about it. It's lip service, it doesn't amount to a damn. . . . Red spruce on the higher elevations are decimated. Here at our home we have two or three good-sized maple trees. They are hit; the branches higher up are denuded. They [the state agencies, APA, and DEC] actually don't know what's the cause. They've been out here liming the lakes. That's a band-aid approach to the problem. I think if they'd concern themselves with that, they could do more for the woods than this picayune eminent domain."

Scientific research bears out his concerns, both in the Adirondacks and elsewhere in the Northeast. Ed Ketchledge, an ecologist working in the Adirondacks, has been monitoring the decline of the high-elevation red spruce for many years. Two prominent ecologists, Gene E. Likens and F. Herbert Bormann, studied the chemistry of precipitation in the Northeast and documented the relationship between air pollution and the decline of great forest trees during a decade of work at the Hubbard Brook Experimental Forest in the White Mountains of New Hampshire. Likens and Bormann found that the change in acidity from the norm of pH 5.3 to the extraordinary range of pH 3.8–4.3 in the Northeast occurred shortly after 1950, at the same time that other scientists had discovered red spruce trees were dying in large numbers in the Green Mountains of Vermont (Mello, 1987). Evidence of correlation mounted as other scientists contributed their research findings (Whittaker et al., 1974).

Forest ecologists Thomas Siccama and H. W. Vogelmann and botanist Margaret Bliss studied the extensive mature forests on four mountains in the Northeast. Their data showed that since at least 1965, the forests had suffered widespread, substantial, and sustained decrease in growth. The growth rates of red spruce and other trees had declined at enormous rates: on Camel's Hump Mountain from 1964 to 1979, there was a 43 percent decline in the amount of standing red spruce wood, and the rate of seedling reproduction declined by about 50 percent. The scientists found that the decline was regionwide, and was becoming worse (Mello, 1987). At elevations of 1,800 to 3,800 feet, sugar maples, American beech, white birch, balsam fir, and other trees were also showing substantial declines (Siccama, Bliss, and Vogelmann, 1982).

The Governor's Commission Report makes just four recommendations concerning air quality: the state should impose emission standards, press for national legislation and international action on acid deposition and global warming, and classify the Park as a Class I (Prevention of Significant Deterioration) air quality area. No funds, personnel, or APA responsibilities are attached to these recommendations. Local people voiced concerns over the relative exclusion of acid rain from the environmentalist commission's agenda. By 1997, the Adirondack Council and the state government were focusing both funds and attention on acid rain as a central issue.

Simmons has seen a lot of changes over time. When he was a child growing up in the Adirondacks, wildlife was abundant. "I remember when I was a kid, and they were lumbering around here a lot; there was all kinds of game, and all kinds of berry picking. Things were, well, they were alive."

Later he often hiked in the High Peaks. He remembers one trip: "We went out in September, six days, on the range trail. We started on Gothics, Haystack, Basin, up to Marcy. We didn't meet a soul the whole trip." Things are different now. "Now they call it a herd path. You go from Marcy Dam over to the trailhead. So many people, you can't stop to take a leak!" he says, laughing and frowning at the same time. "It's for the birds!"

He has also seen the changes development brings. "When we were kids in the Boy Scouts, we used to go over the ridge to Gull Pond — a beautiful little lake, just pristine and wild, nothing on it, not a camp or anything. Now it's been built in. And people have paid thirty-five to forty thousand a lot, per lot. A good-sized lot. I'd just as soon not see [that kind of thing]. In other words, I don't care for overdevelopment — selling off a lot of land for big bucks."

Simmons tells me that some of the smaller towns have disappeared, or changed drastically. In his book he documents the story of Brandon. After Michigan lumberman Patrick Ducey closed his operations there in 1890, William Rockefeller decided to establish an Adirondack estate at Bay Pond three miles south of Brandon, and to include Brandon in his holdings to ensure privacy. About fifteen families were still living in Brandon "and awakened one morning to find that Rockefeller had bought all the land around them and even claimed control of the road that led to the village" (Simmons, 1976, p. 112). A few refused to sell to the Rockefeller agents. Oliver LaMora not only refused to sell but continued to hunt and fish where he pleased and was arrested and was sued. "Pictures of the tall, erect old gentleman with snow-white hair and beard, standing defiantly at the entrance to his humble home aroused wide-spread sympathy" (Simmons, 1976, p. 113).

The landscape has changed, too, as some areas are developed for second homes, and others, once inhabited, return to the woods. Simmons remembers what it was like to be a boy growing up near the woods. "My father was a railroad engineer. We'd get up at five o'clock in the morning, get on a six o'clock train. That was a big deal for us, just to get on a train. And one of my younger brothers went with me, and a couple other friends. Two cents a mile. We went twenty-six miles up to Kildare and Derrick and Madawasca, which was only a flag station. A flag station was no station, just a lean-to. We'd get off out there, they'd just dump us off . . . and there was no way of getting out of there till nine o'clock that night. We were just little kids. And we were a long ways from home; there were twenty-six miles of woods between you and home. And we'd pick berries all day. And then we *did* see a bear every once in a while, and a *lot* of deer. And Indians that were down from the reservation, picking berries too. Enormous big marshes just loaded with berries. We filled packbaskets with them. Oh, those were great trips! I loved them," he says. "Now all those little settlements are gone. Derrick, Brandon, Kildare are all gone. As the lumber industry evaporated, they vanished."

By 1994 an APA economic adviser was working with Tupper Lake to establish a new hardwood mill, managed by a French-Canadian family. But this was only one firm replacing many. The question of what will happen to Tupper Lake remains.

❦ John Stock is tall and gaunt, in appearance and ideology a direct descendant of Gifford Pinchot. Sitting surrounded by books, telephone, and papers, he seems out of place away from the tall, narrow boles of a second growth softwood forest. But his eyes retain the hooded gaze of a hawk, and his mouth sets in a thin line when he expresses his impatience over the management of forest land in the Adirondacks.

Born in western New York State and educated at the New York State College of Forestry at Syracuse University, Stock came to the Adirondacks in 1944 to work as forester for the Emporium Lumber Company at Conifer.

After ten years there, he started his own forestry consulting business, and then went to work full-time for one of his largest customers, Litchfield Park, part of a family-owned conglomerate. The Litchfield family also owns farms, chemical factories, real estate, and investments. Stock is a past president and longtime director of the New York State Forest Owners' Association, and has served as a member of the advisory board on forest lands to the U.S. Department of Agriculture and as chairman of the public affairs committee for several forestry organizations in New York State. He was also a member of the forest industries committee on timber valuation and taxation. In 1973 Governor Nelson Rockefeller appointed him to the Adirondack Park Agency as a commissioner; he served for fifteen years. His friend Louis Simmons said of him, "As member of the Agency he has championed wise forest management and sought equitable solutions to tax problems." In 1994 he served as a consultant to the Blue Line Council, founded by Pieter Litchfield and other wealthy landowners and corporate executives in the Adirondacks.

As a practitioner with positions in organizations in which he is officially supposed to reflect upon his profession and its role in the Adirondacks, John Stock has developed a framework that is more coherent and explicit than most. He uses Pinchot's philosophy of the wise use of natural resources as a guide to develop creative approaches to problems of economics and taxation on forest lands. As an economics-minded manager he is constantly evaluating the market potential of the land; as a forester and philosopher he is constantly evaluating the quality and conditions of the forests on those lands; as a professional forester working for a wealthy elite family, and at the same time living in a logging town and working with many loggers, he has been in a unique position to probe the tensions between social classes. His observant eyes and deliberate choice of words make it clear that he generally keeps his opinions to himself. Now retired, he makes known his discontent with where the Adirondacks seem to be heading, and his criticism of the APA.

Litchfield Park had been purchased in 1893 to be a game preserve, an idea that did not work out at all. The owner imported stonemasons from Italy to construct an elaborate castle within the park, and tried to raise a number of imported wild animals there, including wild boar. Most escaped or died. After that experiment the owner incorporated his "camp" in 1924 to avoid income taxes, and the forests were logged steadily for softwoods from that time on. The family did not log the hardwoods until about 1928, when somebody invented, as Stock calls it, "a reasonable truck tire."

By the time Stock arrived, the softwoods were mostly gone, and Litch-field Park was facing a slow time. But in order to retain their incorporated status, which shielded them from taxes, the family had to prove that some income was being produced by the incorporated holdings, in accordance with the IRS regulation popularly referred to as the "family holding company rule." Unable to cut enough timber continuously, with John Stock's help they diversified, cutting Christmas trees and balsam boughs, harvesting spruce gum, and making maple syrup and natural lump charcoal. For two years Litchfield Park furnished the Christmas tree for Rockefeller Center and once shipped a seventy-foot tree to a Texas corporation. They sold their maple syrup commercially; Litchfield was one of the first to market the syrup in small stoneware jugs, as well as developing a special line of dark, ungraded syrup for the South, where the pale Grade A was considered inadequate for pancakes. Litchfield Park used its hardwood to produce charcoal, but ran afoul of air pollution laws. The owners switched to the sawmill business instead and bought another fourteen thousand acres of land. They operated the sawmill for about ten years until the bottom dropped out of the lumber market.

Stock's diversity of experience has given him a wide perspective on forest management and helped him to develop the economic framework through which he analyzes the costs and benefits of timber operations in the Adirondacks. He is not hopeful. "The economics of forestry in the Adirondacks is very suspect," he says. Part of the problem, he admits, is that higher land values on private land zoned for development have actually made it uneconomical in some cases for timber companies to cut the timber on their lands. He sees significant changes in the way timber lands are managed in the Adirondacks now.

One indication of change is that foreign pension trusts, mostly English and German, which operate under a different set of tax laws, are quietly buying up Adirondack forest land. Once they own the land, they may or may not manage it. Another indication is the increasing interest that timber companies are showing in conservation easements. Through negotiation with the New York State Department of Environmental Conservation, landowners can arrange to sell easements, short of fee title, on portions of their land for public recreational use. This alternative has encouraged a shift away from production and toward recreation. Yet difficulties arise in connection with conservation easements over who pays what percentage of the taxes on the land, leaving many landowners wary of the idea.

New York State tax policy also affects land use practices in the Adiron-

174 dacks. The Fisher Tax Law, now known as Sections 480 and 480a of the Real Property Tax Law, encourages the reforestation of abandoned farmland, and effective forest management practices, by providing an exemption from local property tax on the value of the timber on eligible lands. Passed in 1974, Section 480a continues the traditional severance tax on the value of harvested timber but declares that the assessment of eligible lands should be based on their value for timber production rather than the developable value (Zinser, 1980, pp. 53–54). Small landowners who have forestland may be anxious to get their land certified for management, but when large tracts come under Section 480a, the result can have a major impact on the surrounding towns.

Stock uses the example of Long Lake to illustrate this point. Three big companies own most of the land in the town. If they were to put their land under Section 480a, they would bankrupt the town because the rest of the people would have to make up the lost taxes. "It's an absolute fact . . . and they have just had enough conscience so they haven't done it." Stock raises an eyebrow, "I say conscience, but when you get under 480a you surrender a certain amount of your management procedure to the DEC, which has no experience in managing forest in the Adirondacks." Stock perceives an irony in the fact that Section 480a mandates a certain amount of DEC supervision and management of the private forests under its certification. Yet, because the "forever wild" clause prohibits management of state land for timber or any extractive forest product, the DEC staff has no experience in the management of its own forests for forest products, at least within the Blue Line.

"What will happen to the timber industry in the Adirondacks?" Stock asks me rhetorically. He gives another illustration. International Paper, in Ticonderoga, on the edge of the Adirondacks, is facing economic difficulties. Its mill is completely depreciated, and its pulp is the highest priced in the United States, according to Stock. There has been a serious strike at the Ticonderoga mill. Stock speculates that IP will eventually sell it to an entrepreneur in a leveraged buyout in the same way Diamond International sold its lands to entrepreneur Henry Lassiter, who turned around and resold several thousand acres to the state for a large profit.

One of the biggest problems for the large timber companies revolves around the book value of their Adirondack holdings. The APA effectively decreased the supply of land available in the Adirondacks, so prices went up, and then at the time of the Governor's Commission on the Adirondacks apparently went up again. The land became in many instances more valuable to use for development purposes than for timber management. The companies cannot justify to their boards of directors keeping expensive property when they cannot make as much by getting the pulp off it as they could by selling it. Right now, Stock states, with characteristic grimness, "IP gets over one half their pulp imported." The future of timber production in the Adirondacks, and by implication the future of the Adirondacks, is very hazy, as Stock sees it. He compresses his lips in the faintest indication of anger: "One thousand acres of managed forest provides year-round work for one person. One thousand acres of state land doesn't do anything. . . . It lies there and becomes basically the desert."

We move into a discussion of the rationale behind "forever wild" and the interest groups behind the policy. To Stock, in his framework of economics and timber management, it looks mostly foolish and wasteful. According to his research, 90 percent of people who come to the park never get off the main road, and 90 percent of the Forest Preserve is never visited. He sees those in the environmental pressure groups as falling into certain categories. "[They] have considerably above-average incomes, like to be outdoors . . . take the kind of vacation that the average wage earner can't afford to go on." The average wage earner, Stock says, "wants recreation more concentrated. . . . There aren't that many Joe Blue-Collars who are going to go hiking for a week in the High Peaks."

From his perspective both as a commissioner on the APA for fifteen years and as a forester, he is uniquely qualified to critique both the APA and the Governor's Commission on the Adirondacks in the Twenty-First Century on forest management issues. "Basically, both of them are solutions in search of a problem. There was absolutely no evidence, then or now, that there is a great expansion in the Adirondacks." While the numbers of summer homes are increasing, Stock is certain that the number of year-round residents is declining. Tupper Lake has shown decreases with each ten-year census since 1950, Stock says. He recommends Charles Zinser's book *The Economic Impact of the Adirondack Park Private Land Use and Development Plan.* He quotes Zinser, saying that second homes are a benefit rather than a drawback to the park. Summer homes in some areas are assessed at 150 to 200 percent, which effectively raises local equalization rates, resulting in higher state payments to the towns.

When I question him on the nature of the APA Board of Commissioners and his role on it, he says bluntly, "I was basically for the locals." He expands, his eyes beginning to shine more fiercely. "I was the only person that's ever been on the board of the APA that ever worked for a salary anywhere or ever worked for a profit-making company, either on the APA or the Commission for the Twenty-First Century," which he calls "SAPA," or "Son of APA." While this is no longer true, with John Collins, a local salaried schoolteacher, as commissioner and now head of the APA board, it sets the foundation for the criticisms of inherent elitism that the APA and the Governor's Commission face from many quarters.

"They are not any kind of cross-section of anything, except maybe elitist groups," Stock says, but adds, perhaps in response to the history of complaints against APA procedures that hangs in the air, "The APA actually never hurt anybody. Two people, demonstrably, have been hurt economically by the APA. One, Tony D'Elia, of Loon Lake Estates, was forced into bankruptcy by the APA. The other, Frank Casier, of Saranac Lake, they changed the rules on him in the middle of the game, which cost him a lot of money. Fortunately, he had a lot of money. For the rest of the people, they were an inconvenience. Probably did more good [than harm]."

He underlines his point about elitism with an example from shorefront regulations. "If you can't afford 250 feet of shoreline, you just don't have a place in the Adirondacks." It seems to him that a small, elitist group made the decision that since they don't like to see camps or any other form of human habitation, nobody should see camps; any buildings must be set back from the shoreline and well screened. Stock notes that many people like to show off the variety of historic camps on the lakes. When I comment that some regulations seem to be based on ecological concerns and others on aesthetic concerns, Stock bursts out, "Somebody's *version* of aesthetics!"

I ask him to comment specifically on the Governor's Commission. "Again—nobody ever proved that there was a problem. Druids or hug-a-tree people think [the forest] ought to be completely wild because they like to hike in something they consider completely wild, as long as somebody comes to rescue them if they break a leg. People really want a *managed* wilderness, trails." About the recommendations in their final report, he says, "Some of the recommendations are just basically stupid—like the buried power lines. That means you'd have to dig up every streambed, every wetland, every rockbed." About the transferable development rights (TDRs), which were later dropped, Stock mentions that New Jersey considered them twenty years ago, but that in the Adirondacks, "If you are shifting the tax base from one town to another, it won't work."

In a sample from another regulation under consideration, concerning limits on the number of people using the trail, Stock asks, "Who decides who gets the permit? Someday some famous environmentalist would be turned away and there'd be all hell to pay." In his opinion there is no fair and easy way to accomplish this. First come, first served favors the rich person, who may be better able to plan ahead for a vacation. He suggests considering moving toward the Swiss system. In Switzerland, washed gravel trails, which do not erode, allow larger numbers of people to visit the forests with fewer long-term environmental impacts. Rangers travel the paths, setting up telescopes to highlight aspects of natural history. In addition, no overnights are allowed. These more drastic requirements would change the nature of the American wilderness experience in profound ways, but they point out the nebulous ground between ecological regulations and those that are more strictly aesthetic. While there is some evidence that a very large group may cause more impact on trails than several small groups, what seems to be at issue here is the perception of wilderness. The bulk of the theoretical and empirical literature supports the notion that crowding in outdoor recreation is a normative concept in which perceptions of crowding are influenced by characteristics of the visitors and of people encountered and other situational variables (Manning, 1985).

Stock saves his most scathing remarks for what he regards as the foolishness of leaving so much land "forever wild," without managing the forest. In his view, as he points out, the forests can't be truly wild or healthy unless they are allowed to burn, which is a dangerous proposition in such a patchwork of wildlands and towns. Current fire policies favor putting out all fires, although the DEC is aware of the discrepancy in policies (K. B. Richards, 1985). "How do you get a new crop of trees in an even-aged stand of softwoods? The High Peaks are all even-aged, and people don't stop to realize that they're even-aged because they burned down. You have to cut it down or burn it down. So the High Peaks is going to have to burn in order to get a new crop started. People will be walking in dust and ashes for a number of years, because once it gets started, you probably can't stop it. It's the same in the Ausable. Nothing anybody can do about it."

There is no doubt that the designation "forever wild" and APA regulation promote tourism. But what about the economic impact of tourism on the Adirondacks? Stock argues that the situation is more complex than is usually realized. "The hotels are terribly cyclical . . . a 70-day season in the summertime and 80 to 150 days in the winter. A boom and bust situation. You've got problems you don't think of. In Lake Placid you are looking at $15 million a year in subsidy from ORDA [Olympic Regional Development Association] — no way you can break even on a ski slope, unless you can be an hour from a major city."

Local people find that their children can't afford to stay on in their hometowns. Gabriels and Ray Brook correctional institutions and Sunmount development center for mentally disabled add about $23 million to the area economy. A young person can work as a corrections officer or in a nursing home. Otherwise there seem to be few opportunities other than jobs in tourism, with its inherent instability and dependence on the weather. In addition, many of the businesses requiring capital outlays are started by outsiders or newcomers to the Adirondacks. Few of the businesses lining Main Street in Lake Placid are owned by people who have lived there for more than ten years. More people from outside the park flock there in the tourist seasons, competing with locals for seasonal, usually minimum-wage employment.

"Do you see any way out of it?" I ask.

"No."

I ask Stock about wood products plants, whether they increase the percentage of value added that would occur in the Adirondacks, as the Yellowwood Consulting Group suggested in its report to the APA. Stock again is pessimistic. "There's one furniture plant in the Adirondacks, down in North Creek. All other logs are shipped out. New York has a high and unfavorable compensation for both working in the woods and . . . in the mills. Much cheaper in Canada." He cites problems of poor transportation, problematic bridges, enormous transportation costs, and no railroads. As he sees it, there is not much chance to bring in bigger industries. He thinks that the Adirondacks will have to shift either to government subsidies or to sources of income that many people don't want, including prisons, psychiatric hospitals, and, he suspects, a low-level radioactive waste dump. "Right now there's a law that says one can't be located in the Adirondacks. But any law can be unpassed."

"Do you think if the Commission had been all Adirondackers that it would have been better?" I ask.

"No — that would have been just as bad. You've got to strike a balance. And then there's the problem of who's an Adirondacker. Everyone carries some baggage with them."

Later I read Zinser's book, as Stock suggested. In the preface Zinser credits Stock with continually stimulating his intellectual curiosity. He repays Stock with a cool, deliberate, factually based account which reflects Stock's drive to get at the facts. Zinser provides a complete survey of the net economic impact of the Private Land Use and Development Plan in each of the ninety Adirondack Park towns. In addition, interviews with

local government officials, realtors, and a sampling of employers and developers demonstrate how each group views the impact of the plan.

According to the book, the Adirondack Park Agency Act, passed primarily to control development on the private lands of the park, "represents
one of the most significant pieces of land use legislation enacted in the
United States" (Zinser, 1980, p. 1). Zinser underlines the controversy and
concern surrounding the supposed negative impact of the plan on the economies of the towns in the park, but he also attempts to demonstrate that
this impact has been minimal. The effects have been "moderately negative"
in only three towns and "slightly negative" in another thirty, and there has
been no effect in the fifty-seven remaining towns. On the whole, Zinser
concludes, the economic impact has been only very slightly negative
(Zinser, 1980, p. 240).

Many of the key community people he and his research assistants interviewed believed that the plan had caused a slowdown in real estate and
construction activity. Zinser convincingly shows that an equivalent slowdown occurred in similar mountainous and rural areas of the Catskills and
Tug Hill outside the Park. He attributes the slowdown more directly to the
recession of the 1970s and compares it to a similar decline throughout New
York State and the nation as a whole. It appears that because the recession
coincided with the Park Agency Act's early years, popular opinion, as well
as that of realtors, developers, and others, blamed the act rather than outside factors. These factors included not only the recession but also the
energy crisis, the shortage of mortgage money, high interest rates, a decline
in New York State's population, a decrease in real income, and an increase
in home ownership costs (Zinser, 1980, p. 244).

Zinser also demonstrates that people often blamed the act for problems
created by other environmental legislation and government regulation, including the Wild, Scenic, and Recreational Rivers Act, the New York State
Freshwater Wetland Act, and the New York State Mined Lands Reclamation Act.

He does admit, however, that the plan caused a decrease in land values
of approximately 50 percent on resource management land and 15 to 25
percent on rural use land because of the restrictions on development of
these lands. These two land categories account for 87 percent of the private
land in the Park. The potential for sales also decreased, owing to the larger
lot size requirements. These requirements also disproportionately disrupted
the plans of some elderly people to subdivide their land for their retirement
or to divide it among their children. The lowered land values, in turn, would

have repercussions on the tax base, he predicted, as assessments came into line. At the same time, values in the hamlets were often driven up disproportionately.

Local people certainly recognize the loss in land values, and are quick to blame the APA for the decrease in values and in the number of transfers. Zinser supports the implementation of a compensatory system for landowners in resource management and rural use categories. It is hard to reconcile his recognition of this problem with his statement that only three towns have experienced even moderately negative effects on their economies. He fails to account for the impact, both economic and psychological, on the Adirondack people of the relatively large populations in these three towns. It is possible that Zinser was considering as economic effects only those transactions and sales which had already occurred. But that raises the question whether his book gives a valid picture of economic reality in the Adirondacks.

Zinser also explores the question whether a reduction in the development of large leisure home subdivisions has had positive or negative economic effects for the Park. He concludes that while at first the subdivisions generally benefited local government, eventually their dependence on local services could outstrip the tax revenues the new developments provide. "The net impact on the long-time residents of the area is that their taxes drastically rise. They are forced to sell their property if they cannot meet these increased tax payments" (Zinser, 1980, p. 252). While development also temporarily creates new jobs, often outsiders fill these positions, creating transitional populations for local governments to handle. On balance, it seems that development brings as many negatives as positives to small towns, where services are expensive and infrastructure is minimal.

Looking at the whole picture, one is tempted to adopt John Stock's pessimism. If the APA did not exist and development burgeoned, raising taxes to a point beyond endurance, the locals would be forced to move farther and farther away from their old homes, even while commuting back to work, as has happened in Aspen, Colorado. With the APA, values have dropped on perhaps 87 percent of the private land, and regulations have limited the options local people have had to sell a piece of their land to provide for retirement, college funds, or a place in the Adirondacks for their children. In any case, even as the rest of the country becomes increasingly polluted, despoiled, and asphalt-clad, it looks as if it will become more and more difficult to make a living in one of the few remaining clean, wild areas. Economist Thomas Michael Power suggests that loss of industries and the influx of tourists can be positive for communities, provided they manage tourism creatively, aiming for ecotourism and cultural tourism. His argument that people care where they live, and care enough about it to develop these creative options, is hopeful and beguiling (Power, 1996). Yet his arguments about the positive transformation of these towns from natural resource–dependent communities based on extraction to communities based on tourism and home businesses ring a little hollow. While noting the net gain in population after transformation in some counties, he cannot tell if these are the same people who were there before (pers. comm., 1997). And retirees are not always a positive gain, especially because they may vote against local school bond acts. Their children are not in school there, and they may have no strong ties to local children. Enough retirees in a small community can tip the balance repeatedly, as has happened in some Oregon towns.

❦ The first time I interview Nellie Staves it is totally by chance. Several people from as far away as Lake Placid have told me I should talk to Nellie if I want someone who knows the woods. With some extra time in Tupper one day, I walk into Stewart's and ask the woman at the counter if she knows where Nellie lives. "Yeah, but she won't be there. She'll be having lunch at her daughter's," she says, and proceeds to give me directions to Nellie's daughter's house.

I find Nellie at her daughter's, having lunch. After I explain my research, she agrees to an interview, but not on tape, she says, looking at me suspiciously, as if she thinks I have a tape recorder concealed in my jacket. She has long flyaway gray hair worn in a loose, untidy bundle, and a soft, lined face. She is sturdy and short and looks like a grandmother. She says she is part Abenaki. She sees herself as a citizen of both the natural community and the human community of Tupper Lake; as such, her framework is one of citizenship and responsibility to the communities she lives in.

Nellie is originally from Vermont. Born and brought up on a mountain, where her family lived alone, she and her twelve brothers and sisters walked six and a half miles to school each day. "All we ever had to do was play in the woods — hunt and fish and trap."

Eventually she married a logger and moved to the Adirondacks because of his job. They had one daughter. Nellie cooked in the logging camps in Vermont and the Adirondacks. She used to help her husband scale logs in the evenings. "My whole life has been in the outdoors," she says.

She still hunts and fishes and traps. She traps everything: fox, mink, muskrat, beaver, coyote. "Though now nobody is trapping like they were

182   —the price of fur is so low." The rest of the time she passes her knowledge
on to others in her various roles, including hunter safety instructor and
state-certified trapper trainer. She has been president of the Tupper Lake
Rod and Gun Club, president of the Franklin County Federation of Fish
and Game Clubs, president of the Adirondack Conservation Council, and
delegate to the New York State Conservation Council. She has received
many conservation awards as well as a Citizen of the Year award.

As president of the Franklin County Federation of Fish and Game
Clubs, she has been "very perturbed about acid rain and what it was doing
to trees and waters of our land." Hers is the only federation in the state

Photo 11. Nellie
Staves, hunter, trap-
per, conservationist,
Tupper Lake. Photo
D. Kuklok

which has raised its own money to lime six ponds in its county. Nellie learned as much as she could from the DEC about liming. She also attended an acid rain conference in Albany, which had representatives from twenty-seven countries and states. She learned from all of them, she says, especially the delegate from Sweden. Sweden's practices include techniques for liming tributaries and even the woods. After the conference she collected $1,500 door-to-door. The federation needed one ton of lime per acre to meet DEC regulations (twice as much as Sweden required). After the group success-fully limed the first pond, Nellie collected again until there was enough money to lime the next pond. Nellie persisted and won other contributions for the project. Canada gave her two thousand pounds of lime and one of the commissioners gave her a truck to pick it up in. Now all six ponds have high enough pH levels that they haven't needed to be limed again, and are now stocked with brook trout.

In another project the federation, under Nellie's guidance, took over a county pheasant program that was about to be eliminated. The federation now gets two thousand chicks from the Cornell University Game Farm each year. Nellie oversees the project at Camp Gabriels Prison, where inmates raise the birds under DEC supervision. Franklin County legislators in the past gave money to buy grain for the pheasants. After many weeks of intense care, including medication, pure drinking water, and hand-constructed flyways, the pheasants are given to the federation's six member clubs for release. They are released only on land open to the public. More recently, the Franklin County Federation has had to collect its own funds, since the legislators cut its general and pheasant funds from the budget.

To Nellie the woods are more than just a place to hunt and trap. "The woods are beautiful. There isn't anything that can give me greater enjoy-ment or peace of mind," she says. She expresses her feelings about the woods and her observations through fungus art, etching forest scenes and wildlife on pieces of shelf fungus that she gathers on her walks in the woods. "I hunt deer and rabbits, partridges and pheasant. I don't hunt bear —why would I hunt bear? I have no use for them. I eat them all — I wouldn't ever waste *anything*. I love the animals. I see the deer all summer, and after the deer season it wouldn't enter my mind to kill it. But in season it's altogether different, a challenge. You don't spend time looking at the animal first. But out of season, the Tupper Lake Rod and Gun Club puts on a spaghetti dinner to help Hamilton County feed the deer."

Spending so much time in the woods, Nellie notices changes since the time when she first came to the Adirondacks. "What's happening to the woods?" she asks, shaking her head sadly. "When I was young, you'd never see a lot of trees dead and fallen. In the last ten years you notice how devastated everything is. When we get a windstorm, there's a great tangle in the woods. I see a lot of smaller fungus coming in, and gypsy moths. I'm not a biologist. How am I to say what's causing it? There's a lack of animals now. When I used to be in the woods twenty years ago, you'd see rabbits, foxes, coons. Now in *this* area, around Tupper Lake, I bet you don't see more than one or two foxes a year. The animals are less abundant for trapping. Almost all the animals are down, except beaver, maybe." Another thing she is not seeing in the woods are the berries — raspberries, blackberries, strawberries, blueberries. The raspberries used to be good for a couple years after an area was logged, but now it is almost impossible to get enough for a pie. But, she adds, "I'm not for clear-cutting, I'll tell you that. It's all right to cut some."

The brooks and fishing have changed, too. A lot of brooks have dried up, and many of the remaining brooks are covered with green slime. "There aren't the fish that there used to be either," she says. "That's why we want to lime the ponds and stock them."

Nellie's commitment to finding solutions involves her in some controversial issues. The federation is in favor of the reclamation of ponds, which involves the use of Rotenone, and took 2,495 petitions in support to the DEC. Earth First!ers demonstrated here against the use of rotenone, which kills less desirable species of fish, often those accidentally introduced through bait fishing, in the process killing off some amphibians over a period of several days, until the pond is deemed clear enough for reintroduction of the desired native species. Nellie says that the Earthfirst!ers put two conservation officers in the hospital when the protesters put their canoes across the only place to put in, and sparked a confrontation. An Earth First!er reportedly tried to hold one conservation officer's head under water. One officer was in the hospital three days, Nellie says, and the other was out of work for three weeks. Animal rights groups also filed a lawsuit against the DEC.

Coyotes present another controversial issue for the Franklin Federation, though so far it has not proved as confrontational as the rotenone issue. "They say there are a lot of coyotes, but we're not bothered right here. . . . Right now we're trying to see how many there are in the state," says Nellie. Some people think the coyotes are responsible for keeping the deer population down, but Nellie doesn't know; she doesn't think the coyotes kill as many deer as people say. A shrewd look comes over her face;

she generally reserves her opinion until she sees the evidence for herself. Her own firsthand experience means more to her than reports or rumors. Some people are eager to pass the law that would create a year-round open season on the coyotes. As a trapper, Nellie notes that coyote fur isn't prime in the spring. She can't see wasting coyotes' lives just to get rid of them. She thinks that every county should do its own thing about coyotes, since the population levels seem to differ from one county to another, and the human population's reactions also differ. Essex and Clinton counties have a lot of coyotes, she notes.

Another controversy revolved around the establishment of hunting and fishing displays in the Paul Smith's Visitor Interpretive Center — the VIC, as it is known locally. When the VIC was built, Nellie was on the committee representing sportsmen and sportswomen. She tried to get a display of mounts placed in the center. The mounts were refused in favor of more preservation-oriented displays, so the Franklin County Federation decided to picket the VIC on its opening day. Governor Cuomo was expected to arrive for the opening ceremonies. "Then," says Nellie, "the day before the opening, we sat at North Country Community College with the APA and had communications with the APA and the governor." The APA wouldn't give in. At about 5:30 the governor called and said that the Federation could display its mounts, with reservations. The next day the governor asked Nellie what the Federation wanted. Nellie responded that the group's mandate and the VIC's was to educate, and hunting was a part of Adirondack life for many people. Conservationists and preservationists stood at odds. Woody Cole, then head of the APA board, claimed that the mounts were stuffed with arsenic. The Federation also wanted the display to include a stream with fish in it. The APA put the stream into the display, a shallow rivulet running over stones and sand, but no fish. Eventually the Federation was allowed to exhibit one mount at a time, on a rotating basis. "One mount," Nellie says, with disgust.

As a part of her ethic of citizenship and responsibility to her community, both forest and human, Nellie teaches and organizes numerous classes. She teaches hunter safety and sportsman-landowner relations to all the fifth and sixth graders in the county. Federation members also take the school-children on field trips in the woods. Both the individual clubs and the Federation send children to 4-H camp, and send teachers to a New York State workshop on teaching about the out-of-doors. Nellie also teaches trapping classes and hunter safety to teens and adults. At the Franklin County Fair each year, the Federation sets up displays for citizen education;

the group sponsors conservation field days and sportsman instruction. Nellie is also involved in the annual fishing derbies. Of all these activities she says, "It's the only way to assure that the younger generation can enjoy [them]."

When I ask her about the Governor's commission report, Nellie is impatient. "We know what the Adirondacks are from one end to the other. When they wrote the commission report, we expected to see people all over the streams," doing research for the report. "They went about the whole thing the wrong way. They should have formed a committee with Adirondackers in the first place instead of [leaving them out] and all these groups forming." Irate citizens, protesting their lack of inclusion in the process, or protesting the idea of a report at all, formed more than fourteen groups. Many harked back to the days of protest at the inception of the APA, and some of those who counted themselves old-time Adirondackers rallied to the side of Tony D'Elia and the Adirondack Local Government Review Board, which he ran until his death in 1991. The Review Board, of which Nellie is a member, plans to get an office within APA headquarters to fulfill its official role as watchdog, but this remains under debate, in part owing to the Review Board's vocal criticism of the APA.

But criticism without positive action bothers Nellie. She comments on the grassroots citizens' group sponsored by developer Donald Gerdts. "All this hullaballoo. If they had just taken all that energy and done something constructive . . ." She sees the conservation and sportsmen's groups as doing the most concrete positive work. But she recognizes, with some frustration, that their role is not widely known, and the groups themselves are not as mobilized as they need to be at the regional level.

The Adirondack Planning Commission, however, Nellie has seen as a positive force in Adirondack land use politics; at least it has involved local elected officials in the issues. "I have faith in the Planning Commission in a way," she says, "and I know most of those on the commission." (Some time later the Planning Commission fell apart in the midst of controversy over negotiations with the governor.) Nellie tells me that she will be going as the representative of the Adirondack Conservation Council to the state legislative meetings in Albany, to listen to the debates over several pieces of conservation legislation. She will carry her knowledge of different voices with her.

Nellie does not want to say much about the APA, but her position on the Review Board gives her access to those who are among the APA's most vocal opponents. She feels that the commissioners in general lack wide experience in the woods. She comments that not many locals agree with the opinions of the commissioner, ecologist Anne LaBastille, a Cornell graduate and self-styled woodswoman, who is counted among the commission's resident Adirondack appointments by the state government in Albany. "Don't even ask me about her," says Nellie, but then with her eyes twinkling tells how she and LaBastille disagree over the presence of a Nessie-like monster in Lake Champlain, known fondly to believers as "Champ." "You know, she actually believes in that thing," Nellie says, looking straight at me, perhaps to see if I do too. When I ask her to comment on the knowledge that the trappers and hunters have of the area compared to that of the biologists, she says simply, "They've lived it."

I ask her about her stand on "forever wild." "I look at it two ways," she says. People can use the state land, for hunting, trapping, fishing, or whatever. If the state didn't have it, the builders could buy it, develop it, and post it, and then it might have no recreation on it. Yet Nellie believes that the state has more land than it can take care of. She thinks that the state should clean up the blowdown on the road between Tupper Lake and Saranac Lake. "You look into the woods there and see a real mess. Old trees should be able to be used." She is not against logging, and thinks perhaps the state should do some limited logging, so long as there is no clear-cutting. In a clear-cut, deer and other animals don't have any cover. But shelterwood cuts, where the loggers leave enough trees to protect a hillside, reseed, and shade the seedlings toward the eventual establishment of an even-aged stand, seem a viable option to Nellie. "They have always logged here," she says.

As for the reintroduction of larger wildlife species, Nellie watches the proceedings with great interest. She doesn't think that the lynx program will have much success, and is concerned that the lynx kittens may end up mostly as roadkill. As for moose, she'd like to see them in the Adirondacks. And twice she has seen cougars.

Comparing the values of preservationists — those she sees as belonging to the APA, the Governor's Commission, the Adirondack Council — and conservationists — those she sees as belonging to the fish and game clubs, Adirondack Conservation Council, New York State Conservation Council, and many of the local citizens — Nellie uses the metaphor of an apple. "Now, the preservationist would polish it and keep it on a shelf. The conservationist would split it in half and plant the seeds to grow more. . . . The animals are going to die anyway. It's the same with the trees." She pauses, folding her hands, thoughtfully. "What a great thing it would be if they could all work together, and pool their strengths to do something constructive for the environment."

🌿 "I like to see nice, straight boles when I look at the woods. Trees are a crop, you know, just like corn," says Frank Bencze, swiveling in a hardwood desk chair, the pattern of the grain gleaming in the light from a banker's lamp.

Bencze has been working in woods products all his life. He picked up a formal education in forestry in between jobs. He started out at the Ranger School in Wanakena on Cranberry Lake, in the western part of the Adirondacks. Just ten years before the New York State Ranger School was established on a gift of 1,814 acres from the Rich Lumber Company, Cranberry Lake was described as largely a wilderness, "an untouched and exceedingly beautiful area, its waters abounding in trout and its numerous bogs and impenetrable bays — blocked by standing and fallen tree trunks and driftwood — a haven for wildlife" (Welch, p. 156, 1968). But fires in the dry year of 1908 and logging changed the landscape. Cranberry Lake remains wilder than the other large Adirondack lakes, and is the source of the Oswegatchie River; the entire eastern and southern half of the shoreline is included in the proposed Oswegatchie Great Wilderness. The Ranger School itself is situated a few hundred yards from the boundary of a stand of primeval woods that is part of the Forest Preserve. As a student there, Bencze had opportunities to study virgin old growth forest, rarely found in the Adirondacks, as well as second growth and recently logged areas.

But World War II was in progress, and Bencze soon enlisted in the army. After he was discharged, he worked for International Paper, cruising timber, taking inventory of the volume, in New York, Maine, Vermont, and New Hampshire. After that he worked for New York State for a year, cruising timber, surveying, and locating boundary lines. He went back to college at Paul Smith's for a year and then transferred to Syracuse University, where he finished his bachelor of science in general forestry in two years. Immediately after graduating, he came to Tupper Lake.

"I started out working here cruising timber for the Oval Wood Dish Corporation. They had forty thousand acres of timberland, as well as the mill complex . . . with a large band mill and several lathes," Bencze says. OWD produced flat woodenware products, including ice cream spoons, cocktail stirrers, tongue depressors, and veneer for wooden dishes. They also ran a sawmill that produced hardwood lumber, some of which was used in their own processes. They made a large volume of hardwood flooring, as

well as bowling pins, clothespins, and some other items that came and went
with demand.

Bencze moved up quickly within the company, a progress he describes
in his understated way: "I started out with them cruising timber and scaling
logs, then became the company forester, then advanced to woodlands manager, then vice president of the company." But changes followed, difficult
ones for someone who had invested his life in the forest industry in the
Adirondacks. In 1964 the company sold 25,000 acres to Diamond International Corporation, and in 1965 the plant was sold to Adirondack Plywood,
which was bought almost immediately by U.S. Plywood. U.S. Plywood
converted the entire plant to a veneer-producing mill instead of a sawmill-
veneer combination. Bencze became the permanent manager of U.S. Plywood.

But in August 1969 the company decided to liquidate. Bencze left and
went to a chip-producing plant about thirty miles north of Tupper Lake.
While he struggled with problems with machinery and a fire that burned
the mill down, a plywood corporation purchased a portion of the U.S.
Plywood plant and formed Tupper Lake Veneer. In 1972 Bencze came back
to Tupper to purchase logs for the new owners and head up their forestry
operations. In 1975 he became manager, a position he held until he retired
fifteen years later.

From his years of experience cruising timber and traveling in the Northeast, he offers a perspective on the quality of the Adirondack woodlands.
"The overall quality of hard timber here in the Adirondacks is better than
the quality of timber on Tug Hill. . . . Then as you get out of Tug Hill down
onto the agricultural lands, the quality of timber improves again — deep
soils, more fertile, growing season longer." He comments that utilization
standards have changed dramatically in the last forty years, permitting
smaller-diameter cuts and the use of lower-quality trees. "Unless you really
manicure a piece of timberland, every tree won't be a superb-quality piece
of wood. It's a growing entity, and every individual living . . . is not a perfect specimen." Bencze believes that plenty of good timber remains in the
Adirondacks.

I ask what kinds of cuts he thinks produce the healthiest woodlands for
different uses. "It depends on the site," he answers. "Some of the better
stands of cherry and ash have come off of stands that reportedly were
clear-cut back in the twenties or late teens — the type of cutting that would
be frowned on today, that would be highly criticized. 'Unethical' and so
forth. Yet today it's produced the most desirable stands that we have."

About shelterwood cuts he says, "If you open up too much, beech will take over. Although I've seen nice stands of maple making their way. Depends on the degree of cut."

Often the landowner determines what kind of cut is done. Bencze says his business is with getting the logs; if the land does not belong to his company, he does not want to dictate to the landowner what kind of cut should be made. But he has his own opinions about how logging should be done in the Adirondacks. "I think an awful lot of stands today, if you could get out the overmature old growth trees, you'd be accomplishing about as much good as you could hope for . . . and occasional small ones, the obvious culls, because there are some stands that are still far too dense if you just take out the old growth."

In his opinion the timber businesses in the Adirondacks have done a good job of maintaining the forests in recent times. "A lot of it is a matter of choice. Sometimes it's aesthetic choice, other times it's economic choice. It is my opinion that no matter how you cut these Adirondack lands, they will still sustain and regenerate. It depends on what you want to see as a landowner afterwards, which isn't always necessarily what the public wants to see."

He criticizes the public perception of the forest and forest industries as uninformed. "I get the feeling that the public, the uninformed, uneducated public as far as the woodlands are concerned, wants to set and dictate the policy by which our lands should be managed. The only knowledge that they have is that which they glean through looking at a piece of land, and that is something that is strictly aesthetics. Does it *look* pretty," he says, with mild irritation in his voice. He adds, "And a logged-over piece of land doesn't *look* pretty unless they've done a lot of manicuring, and knocking down of tops and so forth. But that's not economical."

He sees something different when he looks at the woods. "I can look over a cut-over piece of land, and I guess I don't see the tops. I see the remaining stand, and I see the remaining stand as it will be ten, fifteen, twenty years from now. I say, yes, that looks great. Whereas someone else might drive through and say, 'What a horrible mess that is.' "

He also notices the changes in wildlife populations and diversity after logging, recognizing that species respond differently, according to their habitat requirements. Initially, logging may discourage wildlife activity in the immediate area, but after three to five years, he says, there may be more deer and grouse. "Depends more on habitat—like the varying snowshoe hare—got to have lowland softwood swamp type of conditions to begin with." Black bear and other large animals are less likely to be affected, he says, because they cover a big territory anyway. He wouldn't want to guess about songbirds.

When we discuss how much land should be in "forever wild," Bencze says that, from an industrial forester's standpoint, "We have probably *more* than sufficient Forest Preserve acres—we probably have too many." He says, "I'm not totally unreceptive to state ownership or the Forest Preserve cause. I think there are a number of acres that are well served by being in Forest Preserve status. I think we've gone beyond that point."

He thinks that the acquisition of state land is reaching the point of negative returns as the proportion of state land to private land increases. He compares the amount of state land in New York with that in Vermont and New Hampshire, where there aren't any large state-owned areas. "It seems that the general economy of the countryside seems to be more active, vibrant, productive. I think that the lack of the availability of a resource to the area has had a definite economic effect. And I don't think tourism has replaced what we've lost."

Bencze talks about the difficulty of bringing wood products industries into the Park. "I don't think that any concern, large or small, feels comfortable investing any sizable amount of capital in an area where the base for the resource that their livelihood depends upon is being constantly shrunk away from them by state acquisitions," he says. When he first came into the area there were five good-sized sawmills. "Today there isn't a single sawmill left. They've all gone out. Tupper Lake Veneer is on kind of a shaky basis at the moment," he says, and is suddenly quiet, looking out the window.

The problem for investors and wood products industries, he goes on to explain, is not so much the logs available at present as the availability of logs in the future. "Because you just can't set up a wood-using plant or operation, sawmill or whatever you have, on the basis of the timber that would be available for one, two, or three years. It's got to be a long enough period of time to amortize the capital that you're investing into that operation, and with the instability of that land situation, no prudent investor is going to stick his neck out that far."

Bencze argues that, when it comes to making changes in policy, the population in and around the resource area is so small that it has very little if any weight in the state's decision-making process. "We are swung, pushed, pulled, whatever other explanation you may want to use, by New York City and the other populated areas of the state—with the exception of the bond issue." The 1990 Environmental Quality Bond Act, though largely supported in the southern part of the state, was rejected in the north. Adirondackers, opposed to setting monies aside for state land acquisition, especially when the state was in bad financial shape, protested against the Bond Act, and succeeded in turning the vote around. Bencze, like many others, thinks that without the land acquisition issue, the Bond Act, which would also have paid for closing landfills and modernizing sewage systems in rural towns, would have passed. But in his view, "anything else that was pro–Forest Preserve would just go through hands down."

When I mention the APA, he looks chagrined. "I think it's quite obvious [that the APA] really doesn't want too much infeed from the local, the native population." He thinks that the agency would like to cut local representation on the board down to two members, and "if they had their druthers, it'd be none."

As far as the Commission Report is concerned, he says, "There was a lot of lip service to the tune of 'We've got to do something about the economy of the Adirondacks.' The statement was made. You wonder what action will be beyond it. But they again don't seem to feel that there ought to be too much input from the local folks. You read it over and get that feeling. They made up their minds — they know what's good for us, and we should go along with it." Anger surfaces. "We've spent a lifetime scratching out a living," he says.

Bencze believes that many of the decisions about forestland are made on a political basis. "I can remember one sale of a large piece of timberland to the state. It must have been close to two years before some type of economic impact report or statement came out *after* the sale. No less than three or four mills were getting timber from that tract, which was a large tract, twenty-some-odd thousand acres. In the text there, there's a statement that said —" and he closes his eyes, then opens them abruptly, to quote from memory — " 'The removal of this tract from the timber base would have very little economic impact.' "

Even though he has retired, Bencze continues to spend a great deal of time in the woods. His perspective on the forest industries and the forests themselves stretches back to World War II. Bencze has noticed changes in forest health since that time. He has seen a blight sustained by yellow birch, and now the beech blight. He has seen the American elm completely wiped out. And he has watched the decline in spruce at higher elevations, and wonders whether acid rain is the culprit. Probably more trees are lost to natural mortality than to anything else, he says, but he thinks that the predominance of more mature trees boosts the spread of disease. "You wonder if some of this beech dieback did get started in the old growth. . . . Spruce budworm gets started in old growth stands."

He gains much of his knowledge from observation; he spends time in the woods nearly every day. "My sons are actively logging; I look in on their operations. I still look after about six thousand acres of land for the OWD company." He also has a family farm of about seven hundred acres, predominantly white pine, which is managed as a tree farm. His hobbies are hunting and fishing. I ask if he enjoys being in the woods. "Oh, yeah, very much so. I've never got tired of it."

I ask what kind of future he sees for the wood products industry in the Adirondacks. "I'd be just happy to see it hold its own," he says. But a few months after our interview, Tupper Lake Veneer closes, too.

🌿 "How tall is Gary Randorf?" asks an anonymous mock questionnaire on preservationists pinned to a gas station wall. He is very short, and with his round eyes, mild expression, and love of long quiet hikes in the woods, he

Photo 12. A path to the lake. Photo D. Kuklok

194   reminds me of J. R. R. Tolkien's hobbit. Not Bilbo, the finder of wealth
and a magic ring, but Frodo, the protagonist of *The Lord of the Rings*, who
discovers the evil powers of the ring and embarks on a long journey to
destroy it. Gary Randorf, like Frodo, is on a mission, and has been since he
came to the Adirondacks twenty years ago. The powerful force he hopes to
destroy before it destroys the Adirondacks as he knows them is uncon-
trolled development. Yet the issue, even for the Adirondack Council, the
most outspoken and, according to some, the most extreme preservationist
group in the Park, is not completely black and white. Some development is
necessary to preserve the economy of the Park's residents, and to continue
to provide services for the expanding number of visitors. Some industry is
necessary to provide jobs. But if the Adirondack Council had its way,
according to its publications, including its "20/20 Vision" reports, which
outline plans for the future of the Park, development would be strictly
regulated. In the case of Tolkien's ring, it turns out that even the most
moderate use for good purposes carries an inherent danger and inevitably
sickens the wearer. Development in the Adirondacks may carry its own
inherent danger. For some, including both preservationists and home rule
advocates, seeing the issue in black and white makes sense. For others,
believing that the Adirondack Council members see things that way makes
sense.

Gary Randorf came to the Adirondacks after finishing a master's degree
in environmental education and natural resources at Cornell University. He
grew up in Orchard Park in western New York. "In those days," he says,
"we were surrounded by farms. My brother worked on farms, and I worked
on farms. We were members of Future Farmers of America." He followed
his brother to college at Cornell, where he majored in agricultural economics. After graduating, he moved to California for several years, where he
pursued interests in landscape and nature photography. While in California,
he says, "I just got so concerned about how things were getting screwed up
pretty badly." When George Davis, as assistant director for natural resources of the new APA, invited Randorf, whom he'd met at Cornell, to
apply for a job at the Park Agency, Randorf agreed reluctantly. When he
finally arrived to begin work as the APA's natural resources planner, he fell
in love with the Adirondacks.

After two years he became the APA's first Park naturalist. In 1977 he
was offered the job of first full-time director of the Adirondack Council,
which at that time was a watchdog group that participated, on the side of
the APA, in legal actions that challenged the APA Act, as well as in adminis-

trative hearings. After nearly ten years as director, he got an opportunity to follow his love of nature photography and writing when the APA asked him to help with the opening of the new Adirondack Park Visitor Interpretive Center. He returned to the Adirondack Council as acting executive director after two years with the APA, then became permanent director until the book he was working on demanded too much of his attention. He then passed on the directorship to Timothy Burke, former director of the Vermont Deparment of Environmental Conservation. Randorf became senior counselor, and now works half-time in that position for the Council.

"I've had an opportunity that no one else has had—to work for the APA twice and the Adirondack Council twice," Randorf says. "I've had incredible opportunities to do amazing backcountry work for the Park Agency on two different occasions. I did Wild, Scenic, and Recreational River studies for two and a half years. That got me to see the Park, walking or canoeing along twelve hundred miles of river. . . . Then two years ago I worked for the Visitor Center. I cross-country skied all the cross-country ski trails in the Park, wrote them up, and photographed them."

It was as director of the Adirondack Council that Randorf had his most controversial, and most visible, role. For many people in the Park, the Adirondack Council, and especially Gary Randorf, represent extremes of preservationism. For others, including a wide membership outside the Park, the Council and Randorf represent a welcome intensity that serves the Park's purpose to protect the wildlands of the Adirondacks. Randorf describes the five major functions of the Council. One is to monitor the state agencies, including the APA and the DEC. In its educational function, the Council tries to gather information on the Adirondacks and help interpret the Park "so people understand what it is all about and what the APA and others are trying to do to preserve the biological diversity and the landscape." Its third function is to lobby in the state legislature and in Washington, and to keep abreast of what is going on both in Albany and in the nation's capital on issues that affect the Park. The fourth role, when warranted, is to go to court on issues requiring legal action. The council's final function, which emerged more fully and controversially with the Governor's Commission, has been involvement in planning for the Park. "The APA was mandated to do this, but they haven't done as much because of understaffing and the great burden of their project review function," Randorf explains. "We kind of just inherited and took on that work, with our '20/20 Vision' series." But the triangular relationship between the state APA, the privately organized Council, and the Governor's Commission, which put forth some recommendations similar to those in the '20/20 Vision' series, has outraged some of the most voluble antipreservationists in the Park.

Shifting the directorship of the Council to Timothy Burke, a former state administrator, may help the Council clarify its role toward the public. Or it may further antagonize those who believe that state control and regulation have already exceeded any reasonable bounds. Meanwhile, Randorf plans to use his book to promote his own vision of the Park. "Part of it is probably out of frustration of seeing that things have not progressed as far as I would have liked, preservation-wise," he says of his book. "It's a real strong pitch for trying to emphasize how special this place is, and how much is at stake, and that we need to do something relatively quickly to make it the best possible park — make it a real park." He hopes that his book will get more people inside as well as outside the Park to recognize what is at stake. "I hope that it will help some of the locals, just a little bit anyway, feel . . . that there are good things about living in the Park. The book is a celebration of the Park, with a lot of emphasis on its diversity and wildness . . . emphasizing that the wildness is its rarest and most vulnerable commodity, and the one that we could least stand to lose."

Some local people might not agree. But Randorf's reactions to recent controversies over land use management, and his vision for the Park, are more complex, and more closely related to his early farm experiences, than might be suspected from his public statements. His consideration of the value of having a diversity of forest types would surprise many of his opponents. He compares the qualities of privately owned and managed forest with those of the state's "forever wild" Forest Preserve. "I see a great value in having *both* the managed forest and natural, unmanaged forest. There is very little primeval forest in the Park. Some of it is on private land as well as state land, like the lands of the Adirondack League Club and the AuSable Club. . . . The woods that I enjoy most are the woods that haven't been managed. When you manage the forest enough, you get the early successional stages, the shrubs and pioneer species of trees and the berries; it's harder to bushwhack. The open character, the open forest, that you can just roam through, covered with ferns and wildflowers — you can see a real difference."

He tells me about a recent hike into the Hoffman Notch Wilderness. "When you start out you're on Finch, Pruyn Paper Company land that has been heavily logged. All of a sudden you leave that and you go into un-touched State Forest Preserve, and the difference is night and day. You've got this kind of ragged look because they've harvested in there . . . and it will of course come back, but right now the difference is striking." He describes the transition to state forest. "The trail up there is absolutely beautiful . . . a lot of huge yellow birch, white pine, and hemlock. It's pristine. But the forest mixture is ecologically advantageous. The early successional stages of the managed forest attract species like white-tailed deer and ruffed grouse. Pine marten, fisher, and spruce grouse thrive in the untouched woods, so we have the best of both worlds. *That's* what I'm always arguing. We can have both. We have all this acreage — why argue for just one or the other? That's just totally foolish."

The difference in opinion between forest products industries and loggers, sportsmen, conservationists, and locals on the one hand, and the Adirondack Council and other preservationists on the other, rests more on how much land should be in the Forest Preserve, and on occasion how it should be classified to accommodate both mechanized and primitive modes of outdoor recreation. When asked how much more state land he and the Adirondack Council feel is necessary, Randorf replies, "The council and the [Governor's] Commission are very together on that, and through our '20/20 Vision' reports I think we, better than anybody else, have really made the case for which areas still need to be better protected through acquisition or conservation easements to preserve biological diversity, and to round out the wilderness areas so that they are more ecologically intact. In the wild forest areas the challenge is to improve the degree of access." He and the rest of the Adirondack Council see the recreational use emphasized in the wild forest areas; in the wilderness zones, ecological integrity and biological diversity should take priority over human use and enjoyment.

In the first three volumes of "20/20 Vision," the Council makes the case that about 650,000 acres need to be added to the State Forest Preserve. A significant portion of that acreage would help establish the proposed Bob Marshall Great Wilderness area in the western part of the Park, honoring this preservationist's great love of the area. The additional 650,000 acres would bring state-owned land to 52 percent of the park's total acreage. Gary Randorf approves these proportions. "I studied these reports," he says, "and from my knowledge of the Park, if it reaches fifty-fifty, I think that's going to be the ideal situation." But then he adds carefully, "Recognizing that after that . . . [it] may be the economy completely changes, and the forest industry decides it can't stay here any longer because the taxes have gone crazy, out of sight, and there aren't any programs to help." He recognizes some of the local people's unease with the lack of a definite ceiling on state acquisitions. "You know, the people who are on the other side of the preservationists have said, 'Well, how much do you *really* want? You'll never stop. You really want to rule the people out of the Park,' and that's a totally outrageous claim. The exciting thing about this Park is the mixture of people and wilderness. And finding a way to make that work — we're charting unbroken ground."

He realizes that the forest industry also has some concerns about the security of its land base for the future, but he feels that the preservationists and the forest industry are making progress toward a mutual understanding through regular meetings. "What we've been trying to get them to do is to identify what they refer to as the 'Forever Working Forest.' We're saying, 'you identify where those are, and we will go along with you and say, let's keep them out of the Forest Preserve.' " The Adirondack Council, the Association for the Protection of the Adirondacks, and the Adirondack Mountain Club have had many meetings with International Paper, Finch, Pruyn, and Champion, as well as the Empire State Forest Products Association; Randorf feels that there has been a lot of trust, and it is growing.

One solution, which the Adirondack Council spearheaded, is the 1983 conservation easement legislation which allows the state to purchase less-than-fee title to certain lands to provide access for recreation and to extinguish development rights. The 1986 Environmental Bond Act marked the first time that monies could be used to buy less-than-fee interests. But Randorf underlines that in the case of the easements, as in the case of fee title acquisition, the transactions should involve willing sellers — with rare exceptions.

One case in which the Department of Environmental Conservation did press eminent domain occurred on a parcel of land, surrounded by State Forest Preserve, which was owned by Dr. Vince Vaccaro, a dentist residing outside the Park. Randorf thinks that the publicity from that case, occurring at the same time the commission report came out, was the worst thing that could possibly have happened. Vaccaro spent much time pleading his case, writing letters to local papers, and speaking at meetings of local groups protesting the report. He made public his willingness to negotiate with the state, including allowing public recreation access and a promise not to cut the timber on his land. Nevertheless, DEC commissioner Thomas Jorling refused to back down from the use of eminent domain to acquire the land for the state.

Randorf shakes his head. "It scared a lot of people. . . . The unfortunate thing was, people always heard Vaccaro's side; they never heard the state. The state didn't publish anything in the media because their court case was going on. They didn't actually say what their rationale was. There are some fairly good reasons why they wanted to take that land. I don't think they are good enough reasons that they should have. . . . A conservation easement would have been a neat, and to my way of thinking a perfect, solution, and would have avoided all this bad public reaction. I'm sure a lot of people were saying, 'If they can take Vaccaro's, then they can take mine next,' and of course that is what Vaccaro was telling them as well."

But the Adirondack Council and other groups, including the Association for the Protection of the Adirondacks and the Adirondack Mountain Club, sent out a mixed message. "We all supported it. We supported it with some reluctance because we didn't think it was a good, clear-cut — the best case. We were kind of in the position where, if we didn't support it, there would be other cases in the future where there *was* a good justification, and the state would be too timid to go forward. So we were kind of between a rock and a hard place," Randorf says.

The Adirondack Council and other preservation groups support the language in the commission report outlining the rare cases in which the use of eminent domain is preferred. Randorf summarizes their position for me. "Basically, the language is saying . . . if there is an overriding public benefit to be served by preventing the transformation of a healthy, natural re-source–based landscape into something that's completely different — devel-oped — and is a threat to a chunk of land with outstanding resources, then the state can decide to come in and take that land by eminent domain. But eminent domain has only been exercised about twice in the last twenty-five years up here, and it has never taken anybody's primary residence or their home. . . . But the threat is there." He adds, "A lot of the locals are saying, 'Take that language out completely. Don't ever allow the state to take anything by eminent domain.' But you *can't* go that far because there are some times that it's going to be to all of our benefit if the state does, if there's a compelling reason to do so. We think there needs to be a compel-ling reason." But then he sees his error and admits, "What *we* think is a compelling reason, not what Donald Gerdts thinks is a compelling reason. The difference is night and day."

Because the commission report produced a map including planned ac-quisitions for the state, Randorf remarks that some people think that the state is going to march in and take over that land, by eminent domain or other means, which is, according to Randorf, "total hogwash and totally absurd. But they've got it entrenched in their brains." He considers eminent domain a red herring. "I see that issue as clearly one of the people who are so opposed. They feel that they have never been part of the process, and they want to be part of the process. And until they *feel* that they are part of the process, we are going to have this incredible antagonism. Many of the things which they are fighting against, tooth and nail, they would be *for* if they felt they were part of what was going on."

So how to achieve that participation? The local people, through their elected officials on the Adirondack Planning Commission, and now on the Adirondack Association of Towns and Villages, have made it known that they want five members, chosen by the locals, on the APA board. Randorf disagrees with this. He says that there are five local residents on the APA now, and the issue has more to do with who is a bona fide resident. "The governor can appoint people who represent local government, so we don't think any change really has to be made for that to happen. And I've known every single commissioner of the APA. There's been a couple of local government people who have represented that point of view. There have been developers. There's been about ten people on there who have clearly, *strongly* been on the side of local government and local concerns, so I don't think that's really an issue.

"The thing that really muddied the waters, the body that was supposed to represent local interests, the Local Government Review Board — and I was glad to see that some local politicians, including Jim Frenette, and Dick Purdue . . . recently made the same case that I make in my book — is that the Review Board has spun its wheels, and for most of its life had not done what it was supposed to do, and that's advise and assist and monitor the APA and provide local input. But they've spent most of their energy trying to emasculate the APA or abolish it." Randorf argues that because the board existed but didn't do its job, it has prevented, until recently, any other local body from coming into existence. The Adirondack Planning Commission, now defunct, and the new Adirondack Association of Towns and Villages have tried to represent the voices of Adirondack people on participation issues. Randorf suggests that there should be a formal advisory group to the APA, which might include two people from every county, appointed by the local governments, or chosen in any way acceptable to local people.

He recognizes that there is a difference between an advisory capacity and a decision-making capacity, a difference that is important from the local point of view. But he argues that, in spite of being appointed by the governor rather than the local population, the five residents on the APA fairly represent the local point of view. He outlines what we both know, that there are eight citizen members on the APA and three state ex-officio members. Of the eight, five have to be full-time residents of the Adirondack Park. Randorf admits that the governor picked the wrong people for public relations purposes, but he insists that those who were chosen are fair and capable of representing local concerns. "I don't think there's a fairer person in the world than a John Collins, for instance, the teacher from Blue Mountain Lake whose family has been here for several generations. Bill Roden is always on the side of the locals; he's another member. Woody Cole [then-chair] hasn't been in the Adirondacks that long, so I can see it would depend on who you were whether you'd think he was a fair guy or not. I think he's a pretty fair man. I think Anne LaBastille is a pretty fair lady. And that's the four. And John Stock, he was definitely on the side of the locals. So they've had pretty good representation. And when you look at who owns the Park, there's less than 30 percent of the Park that's owned by the people who live full-time within the Blue Line, so they've got pretty fair representation." Using this percentage to judge representation on the APA board perhaps underrepresents local interests, since the APA has jurisdiction only over private land, which represents about 58 percent of the Park.

The issue of representation has sparked an enormous amount of antagonism between preservationist special interest groups and local groups. Randorf feels that there is a great need for mediation. "Some objective party from outside is what's needed. Because there seems to be such incredible polarization, *walls* built between these organizations, which I see as so frustrating, because I really sense, after the debate that has gone on over the commission report, and all the hearings when people testified, that clearly the majority of the people basically want the same thing: to keep the rural character of the Park, open-space character, and they want as little change as possible, with some economic stimulation. They don't want condos and townhouses. They don't want people coming in from the outside and exploiting this magnificent landscape to benefit just a few people to the detriment of the locals. But instead of emphasizing our common ground, we're emphasizing our differences. And some people are making such mountains out of molehills as far as where we're different." But just as with eminent domain, what Randorf and the Adirondack Council see as molehills and what the locals perceive as such may be as different as night and day.

Randorf takes some of the responsibility for the communication problems on himself. He feels that the Adirondack Council could be doing a better job in that area. "We have such a dedicated staff . . . but we can't come up with the recipe . . . to improve communications and start reaching these people. Because after the connection that they made that the [Governor's] Commission and the [Adirondack] Council were one and the same thing, and the Council had drafted all the commission's recommendations and were totally in bed with them, and they were just echoing us and our people . . . [the local] people got so incensed and so turned off at us . . . they started picketing and vandalizing our office. . . . Anything we say now, almost, they will twist in some way because they have gotten themselves to believe that the Council are a bunch of bad people." Gary Randorf's voice, which has been rising, is suddenly silent, and he shuts his eyes for a moment. It is clear that he takes the matter very personally, despite his efforts to define the attacks as irrational.

He says, "I've never seen people so stirred up and emotional. It was hot in the early days of the APA, but certainly not as hot as it was in the summer of 1990 [after the commission report came out]. It was never personal in the past. Then they were against the state and all those bureaucrats, but they didn't single out individuals. . . . It was said at one point that if the commission's recommendations went through the legislature, that Gary Randorf's and George Davis's houses would be burned to the ground." Donald Gerdts and his followers surrounded the house of Eric Siy, Adirondack Council staff member, one day and shouted angry threats. Randorf comments, "[It was] very personalized, and with threats of shooting people. And burning the woods — well, that's been talked about for years — but *shooting* people!"

He argues that when council members try to speak to these angry locals, who are among the most radical supporters of home rule, and engage in a dialogue, they are accused of just trying to smooth things over. When the Adirondack Council was picketed, council members served coffee to the picketers and tried to engage in conversation, with limited success.

Although these locals are among the most radical home rule advocates, and do not represent all, or perhaps even most, Adirondackers, the council is also having problems communicating with other segments of the population. Sportsmen's groups, self-proclaimed conservationists, used to be very closely aligned with the preservationists; they were strongly behind the designation of the areas that are now wilderness, and favored the APA Act, as well as the Wild and Scenic Rivers Act and Bond Act. But the sportsmen's groups opposed the last Bond Act and the commission report. Randorf thinks that the New York Conservation Council has been "unduly influenced by the Adirondack Conservation Council and its 35,000 members." He notes that in a lead article in a newsletter, Adirondack Conservation Council members tried to make the case that the Adirondack Council, and therefore the commission, were anti-hunting. "But we're not anti-hunting. It's not true at all," says Randorf. "I hunted when I was about ten years old. My introduction to the woods was with sportsmen who liked to be out in the woods. . . . And if they shot something, it was to take home and put on the table. They're very good people, but I don't understand why there is such a rift between us now." He remarks that Paul Schaefer, a longtime preservationist and conservationist who was on the Adirondack Council board for many years, seems to be experiencing a lot of frustration. Schaefer got together some of the conservation leaders and some of the Council members to see if they could find common ground. But after what seemed to Randorf a positive meeting, "a few weeks later you see these people blasting the Council and opposing the Bond Act."

Yet Randorf believes that local participation is absolutely essential. "Local people have to feel they're a part of the process, or else there will always be a tremendous resistance. You can pass laws and a lot of things can be done, but . . . you can end up with even more civil disobedience." His definition of what constitutes participation, however, differs sharply from that of the local officials. And while he wants everyone who is a resident of the Park to recognize the great benefits of living there, he also emphasizes that people must give up certain things for the privilege of living in an area of such great wild natural beauty, away from the stress and pollution of urban areas, and with opportunities for so many kinds of outdoor recreation. "The success of [the Park] will be reflected in people living in harmony with their environment. That's what we're trying to do here," he says.

Randorf hopes that the Park will provide an example to the rest of the world. Adirondack Council staff helped to get the Park and the Lake Champlain area designated as a Biosphere Reserve, the fourth largest in the world, and the most populated. Randorf believes that the success he hopes for is very near, and that is why the controversy is so hot. "If it *wasn't* hot, we wouldn't be doing what we really need to do. We need to take the last few steps here to nail this whole thing down and *forever* preserve this Park." He emphasizes how difficult these steps are, calling them painful and controversial. But "they are steps, too, that I believe, if things were under local control, we would never take. There *has* to be overriding state control and state concern. That's not to say that local participation and local decisions aren't part of that. How to weave that together, how to split the whole regulatory scheme so that those things that are truly local are handled locally, and those things that are truly regional are handled regionally — that's what we are trying to do. But we're really struggling with finding the right recipe. . . . We have not found it yet."

The question remains whether the Adirondack Park is going to be a blueprint for other parts of the world or a case study of everything that can go wrong. "It's going to be a blueprint," Randorf says.

❧ The philosophy which he tries to implement in the Adirondack Council's planning for the Park reflects Randorf's personal philosophy as well. "I really see what we're aiming for, and what we're closer to than in any other area in the U.S., is actually living by the land ethic Aldo Leopold espoused. The Indians were living that way initially, so I think we are coming full circle." He echoes Leopold, arguing that we are part of a land community and must treat it as a community of life, not as a commodity to be exploited. He sees his own relationship to the land as that of a steward, entrusted to take care of the land, in the tradition of Leopold, Wendell Berry, and others who have tried both to preserve the land and to support sustainable use.

His belief in preservation is tempered with a farmer's recognition of economic reality. "I do believe that you can only restrict private land so much; beyond a certain point, people deserve to be compensated for it." He says that it was both the Council's position and his personal position that if the commission restricted private land any further, that there should be compensation. He suggests that compensation take the form of tax relief to help support the people who are being asked to act as land stewards for the benefit of the whole state.

But there are other preservationists for whom the concept of steward-ship does not go far enough. Randorf says that to Earth First!ers, steward-ship is a bad word. Yet many who are affronted by the preservation movement do not distinguish between the different philosophies. "To many people, I'm sure that when Earth First! speaks, that's just another branch of the Adirondack Council. It's just another group of preservationists, and they all want to do the same thing, which is drive the people out and make it all a national park or a state park."

I ask him if he defines preservation very differently from the way he defines conservation. "I don't, no," he says, and then adds, after a moment, "I have some problem with labels. Preservation is a harder line, with more emphasis on preserving than on multiple use. It's Muir versus Pinchot."

"And are you with Muir?"

"Yes."

He admires Ray Fadden, a Mohawk elder who speaks every year to the preservation community on Earth Day. Randorf doesn't take issue with anything Fadden says, though at times Fadden is harshly critical of Euro-American beliefs and practices that have damaged the environment. Fadden uses the concept of the seventh generation to get his point across. Randorf says that the idea of taking care of the earth for the seventh generation from now is music to his ears. He confides that the greatest compliment he ever got came from the Mohawk elder. "He called me a present-day Adirondack warrior, and said I needed to be supported. That really meant a lot to me."

❧ The Adirondack Ecological Center, the Newcomb campus of the State University College of Forestry at Syracuse, stands in the shelter of a forest just off Route 28N, west of Newcomb. Most of the center's research projects take place there in the 15,000-acre Huntingdon Wildlife Forest, donated by the Huntingdon family. At any time over sixty projects may be running, with scientists coming from all over the Northeast to participate in the research. Dick Sage, the manager of the center, fits the role of the forester. Tall, thin, and in good physical condition for middle age, he lounges in his chair with an attitude of relaxed good humor, but leaps to his feet with surprising energy on occasion to make a point. He has lived and worked in Newcomb for nearly three decades. As the manager of the center, he works with the theories and applications of the ecological community every day. As a prominent and active member of the hamlet of Newcomb, he also draws from and builds the human community daily. Listening to him speak, I hear him go back and forth easily between ideas of ecological community and ideas of human community. It is clear that the sense of community, of relatedness and connection, forms the frame within which he operates. With a mental agility that matches his physical motions, he leaps into discussions of community problems, transposing his scientific sense of ecology and the expectations of certitude onto hamlet issues with an unself-conscious grace.

Sage feels that the college could play a greater role in the Adirondacks. Ecological Center scientists can provide the research and information that Sage thinks the debate over land use management in the Adirondacks should be based on. He is concerned that much of the decision making is directed by pressures from special interest groups whose goals may be more aesthetically than ecologically informed. For complex ecological reasons, he believes that the Adirondacks, with its wide variety of ecosystems and species of flora and fauna, should remain at about its present ratio of state land to private land.

The critical factor in the difference between the state lands and the privately managed timberlands lies in the amount of disturbance, something that tourists often fail to appreciate. "People go up and down the road complaining about salt killing the paper birch," Sage says. "Paper birch is an early successional stage species; it will not be represented in the vast quantities that it is represented now if the forest just grows and grows and grows. It is not going to be disturbed by fire anymore." Sage, like John Stock, has concerns about the ecological wisdom of the DEC policy of putting out fires on state land. "The only [way] to get early successional stages is by disturbance. Forestry is a form of controlled disturbance, and it can produce those species on the landscape. I'm not saying paper birch won't exist in the Adirondack landscape, but its presence in pure stands that are attractive to people is just not going to exist forever."

But aesthetics are not the only or even the major concerns that Sage has about the lack of early successional stages that a loss of disturbance sites would bring about. "Wildlife species such as pin cherry and black cherry — food sources — are not long-lived and are outlived by more long-lived species that will restrict diversity. The key to maintaining this diversity of wildlife — including 273 nesting bird species — is the interspersion of land that is being disturbed and land that is not being disturbed. What I see now is not an argument for maintaining diversity *within* the Adirondack Park; I see a move to say the Adirondack Park will provide one type, and the diversity will occur across the Northeast where all the rest of the landscape has been disturbed." He shakes his head impatiently. "That's changing the ballgame in my view. The idea was to maintain diversity within the Park."

Some preservationists argue that fragmentation of the landscape comes into play; but Sage counters that people have extrapolated data on a limited set of circumstances, far beyond what the data can support. "I perceive fragmentation to be forest and non-forest — an eighty-acre woodlot and a two hundred–acre field. That's where the data suggest songbird diversity has been affected. It hasn't been between 6 million acres of forested land-scape, part of which is managed and part of which is not managed. They're using that in a totally different argument than the research ever developed. To our knowledge, of the fifty-four mammals [species] that live in the

Adirondack Park, there is not a one of them that requires, for its complete life cycle, unmanaged, old growth, mature habitat. They all require, for at least part of their cycle, having early successional stage habitat available. And they use the bear as an example!" He shakes his head in disbelief.

"I've got a student here that's working on bear. They're only out eight months of the year. And seven months of that they are making their living off managed forest land. One month of the year mature forest is more important to them. Because all the berry species and herbaceous species are on disturbed sites." The bear can live mostly on state land now. The state lands still have some young successional stage forest because of the disturbance history of the last sixty to eighty years, which has included some severe fires. But Sage is concerned about the long-term prospects for such diversity within state lands. He says of the places on state land where there are early successional stages, "That's dropping out very, very fast, and if they don't get it back, they're going to see some major, major changes in wildlife species diversity and plant species diversity in the Park." He argues that many preservationists outside the Park, and some of those within it, do not see the necessity of a combination of old growth and disturbance sites, preferring to provide a habitat for pine martens and other old growth denizens. "But the pine marten isn't going to be all that healthy if he just has foreverness of mature forest, because they feed very heavily on certain things that are associated with disturbance," Sage adds.

I ask how long it takes for a second growth forest to achieve a level of maturity that can support some of these old growth species. Although this topic has not been extensively researched, even in the Pacific Northwest, where it has become an issue because of the spotted owl, Sage has seen some old growth bird species reappearing in thirty-year-old clear-cut stands.

Some people seem to have forgotten the history of the Park's ecology as well, in Sage's eyes. "The perception of some of this management is that the forest is really threatened if you cut a tree. And everybody forgets that the whole forest was burned . . . just devasted, eighty-five years ago . . . but they think its wonderful now." His voice rises. "I just can't fathom this idea that we've spoiled this landscape by harvesting a tree on it, when, by God, you look at pictures of the Adirondacks back in the late 1800s and as far as you could see there was nothing but stumps. And now people think it's the most terrific landscape and ought to be preserved. . . . They lose track of some of those things." But he counters this impatience with support for a balance between preservation and management. He echoes, unknowingly,

Gary Randorf's fifty-fifty proportions; but he doesn't have any perception that the forces at work are willing to stop. "What guarantee do we have?"

He is convinced that the state should not backtrack and take land out of "forever wild" that is currently protected. Nor does he think that in the case of serious blowdowns, as in Tupper Lake, the downed timber should be removed. Yet he would bet that 50 percent of the landscape could be managed under an even-aged system, and probably should be.

What kind of management a managed forest is under matters as much as whether or not it is managed. Sage says, "Some of our recent research with the bear project suggests that the selection system of repeated management, cutting at frequent intervals, is not producing much in the way of plant diversity, beyond what the unmanaged lands produce. You are just not creating big enough holes to get the light regime on the ground that many of these species require."

Some of the SUNY faculty did studies in the Tug Hill area and found that with uneven-aged management, about 20 to 25 percent of tree stems were damaged at the time of any one entry. Theoretically, at least, if some of the stems remain for four or five entries, and reach mature size, they have a good chance of being damaged. Rugged conditions also make it difficult to use the heavy logging machinery without inflicting a fair amount of damage. For these reasons, Sage prefers even-aged management in many cases.

"Our approach is to use a shelterwood cut, where you take out two thirds of the stand the first time around, and then leave an evenly spaced seed source, partial shelter, and shade on it. Then once you've established a stand, come back and take that other third off." After this second cut, the stand will be left alone for as long as fifty years. The researchers at the Ecological Center have found that they need to leave primarily sugar maples as the remaining third in the shelterwood cut, with some white ash and black cherry for seed. In their experience, the other species will reseed themselves, from seed sources on the periphery, because their seed disperses over a wider area. "With this basic approach, we're getting nine to twelve commercial tree species back on the site. A high percentage of it is just sugar maple and yellow birch, which are two bread-and-butter species." But they also get white ash, red maple, black cherry, and both species of aspen and balsam fir, in addition to all the shrubs and herbaceous species. The fifty to seventy thousand stems per acre that they aim for the first few years ensures good form — straight boles, for a forester — and helps support a wide range of species that allows the forester some control over what the future might bring. For the next rotation, Sage and the other researchers plan to add more white ash and black cherry to create more even representation. "We're thinking not only of the current rotation but also of the next," Sage says, "and I can guarantee you that's a hell of a lot longer than a lot of people are thinking about the future of the Adirondacks."

He and his colleagues are talking about "30/20 Vision," not 20/20, he says, paraphrasing the Adirondack Council. "We've demonstrated that we can do this in a predictable way, that we can get results, acceptable results, every time we do it . . . and that providing light through some heavier cutting is a real key. Rather than a stand that comes up 95 percent beech, we've got one that's got quite a diversity of species, one that has a totally different structure in a sense, so it provides an alternative habitat." Sage remarks that some people think that cutting the forest means that all the songbirds present in the old forest will disappear. "Well, some of them do, and some of them make the transition, and there's a whole flock of new species that like that habitat that weren't there before, and some of those are just as rare. . . . You don't want to have the whole Adirondacks in ten-year-old saplings, but if you think about that in terms of what we've got in Forest Preserve land, there's opportunities for all these species out there."

Selective cutting, which many environmentalists have preferred to clear-cutting and other forms of even-aged management, appears to result in lower levels of species diversity. "The real scary part is that some of the research work that's been done [shows that] the real reduction of songbirds is [caused by] selective cutting, because it doesn't appear to be all that beneficial to any of the species. They've sort of got a halfway point that isn't good for anybody." He adds, "Our greatest diversity occurs in shelterwood cuts about ten years after. There are more species nesting and breeding than in old growth." But the selectively cut stand, he notes, had fewer bird species than either of the other two kinds of stands. The red-eyed vireo made it through all the stages. The Blackburnian warbler didn't appear in the early stages of the shelterwood cut, but Sage and other researchers think that it may start showing up when the stand reaches about thirty years of age. The researchers at the Ecological Center have not tracked the stands long enough to know when species that were lost might reenter. They do know that the indigo bunting, which wasn't present in the old growth stand, is very prominent in the brush stage. The chestnut-sided warbler is the most common species. Which constellation of bird species fills the most gaps in conservation terms remains hazy. Preservationists would argue that old growth species are more important, and that there is enough brush and early successional forest elsewhere.

One of the things that concerns Sage most about the wildlife aspect of the controversy in the Adirondacks is that, in his opinion, the concept of wildlife is misunderstood. He approves of calling certain species "animals on wildlands" but doesn't like the connotations of "wilderness animals" because everybody has a different idea of what wilderness means. "If your idea of wilderness is that these [animals] need big tracts of forested landscape, we're done," he says, emphasizing his words with his fist, meaning that the Adirondacks provide sufficient wilderness for these species. If the idea is that big tracts of unmanaged, untouched land are necessary, Sage considers that approach misguided.

Lynx are a good example of what he means. The lynx makes its living by eating snowshoe hare. "Reiner Brocke spent ten years of his life up here proving that snowshoe hare habitat, the best snowshoe hare habitat, was early successional stage conifer stands — young conifer stands. You don't get young conifer stands by protecting the landscape for three hundred years from any kind of disturbance. You get old conifer stands, and that's lousy habitat for snowshoe hare. . . . If you're going to provide the food base these lynx need, you've got to have some kind of disturbance history or disturbance mechanism in place, and to me, the best disturbance mechanism is some kind of controlled or professionally done forestry operation rather than wildfires."

Nevertheless, a lot of what the Adirondacks are today is the result of wildfire. Sage adds, taking a deep breath, a maestro preparing for the final crescendo, "If they're not going to allow wildfires, then they'd better darn well allow management, and they'd better get serious about the even-aged management, because the uneven-aged management isn't really a good duplicator of natural catastrophes." The question remains: How frequent were fires and other natural disturbances before the early logging and the fires sparked by trains created a different pattern over the landscape, one in which hardwoods took over much of forests that had been composed mainly of softwoods? What levels of diversity did those primeval forests support? And will the State Forest Preserve land, in the absence of fire or other disturbance factors, revert to a similar ecology?

Sage describes the region in the past as an advanced forest landscape. "There's a reason they called [people in the Adirondacks] the Barkeaters then; there wasn't anything to eat up here except bark." While moose and probably wolves were more abundant, deer populations were lower. "Our computer models and research show that there was a deer density in the Adirondacks, before the fires and the logging, of about two to three deer per square mile. Now it ranges anywhere from eight to as high as thirty. Right now it might be ten or twelve in this part of the Adirondacks. . . . That's why you don't find any Canada yew or scarlet elder except in places where it's protected. . . . They've eliminated it from the landscape." The deer, like the elk in Rocky Mountain National Park in Colorado, have changed the landscape by virtue of their voracious appetites for certain foods. The management of deer populations in wilderness areas irritates Sage. He challenges the idea of manipulating wildlife populations in wilderness areas: "Why is hunting permitted, why is trapping permitted if it's a wilderness area? It's a quasi-wilderness. It looks like a wilderness in structure, but it really isn't because people are mucking around. You can't muck around with the trees, but you can muck around with the deer."

Much of the Ecological Center's research has suggested that the Adirondack landscape has a low level of productivity for many species, partly as a result of the severe impacts of the climate. Sage thinks that the appropriate exploitation level of wildlife in the Adirondacks is low, and it is being exceeded. "People say the fishing isn't as good [as it used to be]. Well, it isn't! The truth of the matter is, it takes an extremely low level of recreational activity to exploit that resource and depress it." One student did a study of small-mouth bass populations, comparing exploited populations to those that are not exploited. The student discovered dramatic differences in the age structure, the size distribution, and the number of bass. Sage feels that people should practice only catch-and-release fishing in wilderness areas.

And maybe, he thinks, people shouldn't be allowed to hunt in wilderness areas either. "It's all interconnected," he says. "My feeling is that these groups, on both sides, or all sides, although I don't like to pit the preservationists against the developers or the deer hunters versus the bird-watchers — nobody looks at this system in terms of as many of the components as it has. . . . It isn't my little bias versus your little bias. . . . That's the way people do business, but that isn't the way the system is going to come out anything but second-best, in my point of view. When people outright ignore good, solid, environmentally sound research that gives them a perspective that they need because all they care is how something looks on the landscape for a short period of time, that really bothers me. But these are the people making the decisions." He shakes his head, drumming on the desk. One gets the sense, as with many foresters, that to Sage, anything less than thirty years is a short period of time; and thinking in terms of a forest, it is.

He speaks again about the the Adirondack Park Agency commissioners, those who make the decisions. "I think they're being railroaded by some special interest groups that aren't allowing them to make what I perceive to be a much better decision for the future of this Park. There's just too much politics, too much money, too much influence for certain special interest groups to create their vision of the Park at the expense of everyone else's vision, and what I perceive to be at the expense of the most sound ecological vision."

To illustrate his point, he uses the example of the beech blight, which has gone largely unnoticed, except by those who work in the woods. "One third of the Forest Preserve has fallen down in the last fifteen years. Beech represents about 50 percent of the hardwood stands. . . . We know from our research that since the mid-sixties about 80 percent of the beech over sixteen inches [in diameter] has been killed by the beech disease outright, and the disease is holding on in the smaller stems, not causing outright mortality, but with an uncertain future."

The beech disease has taken hold all across the Park, but little mention has been made, other than an article in *Conservationist* which described the disease. Sage tells me, "More trees died than probably blew down in the 1950 windstorm. From beech bark disease. But did you read anything about it? Did anybody say anything about it? . . . People that are running the Park don't even know what it is. Millions and millions of trees died in the central Adirondacks [from] this disease, and you hardly ever heard about it because it was just like a thinning operation—a tree here, a tree there. I got pictures from the air when the disease was at its peak on this property, and just looking at aerial photographs . . . on about a hundred acres, you can count hundreds of dead trees. But there was beech underneath it, and it came up to replace those other beech, and nobody perceived a major change in the system. . . . It didn't change their visual perception of the Park.

"When something like that goes on under people's noses, pretty much undetected, you wonder, do these people really know what's going on in the Park, or are they just in there for their own particular perspective, their own vision." He adds, "I tried to get research money for fifteen years to study this because it had impacts on songbirds and cavity nesters. It is the only major mast-producing tree that we have in the central Adirondacks, because we have no oaks. Every wildlife species out there has beech in their diet. Nobody cares. Nobody even thought it was a problem. To me, as an ecologist, an environmental researcher, a forester, I just can't understand that."

In spite of his disagreements with the way the Park Agency works, he laughs at the situations he finds himself in, mingling an impatience that is closer to disbelief than bitterness, with good-humored irony. But when we discuss the agency's regulation of forest practices and its commissioners' views toward management, Sage speaks in a more subdued voice, and for the first time in the interview he looks sad. These are the issues closest to his own research, and to his role in the town as chairman of a planning board which has been trying for years to get a forest products plant in this tiny hamlet, before the hamlet itself disappears. "We spent almost thirty years here researching how best to manage Adirondack forests. We think we know the answers. But is any of that incorporated into an agency plan? No. I mean, they've got this totally other agenda, which is all driven by aesthetics, not by the environment — the protection of the site, the maintenance of diversity of vegetation on the landscape, the assurance of a good-quality future timber crop. 'We just don't like the way it looks so you can't do it that way.' The truth of the matter is, for most sites in the Adirondacks — and certainly we have a concern for aesthetics too — even-aged management, whether clear-cutting in softwoods or shelterwood cutting that we're recommending for hardwoods, has just been shown to produce a result that is leaps and bounds better than periodic whacking away at the woods, the selection-type cut." He notes that the diversity of species, stand quality, and level of damage to the site all improve with even-aged management.

The agency places relatively few regulations on forest management. The most notable is the requirement of a special permit for any clear-cut on more than twenty-five acres. The process of getting a permit can be slow and frustrating. Sage sees it as a sizable impediment to even-aged management. "Nobody wants to go to the Park Agency to clear-cut on an area that's larger than twenty-five acres because, first of all, it takes six or seven months . . . and they'll come up with some ridiculous set of conditions that tie your hands behind your back . . . because they don't like the fact that you've removed all the trees in a short period of time. It has no ecological basis; it has no economic consideration for the future timber crop. So as a result, people avoid that and do selective cutting, which produces lesser diversity of plant and animal life, greater damage to the residual trees on-site, greater damage to the site by going in every seven to ten years rather than once every fifty years, and a diversity of [tree] species that's limited to two or three species that proliferate under those conditions."

At one of the monthly APA meetings, which last several days, I sat with two representatives from Champion International who were requesting a permit for a clear-cut. They spent nearly all day at the APA office, making a well-prepared presentation, including a meticulous video, and then waiting for the board's decision. The permit was granted, but I wondered, if Champion had to pay two men for several days' work plus travel and the expense of making a video in order to obtain a permit, what was the likelihood that the firm would go through the permit system again? Champion International has since announced that it is reviewing its Adirondack holdings, throwing preservationists into a panic lest the company sell out to developers.

In the end, we come back to the principles of ecology, the sense of a community woven together, warp and weft. I ask Dick Sage for papers on some of the topics we have covered. As he leafs through the papers, he says, "Science starts out and writes a story about 'The Seasonal Home Range of the White-Tailed Deer.' " He pulls one out. "This is 'The Nesting Colony of the Broadwing Hawk' . . . 'The Small Mammal Population in a Conifer Lowland Stand.' " He nods at the papers. "When you've been sitting here for twenty-eight years as I have, all of a sudden it filters through this thick skull — hey, this means something to this, this means something to that. All of a sudden this begins to jell as a sort of philosophy rather than just a bunch of isolated research papers." He gives an example. "Well, it's kind of interesting that every animal that we've ever studied up here has a much bigger home range than any place else I've seen it studied. What does it mean, that the landscape productivity is small? . . . So you're hearing a philosophy, an integration that isn't particularly well written down." What I hear is a philosophy of ecological community in which all of the pieces must be considered together.

In his role as chairman of the Town Planning Board, Sage has experienced firsthand what it means to work with the APA commissioners on the issues that face the human community in which he lives, and the wild community surrounding it. In unusual circumstances, the tiny hamlet of Newcomb was caught up in the midst of a drama over the division of regulation between the APA and local boards, a controversy that made front-page news for days, and challenged the level of freedom in interpretation of the APA act itself. I visited the hamlet of Newcomb many times, and attended several days of APA meetings to get the rest of the story. Sage and the other members of the board demonstrated an enormous commitment to setting out, in a constructive plan, their vision of a community of humans and wild species whose needs are woven together in a single landscape. The story of their struggle to codify their plan is outlined in the next chapter.

8

Newcomb's Plan

THE FIRST TIME I VISIT NEWCOMB, CONSID-
ering it as a possible research site, I am appalled at the thought of
living there. It looks utterly bleak. Heavy snow is falling on a gray
afternoon. It is not yet five, but the sun has already set. The houses, blank-
faced along the highway, without even a sidewalk where one could push a
stroller or stand to chat with neighbors, stretch in a long, narrow strip along
the almost empty road, about fourteen miles coming east from Long Lake,
or about twice that distance west from North Hudson. Not a single lighted
storefront, cheerful inn, or welcoming cafe is visible from the roadway, except
one or two places that are closed. It seems a ghost town shrouded in snow.

Later, when I visit in the summer, camp on the lake, and meet some of
the residents, including Barbara Sweet and Dick Sage, I see a different side
of Newcomb. In summer, tourists drift through, the stores stay open later,
and local people gossip on porches and in the country store at the west end
of town, where one can buy camping supplies, fishing bait, and groceries.
The store owners don't blink an eye when I come through with two small
grubby boys with campfire soot in their clothes and buy nothing but batter-
ies and marshmallows. They are used to tourists.

We camp in the state campground on the lake, and set up our tent next to a sandy beach with a view of the mountains. The weather is hot and sunny, and the other campers, in tents, vans, and RV's, exhibit the inevitable cheerfulness of people who feel lucky to be on vacation, and lucky to have found such a spot.

Newcomb is at the heart of the Adirondacks and the heart of the wilderness: the High Peaks Wilderness throws up rugged peaks to the north, the heavy forests of Hoffman Notch Wilderness lie to the east, and the proposed Wild Rivers Wilderness lies southward. The narrow highway running east to west is the only way into or out of the hamlet itself. Just east of the hamlet, the Tahawus Lake–Sanford Road winds along the Opalescent River until it dead-ends at Tahawus. Originally opened as an iron mine in the early part of the nineteenth century, with two small villages, Tahawus and Adirondac, where the workers and their families lived, Tahawus lost its population when the mine stopped operating in 1858, owing in part to a problematic impurity. It then became the hunting preserve of a private club. But the impurity was titanium. After its uses as a pigment in

Photo 13. Newcomb. Photo author

white paint and as a heat-resistant metal were discovered and World War II made a domestic supply imperative, the National Lead Company reopened the mines. A community of workers grew up again. But in 1962, because of the needs of mining expansion, the entire town was moved to a new site on the outskirts of Newcomb. Seventy-two single houses, fifteen duplexes, six apartment buildings, a school, a church, and a store traveled on the backs of giant trucks to Newcomb, where about one hundred families relocated (White, 1985).

Newcomb itself grew slowly. Buried in the mountains, far from traveled routes, it consisted of only a handful of families in the mid-1800s. By the 1870s, however, hotels and stores were prospering. Sportsmen visited the area. The Finch, Pruyn Lumber Company began lumbering near Newcomb. By the 1890s, Newcomb was in its prime. The lakes, rivers, and mountain scenery drew tourists; the prospering lumber industry sent thousands of logs down the Hudson every season and brought in workers. Two circular sawmills operated in the village. Newcomb established its reputation as a logging town.

In the first few years of the 1900s, a prominent lumberman who was also president of the Board of Education created a centralized school for the town of Newcomb. The school's gymnasium provided the center for public gatherings as well (Fennessy, 1988). In the 1990s the school again provided a central focus for the village. Enrollment had dropped so low, people feared that their school might be closed. The survival of the village itself depended on keeping the school in Newcomb.

In 1970–71, responding to what they felt was the threat to self-determination posed by the Adirondack Park Agency, the citizens of Newcomb set up a Town Planning Board. In 1976–77, Newcomb hired a consultant to begin to pull together the information required to achieve APA-approvable status. The APA divides regulation of development projects into two types: Class A, projects above the threshold for densities in that zone and having regional impact, and Class B, or projects of primarily local impact. Individual towns (townships, in the language of the Adirondacks) can get jurisdiction over Class B projects and developments if they develop a plan for that purpose that is approved by the APA. Newcomb spent a fair amount of money at the time but never got to the stage of a comprehensive plan required by the APA. The work sat on a shelf; it was never adopted by the town board as law because there was no development happening in Newcomb at the time.

The more recent controversy over the Governor's Commission stirred renewed interest. The Town of Newcomb decided that this time it would prepare its development plan with the agency staff sitting right at the table with them. They hired a consultant, paid for by cost sharing then available through the Park Agency. Using the information base gathered in 1976–77, the town eventually compiled enough data to begin writing a plan. The Planning Board surveyed the town through questionnaires about the problems that concerned Newcomb citizens, which included everything from sewage disposal to junk cars; on the basis of the questionnaire, a comprehensive plan was developed. During this time, the Planning Board met with APA staff on a regular basis to be sure that they were developing a plan consistent with the law. After three and a half years of work, the Planning Board submitted the plan as complete; it passed at the local level.

But at the regional level of seeking APA approval, Newcomb's plan got caught in the middle of a controversy fueled by the Governor's Commission report, which almost everyone in the Adirondacks seemed to be discussing heatedly as the summer legislative session drew closer. This controversy centered on how much control local government should have over land use and how much control the state agency should have. If the plan had been submitted a year earlier, before the commission report came out, it probably would have been accepted quietly. A thoroughly prepared plan, which in some cases exceeded the requirements of the APA for Class B projects, it seemed certain to pass. But as a symbol of both local expertise and the rights of local people to determine the development of their town, Newcomb's plan took on a significance that no one could have anticipated.

Because the commission report had been initiated as a result of perceptions on the part of many preservationist groups that the protection the APA offered was simply not enough to keep the Adirondacks free of overdevelopment, many of the Park Agency commissioners were under pressure to be more restrictive than usual even before the report reached the legislature. Agency commissioners and others were anxious to promote their strict regulations with the Newcomb plan, which, if the APA were to approve it, would give the Town of Newcomb the right to make its own decisions regarding Class B projects.

Expecting only a few minor legalistic problems, the Newcomb Planning Board instead found themselves facing questions about the basic tenets of their plan. This was something of a setback. The Planning Board met with various groups that were showing an intense interest in the Newcomb plan, from the Adirondack Council to the Fairness Coalition. The Planning Board also undertook a major reevaluation of the economic impacts that adopting some of the APA's more restrictive regulations might have on their community. After its additional study, the Newcomb Planning Board concluded that in some areas they probably could have done better, but in others, if they imposed the strict regulations on development that some APA members had suggested, major advantages were going to be lost in terms of maintaining the value of their land and the potential to generate income from it. Barbara Sweet, Dick Sage, and others from the Town of Newcomb came to a decision.

Dick Sage, as chairman of the Planning Board, tells the story: "So we came back to the agency and adopted a fairly hard-line policy with them that said, 'Well, we can give a little bit, and we do see some things where we could do a little better job. We'll make those changes, but we're not going to incorporate the recommendations of the Governor's Commission on the Adirondacks in the Twenty-First Century until they are law, because it would just kill us.'

"All of this is predicated on the fact that we have a community that once had 1,200 people in it and a very active mining operation at the Tahawus, which has since closed. We now have 541 people in the town. The census shows that between 1980 and 1990 the population declined by 20.1 percent. We had a school that had 320 some-odd kids, and now has 67, K through 12. We are not only caught up in an environmentalist battle over the Adirondacks, we are fighting for our own very survival as a community. If we lose our school, then we lose the key community center, and the key reason anybody ever had to come to Newcomb. We've never been much of a tourist town. We've always been a mining and a logging town."

The town's Economic Development Committee, of which Dick Sage is also chairman, has been working for years to bring a wood processing plant to Newcomb. Twice so far they have come close, but in the end these plants located in other states. The development committee got the impression that the corporations were hesitant to come to Newcomb because of the perceived possibility that much of the private land remaining in the Adirondack Park was going to be bought up by the state. With the state's economy in trouble, thus creating an unfavorable climate for new plants, as well as weather and transportation concerns locally, businesses don't need the extra "someday we're going to turn this into a great big wilderness and nobody's going to live here anymore philosophy floating around in the sky," Sage comments.

Floating around in the sky is an apt description. The Adirondack Coun-

cil vehemently denies holding this position, as does the Association for the
Protection of the Adirondacks and the Adirondack Mountain Club. Yet
Earth First! and their sympathizers have floated this idea in their *Wild Earth*
publication and in discussions. Locals feel that it is not an empty threat.
"Being a wood using–oriented community, being a mining community, we
are, we think, users of natural resources, and our whole life and community
has been dependent on that. We're sensitive to the environment, and we
think we've done a reasonably good job of protecting the Town of Newcomb. We don't share the wide philosophy of the preservationists that
everything should just be left alone out there on the landscape," says Sage.

On land that has already become part of the Forest Preserve the people
of Newcomb see a lack of management of recreational opportunities, and
this distresses them. The town fought hard to get a second Visitor Interpretive Center, a smaller version of the one at Paul Smith's, located in Newcomb. Complete with indoor exhibits and cross-country ski trails along the
lake, the Interpretive Center should be attracting crowds. But it isn't. Dick
Sage attributes the lack of popularity to a failure on the part of the state to
complete additional cross-country ski trails as promised, as well as a lack
of permanent staff, which has curtailed program development. Sage com-
plains that there is not even a sign in Long Lake to direct people on the
main roads to the Visitor Center.

The Santanoni Preserve is another sore point with many of the townspeople. The preserve was under private ownership until 1970, when the
state bought it. People were eager to have the road into the historic Santanoni Lodge stay open, to support tours or restricted traffic. But under the
"forever wild" policy, conflicting uses in wilderness areas are forbidden;
roads and buildings are to be closed and removed. The road was closed,
and the lodge began to disintegrate. But through the efforts of the Town of
Newcomb, the Adirondack Architectural Heritage, and the New York State
Preservation League, a movement is afoot to preserve the historic building,
although it is not yet clear how this use will be accommodated under the
laws governing the Forest Preserve.

The townspeople see state ownership as a clear path to mismanagement.
"Everything we perceive the state gets hold of falls to ruin, people are kept
out of, and is not maintained," says Sage. "We see all kinds of opportunities
for state trails to be well maintained, to provide cross-country skiing opportunities, to allow more access, and their approach is, 'We don't have the
people . . . we can't take care of it.'" Sage admits that he is expressing his
own opinion, but he stresses that he reflects the feelings of a large segment

of the population of Newcomb. He compares use of state land to use of private timber land. The Finch, Pruyn Paper Company, which has extensive holdings in Newcomb, offers recreational opportunities through leases of their land. More people use paper company land than nearby state land; cross-country skiing, snowmobiling, four-wheeling, fishing, and hunting are permitted.

Newcomb has tried to pursue with the state the idea of promoting the town as a cross-country ski area. Sheltered in the lap of the High Peaks at one of the highest elevations of any town in the Park, Newcomb has some of the best snow conditions in the Adirondacks. But the development of Newcomb as a cross-country ski center requires the development and main- tenance of an extensive trail system, something the state has been unable or unwilling to do. State officials say they can do nothing until they file the unit land management plan. By that time, townspeople fear, Newcomb may no longer exist as a functioning hamlet. Some locals say that what the preservationists, including those on the APA and Governor's Commission, really want to do is to squeeze Newcomb right out of the Park so they can have their woods from one side of Lake Champlain to the St. Lawrence River with nothing in between.

Lately the best thing going for Newcomb has been its school. Fearing consolidation with Long Lake schools if enrollment dropped too low, Bar- bara Sweet, who owns and manages the general store with her husband, and Barbara Kearns, school superintendent, helped activate the metamor- phosis of Newcomb's school into a magnet school which focuses on the ecology, cultures, and history of the Adirondacks. Children have worked with folk musicians to write and sing their own melodies about the Adiron- dacks. Newcomb's approach to solving the school problem, and by ex- tention the community's problem, was written up in the September– October 1992 issue of *Country Life.* The article highlighted the determination of the teachers and townspeople to strengthen the students' sense of com- munity, and their understanding of the wider ecological and cultural com- munity to which they belong. Dick Sage has promised to harness some of the Ecological Center's resources to help the program, whose innova- tiveness has been recognized in Albany. Having something unique to offer, and rebuilding the idea of community, may give Newcomb a way out of its dilemma. Barbara Sweet, in recognition of her actions to help her forest- based community, was one of the citizens chosen for the Northern Forest Lands Council.

✹ When the Town of Newcomb brought its development plan to the APA, in the climate of heightened awareness over local-state control issues, and hardened their case when the APA challenged some of their proposed regulations, they presented their own challenge to the APA. In spite of its small size, the population of Newcomb includes — because of the mines, Finch, Pruyn, and the Ecological Center — many ecologists, resource managers, geologists, foresters, and other professionals whose work is based on natural resources. Many of them know more about the natural environment than some of the agency commissioners. More important, they also have the certification, through degrees and professional titles. The APA had to pay attention. Curiously, the patterns of language, configurations of seating at the meetings, and other rituals retained the patronizing overtones so many locals have objected to.

✹ Chairs scrape and coats rustle as people settle into their seats. The door opens and a blast of cold air sweeps in with a latecomer, Anne Coin, a member of the Citizens' Council. The Citizens' Council represents some of the most avid home rule advocates in the Adirondacks. She extinguishes a cigarette and leans forward in a spasm of coughing. She comes to many of these APA meetings. I recognize others — preservationists, reporters, a realtor who is one of the officers of the Adirondack Fairness Coalition, other local people — though whether they side with preservation, home rule, or both, it is difficult to tell. The last of the commissioners comes in and sits down, spreading a sheaf of papers in front of him. The commissioners sit at long tables forming a square, facing in; on one side they sit with their backs to the audience, closing the square, and closing out the public.

The audience is quiet, intent on the talk in the closed square; in contrast, the commissioners seem relaxed, and their exchange is rapid, almost conversational. They discuss an application for new mineral extraction, and Anne LaBastille talks earnestly about increased truck traffic and minor changes that could be made to ensure the safety of school buses along the route. A letter from Hammond Robertson of the Fairness Coalition and a press release surface. Robertson is upset about disregard for local government and distrust of Adirondackers. He cites comments about a lack of technical expertise in local government.

A number of permit requests are passed: the need for a public hearing for a subdivision in Lake George; a permit for a wooden footbridge onto a peninsula, with a discussion on its visibility from the water. A discussion of Paul Smith's College's new water tower focuses on its visibility and what color it will be painted. A staff member has been to see; the tower is visible only from Lower St. Regis Lake and he says, "It shall be colored a matte, non-reflective dark forest green that will blend with the natural surroundings." Locals laugh; it snows from October to May.

A couple from Keene, relatives of some of the maple syrup producers I have interviewed, want a permit to build on a twenty-four–acre lot they own. It backs onto wilderness land one mile south of the Noonmark Diner, a popular spot for tourists and locals. They plan to cut down five mature white pines, about thirty inches dbh. The commissioners, voicing the opinion that the pines are "critical to the feeling of the property," vote unanimously for a public hearing. During the breaks for doughnuts and coffee and lunch over the three-day meeting, I am able to interview all of the commissioners except Peter Paine, a Wall Street attorney and commissioner since the inception of the APA, who refuses to be interviewed.

On the second day of the APA meeting, the Legal Affairs Committee meets to discuss Newcomb's plan. The room where the meeting is held is far too small; one senses that the APA did not anticipate the level of public interest in what would ordinarily be a dry legal discussion. Present are Barbara Sweet; Neil Woodworth, lawyer for the Adirondack Mountain Club; Woody Coles and several other commissioners; Robert Glennon, the director of the APA; Dick Sage; John Banta and Laura Viscome of the APA staff; Dan Plumley of the Adirondack Council; a representative for Finch, Pruyn, and Finch, Pruyn's lawyer; Newcomb's town supervisor; the editor of the *Adirondack Daily Enterprise;* and several others.

Again the physical messages of the meeting room and its arrangement reflect the inequalities of voice in land use planning. A round wooden table takes up the center of this small room. Coles, Paine, and several other commissioners involved with legal affairs sit around the table, which is spread with papers. Coles and Paine present a curious contrast. Coles, immensely heavy, with smooth, softened features, uses language with a baroque descriptiveness vague in its generalities but relentless over fine points; he is dressed formally, in black. Paine, slim, gray-haired, and athletic, wears a plaid wool shirt with red suspenders; his language, always quick, angling for details, has a precision that is capable of dissecting other arguments. Barbara Sweet, Dick Sage, the Finch, Pruyn representative, and others from the Town of Newcomb who have spent years developing the plan now under dissection, sit crowded together in chairs pulled from various desks, behind those at the table, so that Peter Paine and the other commissioners must constantly talk over their shoulders to the people of

Newcomb. The newspaper editor and I find ourselves near the door. There is not room for one more chair.

Letters have gone back and forth in between APA meetings. Seventeen paragraphs of the plan and three subparagraphs are at issue. It seems a great deal of work. Quickly, most of the discussion slips into legal jargon and the language of town zoning boards. Dick Sage speaks for the Town of Newcomb on the question of the size of shorefront lots: "We did fairly extensive economic appraisal of what it means to do some of these things in the Draft Environmental Impact Statement. It could make it impossible for local people to buy lots or to create businesses. Only the very wealthy could buy these lots." The APA has recommended larger-than-usual four hundred–foot shorefront lots for Newcomb's wild lakes. Dick Sage comments privately that he'd love for them to come down and run some experiments to determine what four-hundred–foot frontage means. Everyone needs that kind of information, he says. "That isn't to guarantee the protection of the resource — it is to guarantee the aesthetics of the resource."

This problem brings up the question of what can be reviewed, since Newcomb's regulations, as stated in the plan, are actually more restrictive than those required by the Park Agency act. The lawyers address this question, the big one that has been bothering everyone: Does the agency have the legal authority to impose conditions on town law when the conditions are already met and exceeded? The APA's standard is the phrase "undue adverse impact," a string of scarcely limited words, defined ad hoc. It seems for a moment as if the town will lose all sovereignty to such a phrase, which can be swept across any circumstance; but the moment passes.

The discussion becomes a positive force, entering into the details of legal addenda and moot points. There is general relief as everyone realizes that a covenant between the powers of the state and local authority is being born, and it is not going to be such a difficult birth after all. But the mood is not euphoric. Each side is compromising more than it wants to. In the midst of a new partnership, while accolades occupy the forefront, old resentments hover in the background. Those seated at the table repeat the phrase "You've done a good job" so often to those behind them that it eventually sounds patronizing. In the hall an APA staffer comments, "These people will get what they want, if you let them." Newcomb Town Board members seem glad that the ordeal is winding down but frustrated by the extra work and by what seem to be extraordinary expectations from the APA.

After their return to the larger session, Commissioner Elizabeth Thorn-dike makes three points formally to the gathered board and the audience. The first is that the APA recognizes the ability of Newcomb, more than any other town, to do its own planning, but also that the state agency has more clout than the Town Board. They need to continue to work together. Her second point, worded carefully, is that the agency will base its decision on the current body of law. The Legal Committee, she says, is working on both the letter of the law and the spirit of the law. Her third point is simply that the low-intensity use area is what everyone is concerned about, and this is the place where there will be different interpretations of the Adiron-dack Park Agency Act.

Finally, the board votes. Newcomb's plan passes. The vote, in the tradi-tion of a board that knows it will be criticized whatever decision it hands down, is unanimous — for reasons, one suspects, of solidarity.

Dick Sage, commenting on the process of writing the plan, says, "I had visions at one time that we were going to design this town to the hilt. We know our soils. . . . I'd like to specify what soils somebody can build on . . . and if someone's going to have a development on Third Lake, it's going to be a cluster development, right here. Our consultant said no, you can't do that. You do it with these broad guidelines and back door techniques. You've got to have one principal building per eight acres, and these fancy zones that the Park Agency had drawn, that include all kinds of areas you'd never want to put a building on. . . . It works on a broad conceptual level but leaves you in a general gray area." He shakes his head slowly. "I wanted to come up with something that would tell somebody up front that they had a 90 percent chance of success in doing something here, rather than all kinds of fuss, and find out somebody didn't like their plan and turned it down. . . . I was really naive. I thought that's what planning was. Costs everybody money and wastes a lot of time. It was kind of a rude awakening for me."

❧ Sage had tried to use the language of ecology, of community and specific interdependencies, in a realm where the languages of zoning and aesthetics, of bureaucracy and negotiated compromise, are dominant. Which language speaks for the future of the Adirondacks most clearly and which language has the greatest political clout are not necessarily the same.

The language of ecology speaks at the level of species and communities and relies on an understanding of the natural laws operating within ecosys-tems. The test of its success is simply in the continued reproduction of species and natural communities in ecosystems. It is this language which speaks most clearly for both scientists and holders of indigenous knowledge.

The language of zoning reflects human needs and the artificial boundaries imposed by human systems where these systems increasingly meet the constraints of the natural landscape. Its success is represented in political terms — regulations acceptable to the majority of citizens. The ability of zoning to maintain the landscape is inexact.

The language of aesthetics reflects the complex values and different worldviews of particular groups of human beings. It can also be the means by which one class or group imposes its values upon another. It may or may not relate directly to the successful reproduction of ecological systems.

Photo 14. Leaving Newcomb. Photo author

9

Battles and Bridges

THE RAIN HAS BEEN POURING DOWN ALL afternoon, a chill rain that numbs any exposed flesh and drenches through rain gear. In a momentary lull we manage to get the tent up and dinner started. The children play noisily, oblivious to the cold, as happy as ducks in a liquid sky. It is too cold for the rich smells of mud and spring buds to emerge, but the afternoon is silver-toned. This is our first camping trip since fall, the first time sleeping on the hard ground among the sounds of the pines since the snow melted.

On one side I can hear the spring peepers out on the lake; on the other side I hear the guitars and voices of Earth First!ers, their singing puctuated by wolf howls. Earlier I thought I heard several of them giving imitations of owl hoots.

Laura Rappaport, reporter from the *Adirondack Daily Enterprise*, has come camping with us at Lewey Lake State Campground after we had both heard rumors that there would be a confrontation between the Earth First!ers and Don Gerdts' Citizens' Council of the Adirondacks. We are both eager to interview some of the Earth First!ers, for different reasons.

We walk over to their campsite, where a dozen or so are standing around the picnic table, preparing dinner. We listen to their explanations of who they are and why they are in the Adirondacks. It is a heterogeneous group, mostly from outside the Park: a bearded man with streaks of gray in his ponytail who recites scientific facts; a tall young man with an angular jaw who leans forward with intensity to say, "We're just normal, concerned people"; a slender woman who says that she is an actress in New York City but is also interested in herbal medicine; a chemistry professor from St. Lawrence University; a thin black man with a cross earring and startled, mild eyes; a very young blond woman; a young man with long dreadlocks, cooking on a Coleman stove while chatting conspiratorially with us; a red-haired woman in a hand-knit Icelandic sweater, chopping zucchini; and, among others, a silent man with a large bruise over his right eye, a cigarette hanging from his lip, who slips away into a tent before we can ask him any questions.

I find myself wondering if he is the one responsible for pouring sand into the gas tanks of several Ticonderoga logging trucks. Laura asks the other Earth First!ers the same question, but they say they don't know who took action. Although Earth First! stickers were stuck to the trucks, the members say those stickers are widely available, and anyone could have used them. Maybe it was someone trying to make Earth First! look bad, one member suggests. In any case, another argues, they are a movement, not an organization, and are not responsible for one another's actions.

A discussion of deep ecology and the basis for Earth First! grows lively and gradually involves most of the group. We are bombarded with the spiritual ecological philosophy and its manifestation in scientific-sounding data about the damage done to the natural environment. Finally, we go back to our own campsite for a spaghetti dinner. The temperature is so cool that the spaghetti is cold as soon as it hits the plates. Fortunately, the cold keeps the blackflies away.

Afterwards the chemistry professor comes over, and the three of us talk and argue for over two hours about the Earth First! group, the Adiron-dacks, and the Governor's Commission report. He is one of the most outspoken of the group; together, he and his wife edit the Earth First! journal. Among other things, he notes that no Earth First!er could claim to speak for the entire movement, and that some would readily risk injury or death for their principles. He is against capitalism, but doesn't flinch when we remind him that the Governor's Commission includes some of the wealthiest people in New York State, as well as some who have made or inherited their wealth from large corporations whose work is detrimental to the

230 environment, such as Exxon. The commissioner who is an editor of the *New York Times* writes his editorials on paper made from trees cut in the Adirondacks. This information is new to the chemistry professor, but he is not bothered by it. He just wants to know the commissioners' philosophy. "Are they for Big Wilderness?" he asks. He personally hopes for the return of the lynx and the wolf.

There is a wild, stern light in his eyes; he reminds me of pictures of the abolitionist John Brown, whose farm is near Lake Placid. The chemistry professor's arguments are cagey and articulate, and some of them are based on a comparison with abolitionists' arguments about the rights of humans wrongfully held as property, but in the end, the news reporter and I let the topic drift away, a criticism implied, when our eyes meet, of this Earth First! philosophy which refuses to negotiate, refuses to see that the argument involves more than Big Wilderness, and includes a belief that regional needs should completely dominate the local perspective. "No compromise in defense of Mother Earth!" is the Earth First! slogan, and it fits the individual members, mirroring the hard light in their eyes. They plan to

Photo 15. Indian Pass in the High Peaks. Photo D. Kuklok

meet in the morning to discuss the commission report; although a number of them have not read it yet, they believe that it does not go far enough.

Yet their understanding of wilderness has a different, more purely ecological and spiritual basis from that of the commissioners, the Adirondack Council, and the APA. In some ways their mission to rescue wilderness for its own sake, rather than for the way it looks or for their own ability to use it for recreation, is more selfless than the arguments of the mainstream preservationists. The aesthetic concerns of the commissioners for earth-tone houses, screened paths, and bordered roadways are laughable to the Earth First!ers at Lewey Lake. Either the Park is wild or it isn't. The animals can tell you, they say, and it's the animals' view that matters.

❧ The views of animals and Earth First! members, whether or not they are similar, represent only one angle of this complex polyhedron of visions of land use in the Adirondacks. The multiple worldviews represented by different land use schemes conflict on various levels. In one sense, they constitute a battle of cultural views. On another plane, this is a struggle of class values, between privileged upper-class preservationists, including those who have rebelled against their privileges but maintained the essential worldview of a class with the power to control decision making, and the relatively less powerful, less wealthy, less privileged working and middle classes who struggle to assert their right to a voice in decision making.

The struggle is also between the aesthetic tastes of urban and rural Americans. Urban Americans today live in artificial, human-constructed surroundings, among a surfeit of examples of human destructiveness toward the environment. Their aesthetics have developed based on the presumed toxicity of humans in the human/nature relationship. Rural Americans, including those in the Adirondacks, live in surroundings in which nature still predominates. Their daily lives are filled with difficulties created by natural forces — wildlife, snowstorms, flooding. In addition, their relationship with nature is a working one; jobs and subsistence often depend directly on successfully maneuvering within the context of the natural environment, successfully predicting natural events and coordinating actions with the invisible rules of the wild. Many rural Adirondackers whose livelihoods depend on the natural environment believe in their own rights of usufruct as members of an interdependent human/nature relationship. Yet the point at which usufruct rights slide into destruction remains blurred, complicated by the application of different aesthetic as well as ecological standards.

The land use views of sportspeople overlap with those of rural people in the Adirondacks, but not completely. As conservationists, both groups stand for protection as well as use, though levels of use are often particular to specific game animals, and to whether sport or subsistence is the operative factor. Those for whom the balance tips in favor of meat for the table may prefer management that increases numbers of deer and fish; those for whom sport is the ultimate goal may prefer the more preservationist kinds of management that favor rare, bigger fish and old bucks with many points.

The issue of table meat versus "wilderness experience" may map fairly accurately onto the insider-outsider spectrum of the debate. Those who live permanently within the Blue Line and have jobs that depend on economic stability there develop different worldviews and attitudes toward land use management from those who come to the Park for sport and other recreation, including use of summer homes and desirable retirement locations. The insiders often develop an ingrained resentment of wealthy vacationers who come to the Adirondacks for leisure pursuits but try to dominate land use decisions that fall most heavily on year-round residents who work inside the Park's boundaries.

From a cultural point of view, for those who have shaped their lives within the cultures of logging, trapping, hunting, and other forms of natural resource use, the imposition of the land use decisions of an outsider culture threatens to obliterate their way of life. In this sense more than any other, the land use issues in the Adirondacks echo those of colonialism and neocolonialism in the Third World. With high rates of poverty and unemployment and export of raw natural resources, combined with the loss of control over development that local governments are experiencing, the Adirondacks could qualify as a not-so-small Third World within New York State. As in Appalachia and rural Oregon, the exploitation of the natural resource base by large external corporations, and the removal of raw products from the region with value added outside the region, lead to an economic and political colonialism rarely recognized as such (Beaver, 1986).

At another level, the debate is over private ownership rights and public welfare rights. Those who live on the land targeted for public welfare often become more conservative to protect their ownership rights; these rights are defended as a matter of principle, based on the importance of traditional private ownership in a democracy as a means to self-supporting independence. When ownership rights are challenged or constrained, many advocates feel that freedom itself is being threatened; hence the references to the Constitution that flavor the talk of many of the home rule and private ownership advocates, especially those who feel that they are already partly disenfranchised because of the relative voicelessness of their class in societal decision making.

The core of the argument, which blurs the boundaries between public and private land, is the issue of usufruct, the right to use the land and its products. The "forever wild" clause forbids plant harvesting of any kind, including firewood, maple sap, even large quantities of berries. Increasing regulations on private lands can keep a family from building a home for a son or daughter. Because the majority of New York State citizens have the right to set the allowable uses for land, public or private, within the Adirondacks, recreational and aesthetic needs have preempted subsistence uses. The battle over private versus public ownership also involves the worldviews of the private industrialists, corporations, developers, and other large landowners, such as those on the Blue Line Council, whose wealth is tied up in private ownership. Their political allegiance to private rather than public ownership and management of the land may affect many jobs, and through them the economic health of hamlets and villages whose residents depend on these jobs.

These different angles and facets of the Adirondack land use issue become frozen into position, especially where the proponents of different views have difficulty interacting and negotiating or even understanding one another. Each side develops its own symbols and the signs, both literal and figurative, that represent its position to others.

❧ In 1989 the Department of Environmental Conservation placed boulders at the entrance to the wilderness section of Crane Pond Road in Schroon, a 110-year-old town highway that cuts 1.8 miles into an area now designated as wilderness. The DEC closed the road to motorized traffic to bring it into conformance with the surrounding Pharaoh Mountain Wilderness Area. It had been open to cars as a "primitive corridor" until changes were made to the State Land Master Plan two years earlier. While it is ultimately the APA that determines additions to the master plan, it is up to the DEC to enforce them. In May of that year citizens removed the boulders in the presence of the state police, and later paraded one of them to the State Capitol in Albany, painted with the words "stones of shame." The DEC stopped enforcing the closure, although the road remained officially closed.

On Sunday, September 2, 1990, Earth First! members blockaded Crane Pond Road in an overnight encampment. The group of twenty or so included representatives from many states. About a hundred townspeople turned out to confront them. Warrensburg supervisor Maynard Baker got into an argument with one of the Earth First!ers and hit him in the face, and they fell to the ground together. After the confrontation, the Earth First!ers packed up and left. Later, the Earth First!er who was hit filed charges against Baker.

On Thursday, September 6, Don Gerdts and members of his Citizens' Council announced plans to throw up a roadblock on the Crane Pond Road. Gerdts said, "We're going to stop Earth First!, the DEC, misguided preservationists, or any other radicals who want to interfere with public access to the road." Gerdts and his group planned to set up a barricade of automobiles and maintain it around the clock, seven days a week, to protest the closure of the road and interference from preservationist groups outside the Park, although "regular citizens" would be allowed access. Gerdts was concerned about the presence of other Earth First! members in the Park, saying, "The Adirondack Minutemen are on the alert. We can have two or three hundred volunteers there in half an hour if there is trouble" (*Adirondack Daily Enterprise*, September 6, 1990).

On the same day the Adirondack Planning Commission resolved that the DEC should reconsider its policy of closing off all existing roads into wilderness areas. The commissioners voted unanimously to support maintaining access to existing roads into the wilderness, specifically at Crane Pond and two other closed and barricaded roads. The commission hoped to force a discussion of the Crane Pond Road issue with the governor.

On Thursday, September 20, the Adirondack Planning Commission called on the DEC to come back to the negotiating table to discuss closure of the road. Meanwhile, some Schroon Lake residents began repair work on the road. The DEC decided not to enforce closure until the matter was resolved in court in a lawsuit filed against the state by the Town of Schroon.

On Wednesday, September 26, the Franklin County Legislature backed the opening of Crane Pond Road. Jim Frenette, a county legislator, said, "The roads [closed under the master plan] are short, and closing them doesn't add significantly to the wilderness areas. Closure only reduces access for many citizens. There is no practical benefit" (*Adirondack Daily Enterprise*, September 26, 1990).

On Thursday, November 30, a group of thirty masked men armed with deer rifles gathered at the entrance to Crane Pond Road. Don Gerdts, describing them as the Adirondack militia, stated that they were there to protest the closure of the road. "There's no question that these boys are willing to do what they have to do. They've been abused by the state and the APA and they have no more patience" (*Adirondack Daily Enterprise*, November 30, 1990).

On Thursday, April 4, 1991, the State Court of Appeals announced that it would not hear an appeal brought by the Town of Schroon on the DEC's closure of the road. Although the court had upheld the state's right to close the road, DEC officials had no plan to enforce its closure. Home rule advocates said that the road had been open for a hundred years, and that the region was not a "wilderness" but had in fact been logged several times. Gerdts was quoted in the newspaper as saying, "Whatever the state forces us to do, we will do. They're not going to get away with [closing the road again]. The atmosphere here is tense, and the Adirondack militia is on a twenty-four-hour alert." He warned that if Earth First! showed up, they should be prepared to defend themselves.

Earth First! activist Jamie Sayen, who had been arrested and charged with assault for trying to block a pond reclamation effort in which two DEC officers were hurt, said, "We certainly hope the DEC will enforce its own laws," and later added, "The situation back in September was DEC had closed the road and Gerdts and his gang had illegally reopened it. Earth First!, a supposed outlaw organization, was in the position of enforcing the law" (*Adirondack Daily Enterprise*, April 5–7, 1991).

❧ During all the activity of September 1990, I go down to the area to interview a restaurant owner, fisherman, and past president of the Adirondack Conservation Council. I meet him in his restaurant, where there are stacks of Tony D'Elia's book *The Adirondack Rebellion* for sale at the cash register. The owner comes around from behind the counter, dusts off his hands, and sits down at a table covered with a red-checked tablecloth. He tells me that he has spent summers here for thirty-six years, and has lived here for twelve; he has written a chapter in a book on fishing in the Adirondacks. He is totally against the Governor's Commission report, primarily because there has been no local input. He notes that Crane Pond was added to the Pharaoh Wilderness area twenty years ago. Fishermen had been using motorboats on the pond. When these were no longer allowed, they used electric motors until they were no longer allowed, either. Then the road was closed. There are five or six good trout ponds beyond Crane Pond; fishermen used to be able to boat through Crane Pond and then walk to them. It seems to him that the preservationists want to get rid of the sportsmen and reduce traffic, and they have accomplished this by hurting

the sportsmen. He notes the Citizens' Council "checkpoint," now in operation, and says, "I am totally in favor of the whole action — it's more like civil
disobedience to what seems like a totally unjust situation." He adds that a
lot of trappers used to use the road. They worked full-time jobs, and would
go in to check traps or set them after work; something they wouldn't be
able to do without the road. Hunters, too, could get in quicker for a day's
hunting. He estimates that about 75 percent of families in the area include
a sportsman. "I love trout and venison," he says. "It's a delicacy that I count
on every year."

About hunting he says, "As far as a *necessity*, that's passé. But it is always
true, it takes the edge off. We're talking two hundred dollars worth of meat.
These people up here don't make a lot of money — five or six dollars an
hour average, town people maybe seven. Service industry, if they are lucky,
make five." He believes that the only thing the Crane Pond Road designation changes is access. To talk about preserving wilderness — he shrugs, "*Is
it wilderness?*" Crane Pond used to be the original settlement in this area.
By calling it wilderness, the state is "trying to create a situation — dreams
— that don't exist anywhere else." He is not against protection of the woods.
"I'm a sportsman. We've done more things to preserve the woods and lakes
than anyone else." But he believes that the hidden agenda of the state is to
eliminate people within the Blue Line. We talk awhile longer about the
commission report and what it means to him as a sportsman and a resident.
At the end of the interview he gives me a generous list of other people I
should talk to, friends and sportsmen, including several state officials, who
share his views, and a copy of *The Adirondack Rebellion*.

When I interview the preservationist Gary Randorf, he says that he is
a strong supporter of wilderness in the Park. "I get frustrated by the local
government and the local people's attempt to unduly and unfairly influence
how state land is managed and where roads are closed. The closing of
Crane Pond Road — that's a statewide issue to be decided by the people of
the state, through public hearing or whatever. So I get very frustrated when
the Adirondack Planning Commission wants to sit down with the DEC and
talk about improved access to state land. Representatives from all over the
state should be sitting down. . . . Some people would like to say, well, let's
ignore the local people and get the support of the rest of the state and to
hell with the locals. But that's just not going to work. It's clearer than it's
ever been that they're *not* going to *stand* for it anymore." Randorf says that,
personally, he thinks there should be a compromise, such as closing the

road a half mile from the pond, but he doesn't know if the Adirondack
Council would support that. "This is like the line in the sand."

On March 24, 1992, the newspaper article about Crane Pond begins,
"During the last few years, Crane Pond has symbolized the conflicting
viewpoints over use of the Adirondack Park more than any other location."
It quotes DEC Region 5 director Thomas Monroe as saying, "The road
remains barricaded as a matter of law but will not be chained and people
will not be ticketed as a result of driving to the parking lot" (*Adirondack
Daily Enterprise,* March 24, 1992). In other words, it is a stalemate.

Crane Pond Road, frequently in the news and in the minds of Adirondackers, accretes more and more meaning as a symbol in the debate over
land use in the Adirondacks. On the surface the issue is access — for the
sportsmen, for the handicapped, for the elderly and children and anyone
else who cannot or would rather not walk the 1.8 miles into the forest. On
a deeper level the issue is wilderness itself: what it is and whom it is for.
The Earth First!ers and other deep ecologists see each wilderness as a
biome for a spiritual mega-nature to reproduce itself in. It is for the animals,
the plants, the water, the air, the biota in its interconnected, life-driven
form, minus the human beings. A road into a logged forest may not *be*
wilderness, but it has wilderness *potential* and as such is worth fighting for.

For the more mainstream preservationists directing the Adirondack
Council, the APA, and the Governor's Commission, the wilderness is for
the flora and fauna, but it is also for the tourists, specifically the wilderness
travelers such as backpackers who appreciate nature in its most untram-
meled form, without the aesthetic disturbances caused by human technology. For them, access is a deflected issue because the areas labeled "Wild
Forest" are supposed to accommodate those who cannot or will not walk
in, or who prefer motorized access. Yet they also have the least clearly
defined or most flexible concept of wilderness — as an area where there is a
minimum of permanent human structures, and wild flora and fauna currently predominate, regardless of the area's history.

For the home rule advocates and their supporters, including many
sportspeople, Crane Pond Road functions as a symbol of their right to use
wildlands as a resource. As local people, they see the history and tradition
of particular areas of land playing an important role in spiritual ownership
and usufruct rights. In defining wilderness, they look for historical and
present-tense markers of human manipulation of the environment in that
area, including past logging and road building. For these residents and

resource users, the future restoration of the area as wilderness, while not inconceivable, is still an imagined outline rather than a reality in the context of historical human occupation.

At Crane Pond Road the representatives of the different worldviews involved in the Adirondack land use issue met and outlined their positions. They asserted them with the threat, and the reality, of violence as a force to maintain their separate identities. The confrontations at Crane Pond Road, and the extremes of the debate represented there, solidified the positions, marking them clearly for everyone to see. The escalations into violence, into "us and them" thinking, demarcated the differences and did nothing to bring about interactive problem solving or compromise. All sides refused to budge. But while more mainstream preservationists, such as the Adirondack Council and the Governor's Commission on the Adirondacks in the Twenty-First Century, have criticized such stances as counterproductive and maintained their own willingness to work together with local government, they contribute to such polarization by turning a blind eye to the meaning of democratic participation. George Davis, executive director of the Governor's Commission, presented its report and findings to Adirondack citizens at a meeting a month after the report came out. That meeting serves as a window on a different form of "us and them" thinking.

❧ The sky darkens in the tall firs and pines around Paul Smith's College. Cars of all descriptions — new and old Ford pickups, new and old BMWs, Volkswagens, and Chevrolets — pull into the parking lot, as George Davis, executive director of the Governor's Commission, prepares to make a presentation on the commission report. Already a dozen protesters with signs have gathered on the stairs leading to the entrance.

"Live Free or Die — Protect our God-Given Rights"
"Send Mario Back to the Grocery"
"Bug Huggers Go Home"
"Liars and Land Thieves"
"APA No Way"
"B.S.!"

These are the representatives of Don Gerdts' Citizens' Council and some from another home rule group, the Solidarity Alliance. Eventually everyone files inside the gymnasium, even the sign carriers, and they sit in the bleachers. At first glance the room seems divided roughly in half. In the stands on the right-hand side, as one enters, there are about fifty people, many holding signs, two with flags, one of which is upside down, the universal sign of distress. There are more in the next section of bleachers who seem to have aligned themselves out of sympathy with the sign carriers. Those more supportive of the commission report and the APA, including a member of the Adirondack Council, are seated on the left. But the comments prove that the situation is more complex.

Davis, a clean-cut man of about forty with closely cropped hair and wearing a button-down shirt, faces the people in the bleachers. He is tense, like a runner before a race. He begins by telling the audience about the note he kept pinned above his desk during the commission's year-long tenure. It outlined the three basic principles that the commissioners followed: first, to preserve the Adirondack Park; second, to treat private landowners fairly; and third, to improve the quality of life for residents.

A brief slide show defines, as he says, "what the commissioners would like the Park to look like in a hundred years for our great-grandchildren." Then Davis explains statistics on development, stating, "You will not find the word 'crisis' anywhere in this report." The "crisis" word, which did show up in "20/20 Vision" reports and in the newspaper information on the progress of the commission at midyear, had sparked contentious debate Parkwide. The Adirondack Council reports featured pictures of real estate signs and new developments; others, including John Stock, who make it their business to study the situation, insist that the Adirondack Council and the APA and other preservationists are exaggerating. George Davis has built a crusade against what he sees as a steep trend in development, signaled by the number of permits requested, and supported by trends in subdivisions and upward trends seen by the tax assessors. Others have responded that it is the fear of increasing regulation that has prompted anyone who plans to build in the next ten years to apply for a permit now. At this presentation George Davis says, "It is up to each individual to decide at what point it is a crisis."

People in the audience hoot, and someone calls out, "Do you love the Park?"

"Yes, I do!" Davis shoots back.

"Not more than we do," shouts another member of the audience.

The commission report has proposed a reorganization of all aspects of state administration. Davis explains the four-part plan, including expanding the Adirondack Park Agency into an Adirondack Park Administration; restructuring the DEC and consolidating its regions to match Park boundaries, as a new Adirondack Park Service; organizing local governments; and an Adirondack Park Community Development Corporation to deal

240   with issues such as sewage, water, and affordable housing. But despite the commission's efforts to address local concerns, it is clear from the tone of the report and what Davis is saying that its emphasis is primarily on the environment, aesthetics, and the control of development.

Heckling from the audience increases as others call out, "Let him speak!"

Davis discusses the commission's support for the forest industry, health care, the local economy, affordable housing, and local government services. When he gets to the construction moratorium, calling it the "biggest red flag of the report," and stating that it could undercut construction by 30 to 40 percent, the stands on the right erupt. People bang on the stands with their signposts, accompanied by whooping and booing which continues right through Davis' discussion of conservation easements. He manages to finish, downplaying the importance of eminent domain, and stating, "Local people best know where development should go in their communities." But the air is charged with hostility.

The questions start. A woman reads a prepared statement on Paul Smith's College, saying, "Where we are tonight is an important part of the Adirondacks. Why did the commission ignore it?" Clapping breaks out. Someone asks, "How many town supervisors are here tonight?" A count is taken: one out of eighteen. The Peru town supervisor, the one present, whose town is currently only partly within the boundary of the Blue Line, stands up to make a statement. "I woke up Sunday morning, and read in the paper that the entire Town of Peru was included in the map of the Commission on the Adirondacks in the Twenty-First Century. I was very concerned about that. I almost choked on my coffee! Why was there not any forewarning or any public participation? And what was the reason for including the land in this boundary?" He continues, "You say you want a partnership with local government. Why were there no local government officials on the commission?"

When Davis responds that the commissioners were picked for their intelligence, boos and laughter erupt from the audience. People ask about the effect of the moratorium on construction: What happens to the 35 percent of contractors whose work will be eliminated? Then half of the people in the bleachers on the right, the sign carriers, parade out of the gymnasium.

After their departure, a Saranac Lake resident says that Paul Smith's College should be ashamed that only George Davis was allowed to speak.

"For years we have heard about the 6 million–acre Park — three and a half million acres is private property, not Park," he says. "By what stretch of the imagination could a man call three and a half million acres 'Park' because somebody drew a little blue line around it?" Davis answers that the New York State government created the Park by an act of the legislature.

An administrator from the Board of Cooperative Education Services (BOCES) stands up and asks, "Did you consult me? Did you consult BOCES?" Davis answers cautiously, "We may not have." Someone shouts from the stands, "Got a real thorough report!"

Another man, white-haired, wearing a red-and-black-checked logger's jacket, stands up, with a list of questions in his hand. He reads from his sheet, and elicits from Davis the following figures: the commission used $600,000 of taxpayers' money and over $400,000 in donations. The 20,000 copies of the commission report, a soft-cover eight-by-eleven book with glossy full-color photos, were printed at a cost of two dollars per copy. The old man looks up. "That's over a million dollars that has been used to beat us," he states matter-of-factly, and sits down. A loud round of applause and whooping greets his comment. "George Davis, who elected you?" someone shouts.

Then a woman sitting with members of the Citizens' Council goes into a rambling harangue ending with references to the Fourteenth Amendment, and demands to know, "Are you communist or American?" Davis replies, "I don't believe we have done anything illegal." And in a sudden shift from the jumbled rhetoric that she seemed to have swallowed whole and spat back at him, the woman asks, in her own voice, looking directly at Davis, "Are we not a part of nature? Do we not have the right to survive?"

George Davis continues, but the audience is quiet, digesting that blunt statement of the fundamental difference between the viewpoint of the preservationists, especially those from urban and suburban backgrounds, and the viewpoint of much of the local rural population. Many preservationists, such as Davis, see humans as something apart from nature, too degrading or defiling to be considered a part of it. Wilderness is wilderness only when it is completely free from human impact. But many locals see themselves, if not exactly as a part of nature, as having a right to a place in nature. For them, wildlands and humans are not mutually exclusive. More frustrating for many locals, including government officials, is their exclusion from the decision-making process about the lands where they live, at a level where it counts. The questions continue.

❧ The Davis presentation is only one of many meetings and presentations occurring around the Park, as each of the many groups tries to define itself and its positions, and campaign for those positions. Davis presented the views of the mainstream preservation interest groups, from the Audubon Society to the Adirondack Council; other meetings present other views. Which views are those of insiders, which are those of outsiders, and which are those of the Adirondack residents is not always clear.

❧ The Holiday Inn conference room in Lake Placid is packed on this spring night in 1990 for an introductory meeting of the Adirondack Fairness Coalition. Dark blue folders are handed out at the door, holding about twenty pages of a cleanly typed information packet, including statement of purpose, map, letters, membership form, list of state senators and assemblymen, a copy of a letter from the Adirondack Council to the Governor's Commission, and a two-color newsletter. It is a professional job. So is the meeting, the speakers in dark suits talking from a podium with microphones, and finishing with a high-quality slide show accompanied by music. There is a big crowd here, young and old, well-dressed lawyers, and old-timers in flannel shirts and boots. Many are middle-aged business people; at two hundred or thereabouts, it is a significant showing in this village of three thousand, though some people have come from the surrounding hamlets.

The Fairness Coalition (organized by three real estate attorneys, the founder and at that time president of Lincoln Logs log homes, and the supervisor of the Town of Schroon), lists five primary positions: that since the Adirondack Park Agency Act is one of the most restrictive land use regulations in the nation, there is no need for additional regulation; that local government should fulfill its important function in land use regulation and planning as set forth in the statement of legislative findings and purposes of the original Park Agency Act; that there should be no new bond issue; that New York State must guarantee reasonable access to the Adirondacks for all vacationers, hunters, fishermen, campers, the handicapped, and others; and a pledge to disseminate an accurate picture of the current state of the Adirondacks relating to land use, land use classifications, and the local economy. In March 1993 Frederick Monroe, one of the real estate lawyers, and the Fairness Coalition's most quoted representative, states that their positions remain unchanged since 1990, except for that on the Bond Act, which failed. Their board of directors has grown to fifteen, and includes the organizer of North-East Loggers; Glenn Harris, former assemblyman from Long Lake; a banker; Joe Rota, the director of the Local Government Review Board; a stockbroker; two store owners; another town supervisor; and several others. Their executive director is realtor Susan Allen.

The speakers say that they have formed the Fairness Coalition because they are concerned that the commissioners' report may be harmful to the people of the Adirondacks. It quickly becomes clear that the Fairness Coalition is positioning itself in direct opposition to the Adirondack Council in an openly adversarial role. The speakers talk at length about the Adirondack Council, citing its annual budget of $1 million and a staff of sixteen; they state that the Governor's Commission is funded by some of the same sources that support the Council, and has connections through George Davis and others to the Council. They assert vehemently, several times, that there is no development crisis in the Adirondacks, as the Adirondack Council asserts. Their own research has shown that much of the development is taking place just outside the Park because of restrictions within the Park. During the slide show the cool, measured speech of attorneys gives way to more passionate rhetoric: "They want to preserve every rock, every tree — if they had their way they wouldn't even let nature change. . . . They really want the people out of the Park. Will they take away our right to hunt or fish? . . . We feel we have an emergency — a people emergency. They are trying to take away our way of life."

The third speaker is an attorney from Glens Falls. He says that he joined the Fairness Coalition primarily because he believes in careful change, evolution not revolution. The balancing act of the APA is still intact, he says. He names two large developments that the agency has controlled. One is Gleneagles, the proposed development of the historic Lake Placid Club property, which is in the process of applying for a permit. In spite of a two thousand–page report on the development, the agency has come back with many questions. Gary Randorf, the speaker notes, has praised the agency for a course of action opposed to Gleneagles. The second, the Patton development, has been beaten down by the APA a number of times, he says. He condemns the "creative jurisdiction" of the APA, which exists not in the act but in the hearts and minds of the commissioners. He also challenges the APA to reveal the nature of all the permits it says people are requesting. He believes that the majority of these permits are very simple, and cites the example of a five-acre parcel given by a mother to her son. Many people believe that the sharp rise in requests for permits is a result of the regulations: fearing further restrictions, people are seeking to establish grandfather clauses or complete the paperwork necessary to subdivide, if desired, at some later, unspecified time.

The fourth speaker, the supervisor from the Town of Schroon, denounces the proposed moratorium. The fifth speaker, the president of Lincoln Logs, says that the people of the Adirondacks are under siege. He lists the Fairness Coalition's plans for disseminating accurate information, assembling a formidable membership, gaining a voice in Albany, and responding to the Governor's Commission. He ends by aligning himself with Adirondackers, calling himself and them "confirmed rugged individualists."

The audience responds to the speakers with impassioned comments. An older member of the Citizens' Council speaks at such length that she has to be asked to allow others equal time. A fourth-generation Adirondacker who works in radio says, "I hear it from my listeners every day — we are very discouraged." Another speaker asks where the state was when the loons were disappearing as a result of acid rain or when the brook trout were threatened. The comments from the audience go on and on. Often there is clapping, shouts of approval. When Dan Plumley of the Adirondack Council stands up, there is hissing and someone shouts, "Sit down!" Plumley speaks moderately but accuses the Fairness Coalition of making heated comments. There is no clapping.

Finally there is another slide show, this time superimposed stills of Minerva, the colors of the town fading into the faces of the local residents. The speakers announce that they want to celebrate the people of the Adirondacks. The accompanying music sings, "I was born in a small town . . . people let me be just what I want to be." Pictures of children playing, small attractive homes slide by.

The orchestration mesmerizes. The professionalism and planning equal that of any environmental group in the Park. These lawyers, realtors, and business owners quickly become a potent force in the controversy, winning support from many local people. It is clear that they have struck a common chord. Yet as I leave, I find myself wondering who these voices really represent.

Some would say that Donald Gerdts and the Citizens' Council represent the voices of local people. Yet Gerdts himself is an anomaly. A small-time developer who had moved to the Adirondacks from Long Island less than ten years before, he has fomented a movement of angry Adirondackers voicing opinions that are a mirror image of the extremes of the preservation movement. They speak of the right of sovereignty, or home-rule. They link governmental controls of private land with communism, and frequently refer to their constitutional right to do what they want with their land. Their actions follow the traditions of civil disobedience: they stage protests and rallies at the State Capitol, and form a motorcade slowdown on the Northway, the major highway that runs from Albany to Montreal.

But, finally, their actions verge on violence. Guns appear; threats to individual Adirondack Council members are made; speakers at meetings are heckled. Many Adirondackers abhor the violence; and many more deny that Gerdts speaks for them. Yet the rights of individuals to determine the use of their land speaks potently for many. Republican State Senator Ron Stafford, whose North Country constituency helped defeat the Bond Act and encourages Stafford to vote against Adirondack legislation, holds to the principles of individual freedom in land use, and has even suggested that the APA be dismantled. Gerdts speaks for some; nevertheless, within his own group there are growing rifts.

At the other end of the spectrum, the Residents' Committee to Protect the Adirondacks has evolved in support of the commission report and the APA. Some members have lived in the Adirondacks all their lives; others are the sons and daughters of people who spent their summers in the Adirondacks, and as adults came to live there year-round. Some are graduate students working at research centers in the Park; others are guides or carpenters. Many have a high level of formal education, and most share a preservationist vision of the Park.

Their newsletter, *Adirondack Voices*, is detailed and well researched. One article supports the APA by citing the Maine Land Use Regulatory Commission, which manages the use of land in nearly one half of Maine. Unlike the New Jersey Pinelands Commission and the Columbia River Gorge Commission, the seven members of MLURC are appointed by the governor, subject to review and confirmation by the legislature. Four of the members, according to statute, "shall be knowledgeable in at least one of each of the following areas: commerce and industry; fisheries and wildlife; forestry; and conservation. At least two members shall be residents within the commission's jurisdiction." In comparison, *Adirondack Voices* notes, "5 of the 11 APA commissioners must be resident in the regulated area. In both cases the local area has no formal input into the Governor's selection." The writer uses the MLURC example to suggest that regulation in the Adirondack Park is not extraordinary, and in fact residents have more opportunities for participation on the regulatory boards in the Adirondacks than in similarly regulated land in Maine.

Perhaps the article was also intended as an answer to an article in the Fairness Coalition newspaper a year earlier, that cited examples of local representation on the New Jersey Pinelands Commission, which has fifteen commission members, seven locally appointed, seven state appointed, and one federally appointed, and the Columbia River Gorge Commission, which has 12 voting members, 6 locally appointed and 6 state appointed.

A third newspaper, *Adirondack Echoes,* published by the Adirondack Conservation Council, is not pro-development, nor does it advocate closing the APA; instead it skates between the Fairness Coalition and Don Gerdts in its attitudes toward regulation and the commission report. The self-proclaimed "voice of Adirondack Conservation" dealing with sportsmen's issues, it raked the preservationists, from the APA to the Adirondack Council to the Governor's Commission, over the coals in its winter issue of 1991 for "elitism," "imperialism," "secrecy," and a narrow "wilderness philosophy." Throughout the long, detailed articles, the writer, a retired businessman and conservationist, gave a historical account of the involvement of preservationists in park regulation since the beginning of the APA.

He describes the commission members: "The leadership core of the commission included arch-preservationists Peter Berle, George Davis, Richard Lawrance, and Harold Jerry. These fellow travelers, originally involved in the first Temporary Study Commission and the APA, utilized their cohorts on the APA and their public relations organization, the Adirondack Council, to prepare the public for acceptance of their preconceived plans for the Adirondacks." The article ends: "The irony of the current situation is that Adirondackers' love of their land exceeds that of their 'masters.' Adirondackers want controlled growth and environmental protection, but they also want to earn a living while maintaining their democratic right to control their future and utilize renewable natural resources. When the final 21st Century Commission legislation is passed, who shall prevail . . . the 'peasants' or the 'masters'?"

🐾 Other groups form. One is the New York Blue Line Council, a coalition of statewide groups with Adirondack industry and property interests, started up in 1990. Its leaders include Robert Flacke, former commissioner of the DEC, past chairman of the APA, and the member of the Governor's Commission who wrote a dissenting report; Pieter Litchfield of Litchfield Park; some representatives of forest industry; and several large landowners in the Park. This group, made up of many wealthy and powerful individ-

uals, advocates property owners' rights along with conservation. But when
I speak with a key member, a different concern emerges. He says that their
real concern is process, and to emphasize a participative process for all
concerned.

As the debate escalates and the groups multiply, some try to break the
growing deadlock. Richard Purdue of the Adirondack Planning Commission is one of these. On July 19, 1990, in Lake Placid, in a room in the
same building that houses the Lussi Rink, where skaters tried for Olympic
gold in the winter of 1980, the Adirondack Planning Commission holds a
meeting to try to bring together some of the voices of the Adirondacks.
Purdue, supervisor of the Town of Indian Lake, a Princeton graduate and
former employee of the CIA who has lived in the Adirondacks for over
twenty years, has organized this meeting to get input from fourteen different citizen groups active in Park land use issues.

As the Adirondack Planning Commission moved from working to get
more local representation on the APA to negotiating with the governor on
several other land use issues, more local input became critical, both to
provide true representation and to build consensus. Consensus on any of the
issues would provide some clout for the Adirondackers, an almost inaudible
minority voice in the legislature. It would also protect the Planning Commission from divisive pressures already making themselves felt within and
outside the Planning commission. But consensus is not about to come from
this meeting. At best, it represents an uneasy truce among a heterogeneous
group, a momentary silence in the battle when words can be spoken, and
perhaps listened to as well.

Purdue introduces members of several county governments, as well as
Mike DiNunzio of the Adirondack Council; Bill Johnston, Essex County
planner; and Jim Frenette. They are here mostly to listen to the spokespeople from fourteen groups, and to comments from the audience. They sit
facing the audience.

Fred Monroe, chairman of the Adirondack Fairness Coalition, steps up
to the microphone to speak. He identifies the Fairness Coalition as a grassroots organization with 1,500 members which desires a balance between
the preservation of environmental quality and reasonable growth. He argues that the pure wilderness movement has given inadequate attention to
the needs of people. He concludes by reiterating his group's position that
there is no development crisis in the Adirondacks.

Other groups follow. Melinda Hadley, secretary of the Local Govern-

248   ment Review Board, reads a report detailing a list of letters sent to the governor, and the lack of response. Leaders of several branches of the Solidarity Alliance speak from prepared statements. Howard Aubin of the AuSable branch, owner of a small sawmill, makes an impassioned plea for home rule, citing the Constitution. He says, "What you are calling the 'back country'—it's our home. AuSable Forks is much different from Lake Placid or Lake George!" Someone else speaks for the Solidarity Alliance in Elizabethtown. When an Alliance member says that people can judge the strength of this movement from the defeat of the Bond Act, loud clapping breaks out in the room. Another Solidarity Alliance member speaks out for the branch in Crown Point, saying that members are unhappy with the Planning Commission because its policy of negotiating "for the people" prevents legal battles on constitutionality. "We will not recognize the Adirondack Planning Commission!" People in the audience begin chanting "Good!" and clapping. The speaker criticizes the Planning Commission for closed-door meetings with the governor, and urges everyone to recognize the individual citizen as sovereign.

Gerdts himself, looking tired and heavy around the eyes, speaking for the Citizens' Council, says that he does not recognize the Planning Commission, and so will make no public statement. He sits down abruptly. The intensity with which people are leaning forward in their seats hints at confrontation; but the heat of the day and the room's stuffiness seem to stifle it.

Aggrieved landowner Vincent Vaccaro, a dentist from New Jersey, passes out copies of his letters to Adirondackers and legislators with a heading that reads, "Concerned Citizens of the Adirondack Park: concerned citizens united for the protection of the rights of private landowners and residents within the Adirondack Park." Vaccaro takes the microphone, speaking openly about his love for his land and his fight to stop the state from taking it by eminent domain. He is willing, he says plaintively, to place conservation easements in the deed to his property forever prohibiting subdivision and development, sell some of it to the state, allow public access, and give the State the right of first refusal should the land come up for sale in the future. Purdue comments that the Hamilton County Board of Supervisors unanimously adopted a resolution supporting Vaccaro.

Dave Morrow, a tall man in his late twenties or early thirties, dressed in sweater and loafers of the kind seen in L. L. Bean catalogues, speaks for the Residents' Committee to Protect the Adirondacks. He says, "We represent a set of views of residents held by a silent majority that have received no expression so far." He announces that this is the group's first appearance, and he introduces it as a grassroots organization of natives and newcomers alike who wish to protect open space and ensure economic viability and a special way of life. His presentation is well organized, and Morrow is a clear and forceful speaker; the reporters in the room focus attentively as he lists the group's positions. He argues that the people with the biggest stakes are the residents. "However, this area does *not* belong exclusively to the Adirondackers. It has national and international importance, whether we recognize it or not." He ends by stating, "We abhor the threats of violence and the unnecessary resort to civil disobedience" and urges all groups to join the Planning Commission, saying, "There is a place for closed-door sessions."

A member of the Adirondack Landowners' Association speaks out against state acquisition of private lands and the acquisition of easements which grant public access. Mike DiNunzio of the Adirondack Council says that he is here "to listen and to learn," and not to discuss whether there is a crisis or not. Dave Gibson of the Association for the Protection of the Adirondacks speaks next. He says that there is a need for more forums of this kind. Although he sees no common agenda now among the groups, there may be in the future. He urges patience and the willingness to engage in constructive debate.

Bob Stegeman, director and chair of the Empire State Forest Products Association, speaks earnestly about the needs of industry. His association is concerned about the commission's recommendations and the uncertainty of their effects on land use and the ability of forest industry to survive in the future. If the forest industry goes, so goes the Park, he says, but the process works both ways. He lists his group's major areas of concern: state land acquisition; conservation easements; protection of land values; the takings issue; and the effects of recreation on forest industry. He is disturbed by the commission report's proposed "superagency," which would subsume the DEC and put an expanded version of the APA in control of the Park. He hopes that there would be checks and balances.

Pete Simmons, an older man in a suit and tie, speaks for the Tupper Lake Shorefront Owners Association. He is dismayed at the glibness of conservationists who say that they want to save these lands for their grandchildren. "They really," he says indignantly, "want to use our land at our expense." He argues that the preservationists are a small minority of elitists.

250   His and others' taxes will be going up after equalization, thanks to the APA. He hopes, he says, that the governor will respect private property and the historic role of local government.

The final speaker, a member of the Adirondack Blueline Council, states that this group's purpose is to determine the facts.

The meeting closes. Whether other meetings will bring any form of consensus is, at that moment, doubtful.

❧ On a summer evening Laura Rappaport, the chief reporter on Park issues from the *Adirondack Daily Enterprise,* and I drive down to Blue Mountain Lake to the Adirondack Museum to hear Craig Gilbourne, director of the museum, speak about his role on the Governor's Commission on the Adirondacks in the Twenty-First Century. The museum itself houses a historical library, artifacts of Adirondack life from railroad carriages to nineteenth-century logging equipment, a blacksmith's shop, and farm implements. There are several buildings set out on green lawns. Admission costs eight dollars, but one day a year residents can get in for free.

The sun is still shining, the mountains casting long blue shadows across the lake, as we go inside. About 50 percent of the audience is gray-haired. Gilbourne, himself gray-haired, stands in front of a packed room and describes what it was like to work on the commission. In January 1989 the commissioners met with Governor Cuomo to plan their work for an April 1, 1990, deadline. This schedule was far shorter than the nearly three years that the Temporary Study Commission had had; the budget of the Commission for the Twenty-First Century was also far smaller. There were fourteen commissioners, including the chair, Peter Berle. Gilbourne characterizes them as "a good working group." Claire Barnett of Westport; John Bierwirth, Grumman Aircraft CEO; Sarah R. Bogdanovitch, a forester, graduate of Paul Smith's College, and a Rockefeller; Robert A. Boice of Cooperative Extension, also a fisherman and hunter; Bob Flacke, onetime commissioner of the DEC, owner of several motels in Lake George and proprietor of Fort William Henry; Harold Jerry, director of the Temporary Study Commission; Reed Kingsbury, from a Rochester newspaper; Richard Lawrance, member of the Temporary Study Commission and onetime chairman of the APA; John Oakes, columnist for the *New York Times,* and chief editorial page editor, in his seventies "a fearless one as far as dealing with a lot of flummery"; Harvey Russell of Pepsico, the only African-American on the commission, who believed that human issues were at least as important as preservation issues; James F. Smith of the Orange and

Rockland Power Company; Ross Whaley, president of the State University of New York College of Environmental Science and Forestry (CESF); and Gilbourne himself. George Davis was executive director of the commission's staff of fifteen. There were also many advisers, consultants, and interns.

Gilbourne remarks that what the commission was trying to accomplish was more philosophical than a matter of fine-tuning. That job, he says, belongs to the planners. He argues that the state must have a clear statement of policy with regard to the Park, which it does not have now. Development efforts should be encouraged if they are appropriately scaled and properly sited. The state should assume some financial responsibility for the difficulties faced by the rural population as a result of state policies that have had a negative impact. And environmental considerations should be set ahead of any others in the Park.

Gilbourne also talks about the ownership patterns in the Park. Thirty-seven corporations and individuals own tracts of two thousand acres or more. Five hundred and sixty-five owners, mostly in resource management and rural use areas, own parcels of five hundred acres or more. Also, he notes, the forest industry owns twice as much land as it did a few years ago; there is a trend toward a concentration of ownership in the hands of fewer people.

After outlining the basic considerations leading to the recommendations, Gilbourne opens the floor to questions, but not before expressing his "personal quirks" regarding the outcome of the commission. In contrast to Harold Jerry and John Oakes, who thought that the report was not restrictive enough toward development on the parcels of two thousand acres or more, much of it owned or managed by industry, and who also thought that the commission went too far in subsidizing the forest products industry, Gilbourne thinks that the independent jobbers to whom forest industry contracts out its jobs have a hard life, and trying to keep them in business is important. He says that statistics on the number of people involved in logging in the Adirondacks are artificially low because the Department of Commerce does not count independent jobbers.

While responding to questions, Gilbourne says something that startles the reporter and me so much that we look around at the rest of the audience to see if they have heard it too. We shake our heads as if to knock out a buzzing in the ears; we can't quite believe it. But he says it again, a little differently. He comes very close to suggesting that people with second homes in the Park should be able to vote in the Adirondacks as well as in

252 their primary places of residence. After all, he argues, they are paying taxes here too.

The last question comes in three parts. "What do you perceive as *your* role?"

"A very strong understanding of historical perspective."

"What gave you personally the greatest satisfaction?"

"I'm still waiting. The governor is a loner. He is very intelligent, but he doesn't assume leadership. . . . He's very adroit, a lawyer."

"What would you change?"

"I would have changed — made preparation for the wild storm of protests. I would have had tapes. More presentations."

🌿 Many people, both preservationists and state officials in the Park, speak scornfully of the home rule advocates' claims that preservationists wish to push the people out of the Park and create a vast wilderness populated only by the loon, the cougar, and the wolf. Yet in 1993 a publication arrives in my mailbox, sent by what organization I do not know. It is titled *Wild Earth: Special Issue,* and headlined "The Wildlands Project: Plotting a North American Wilderness Recovery Strategy."

Inside, on the masthead, I find many familiar names: Earth First! activists, including founder Dave Foreman, who is listed as the executive editor: John Davis, whom I met on our camping trip, editor of the Earth First! journal; Reed Noss, the forest ecologist who has sailed to the forefront of the Pacific Northwest debate over old growth; and others who are well-known Earth First! chroniclers and deep ecology writers. Included among the editorial advisers I find Roderick Nash, Bill Devall, and Dolores La Chapelle; Christopher Manes, also of Pacific Northwest old growth forest fame; Gary Nabhan, whose groundbreaking agro-ecological research in the Southwest has inspired many; George Sessions; Arne Naess, the Norwegian founder of deep ecology; and others, including Bill McKibben, author of *The End of Nature* and a resident of the Adirondacks.

The articles present regional analyses of wildlands left in each area, together with plans for recovering the ecological unity of these regions through protective policies. Among them is "A Proposal for an Adirondack Primeval" by Paul Medeiros, a Cornell student. If the home rule advocates in the Adirondacks ever saw this article, they would feel their worst fears justified. Violence could result, and certainly violence to people's ideas as the two most polarized worldviews of the human relationship with nature meet and clash. Those who see humans as central and of primary impor-

tance, with nature as a set of resources to be used, and those who see nature
as primal and primary with humans as "a cancer," an inappropriate evil to
be eradicated from wilderness wherever possible, would collide with the
force of an atavistic battle over this most fundamental relationship. At risk
in such a collision would be the less loudly expressed worldview of those
who believe that humans have a right to be a part of nature long as they
respect its integrity: the woodspeople and others who value the woodspeople's views and lifestyles, and the mutuality they represent.

The "proposal" ends:

> "We must ask ourselves: What are the Adirondacks for?
> Are they a playground for the New York elite and their out-
> board motors? Are they a home for a special rustic breed with
> jeeps and rifles? . . . The Adirondacks represent one of many
> bioregions not meant to be permanently inhabited by the spe-
> cies *Homo sapiens.*
>
> The Adirondacks do not belong to modern humanity, nor
> modern humanity to the Adirondacks. We are not worthy to
> walk among the ghosts of towering pines and hemlocks. We
> are not ready to share our foot paths with the cougar and the
> wolf. Only when humanity can learn to give what it has taken
> from the Adirondacks, will we find our place in those moun-
> tains. And in those days, the maps will read:
> *This country by reason of mountains,*
> *swamps, and drowned lands is*
> *impassable and uninhabited.*
> —*1775 Map of Northern New York*
>
> (Medeiros, 1992, p. 41)

The morning after our overnight at Lewey Lake it is still pouring rain.
The Earth First!ers emerge from their tents looking groggy, several hours
after a gray, watery daylight first hits the campground. Eventually they
decide to head down the road to a diner in Long Lake, where they can
discuss the commission report over a hot breakfast, and dry out.

10

Views of the Forest

THE USEFULNESS OF "FOREVER WILD" AS A designation for new land acquisitions has been exhausted, according to many local administrators in the Adirondacks, foresters involved in timber management, and others. Regulation of privately owned lands, as an alternative to preservation through "forever wild," has created tensions and problems that are not yet resolved. The APA is welcomed by some, grudgingly accepted by many, and deeply resented by others. As of 1997, the recommendations of the Governor's Commission on the Adirondacks in the Twenty-First Century had not yet successfully made their way through the New York State Senate, despite former Governor Cuomo's and others' attempts at revisions and behind-the-scenes negotiations. The Northern Forest Lands Council has had limited success in pushing its legislation through Congress. Yet many local people agree that it is important to protect the Adirondacks from development at levels that would damage the natural environment and, for both the locals and visitors, spoil the wild character of the Adirondacks.

Problems surround almost every aspect of the attempts to discuss the situation. Different agendas, different definitions of wilderness, different senses of whom it is for, different understandings of where the boundaries lie between private rights and responsibilities and public rights and responsibilities for land that is privately owned, different aesthetic and ecological values, class and cultural differences all interrupt the dialogue. The conversation about land use in the Park has been taking place for over a hundred years, at a meta-level that includes voices representing many different positions and many different times and places in history. It is possible to see where and when certain voices have dominated. Out of the conversation have come many suggestions. Gradually, the surviving options develop into concepts and are effected as solutions. Once a concept has been implemented, it gathers a weight and a reality of its own. Other options seem to fade into a shadowy past tense, only to spring to life again in moments of crisis.

Local people, some of them the great-grandparents of present-day local citizens, were forced into the park concept, willingly or not, a hundred years ago. In this current moment of crisis many local people are adamantly advancing suggestions ranging from a return to home rule and the end of the APA, to increased representational participation in decision making, beyond mere advisory capacities. The major demand remains that of filling the five seats on the APA Commission with local people chosen *by* local residents rather than by a distant governor. These demands must not be ignored as they have been, for two reasons, one practical and one ethical.

On the practical side, if the numbers of local people, even as few as 130,000, who react negatively to increasing regulation continue to be ignored, they will continue to agitate against preservationist concerns, especially insofar as these are perceived to originate from wealthy outsiders, who also represent the class most responsible for exploiting and degrading the environment worldwide. The agitation of local populations has serious consequences at local, regional, and even national levels.

At the local level, opposition can stalemate processes that could be negotiable, such as the closing of the Crane Pond Road, when people perceive these processes as excluding them. At the regional level, the people of the Adirondacks have proved, with the 1989 Environmental Bond Act, that they can seriously influence the outcome of a state-level vote on issues that affect other parts of the state as well. At the national level, their strong reactions to land use reform and the preservation and conservation of wilderness, wild forests, mountains, and waters reverberate in other communities facing similar land use issues. From logging towns in the Pacific Northwest, to the communities surrounding Yellowstone National

Park, to the southern Appalachian communities mingled with the Cherokee National Forest near the Great Smoky Mountains National Park, the increasingly pressured stances of these communities serve as models for each other.

Networks of property rights advocates are springing up among these communities, yet local perspectives and a focus on the home community remain much stronger than alliances with national causes. While property rights issues, appearing in "takings" cases across the nation, may provide a vehicle for expression of the fears of some local people and serve to bind them into a larger national group, many take pains to disassociate themselves privately from national agendas. Where some researchers have seen local or rural populations claiming some of the symbols and terminology of capitalist industries, interviews in the quiet of the home and the forest reveal deep class rifts that prevent any but the most superficial adoption of industry rhetoric by working-class individuals.

Those from urban backgrounds with preservationist interests at heart often seem condescending toward the intelligence and knowledge of local populations. People in these rural communities may average fewer years of formal education than in the environmental community, may have lower incomes, and may be perceived as more "working class." But they may also be closer to nature on a daily basis and thus better informed about local ecosystems. Especially where changes over time have been localized, indigenous knowledge, aware of several generations of information, may provide more realistic pictures of natural and human-induced trends. Agencies tracing the history of salmon populations and water levels in small tributaries in the Pacific Northwest, in valleys where farmers and ranchers have lived for generations, already benefit from working with indigenous knowledge holders in local communities.

Environmentalists have consistently underestimated these communities. It is naive to assume that the extremes of the local groups will not mobilize at a national level, as in fact they have already done through the Wise Use movement, to battle increasing land use restrictions and state and national controls. The polarization of preservationist special interest groups and local groups which may include preservationists, and certainly include conservationists, is unproductive and may result in severe damage to the environment as the sides become more and more frozen in stances that do not permit real communication or negotiation. Bargaining, in which different sides exchange non-mutual benefits, is no substitute for principled negotiation, in which the good of the whole is considered.

Mediation, which could be useful in the process of resolving conflicts at the local and regional levels, cannot be productive unless all parties are able to listen effectively to one another. Rigid stances, resulting in posturing, such as that of Earth First! and Senator Ron Stafford, effectively close off this option. Those with rigid stances refuse to engage in a dialogue in which the words of each may change the ideas of the others; and by using threats and nonnegotiable symbols, participants raise the level of confrontation to one that drives the other parties involved to take rigid stances also. Negotiation comes to a halt, and organizations that rely on negotiation as their main tool, such as the Adirondack Planning Commission, disintegrate, thus jeopardizing future possibilities for communication and negotiation. Collaborative processes that allow all to participate in decision making show more promise, yet even the Clinton Forest Summit in the Pacific Northwest, held in 1993, failed to sustain such an effort (Walker and Daniels, 1996).

In addition to blockading any efforts to work together toward land use regulations, posturing also escalates violence and confrontation in the event of forced changes. As people assume positions in which communication is strictly self-reflexive rather than interactive, the ability to empathize with individuals in other groups, which normally curbs violence, is lost. An "us and them" way of perceiving the conflict evolves. As the "Minutemen" and other Revolutionary War metaphors of Anthony D'Elia's *Adirondack Rebellion* demonstrate, and as the language of the Earth First!ers and other preservationists who refer to themselves as "warriors" protecting "virgin wilderness" and "Mother Earth" demonstrates equally, the primary mode of conduct becomes war. Real violence to individuals through personal attack, both verbal and physical, becomes possible. Such violence has already broken out in the Adirondacks, from several sides; both Earth First! and local groups have damaged property, and through threats and actions, have initiated violence against individuals. These actions become reasons to perpetuate further violence.

The burning of ecologist and APA commissioner Anne LaBastille's barn, as well as a tire-slashing, were presumably motivated by local anti-preservationist sentiments. And damage to the environment, the common concern of all sides, becomes a real threat through accidental or purposeful human activity; burning the woods is now threatened frequently, and is alleged to have happened in the past, although many preservationists deny this harsh reality. For those who truly care about the environment and the wild spaces of the Adirondacks, including both local people and members of preservationist interest groups outside the region, the importance of deescalating the confrontation and reopening the conversation is paramount.

The ethical reason for not ignoring local concerns and needs holds even deeper significance. Valuing other human beings results in respect for their point of view. But historically it has been shown over and over that in certain situations, whole classes of people have been categorized as "less than equal." In a democracy this categorization can affect those in a minority, or those who are perceived as having less power.

In the case of the Adirondacks, there has long existed a class division as extreme and long-lived as any in the United States. Those who own large tracts of land in the Adirondacks, who are often visitors rather than year-round residents, and many of whom hold preservationist values, come from some of the wealthiest and most prominent families in the Northeast. Many of these families gained wealth from exploiting natural resources, often with little concern for environmental aftereffects. The split within this wealthy class over preservation and exploitation may extend to splits within the prominent families, and even within individuals who attempt to have their cake and eat it too. Some of these people earn money from environmentally destructive industries but would like to keep their vacation lands pristine. The people who live year round in the park have historically been the caretakers, servants, and providers of goods and services for the elite. A despicable recent metaphoric convention terms these lower-income residents "the little people." The inference is clear: class stratification entails inequalities.

The marginalization and recategorization of a group of people as a separate class which can be treated differently — in this case, as some locals argue, as second-class citizens — creates inequities. These people are patronized, presumed to be less intelligent than their wealthy neighbors and less capable of making land use decisions, and are not included in the process of decision making. Indian Lake Supervisor Richard Purdue tells this story: at one meeting where he and his wife were sitting in the audience, an environmentalist from outside the park turned to Purdue's wife and, assuming that she also was from outside the park, said, "These locals are really stupid." Purdue feels that this sums up the attitude of many preservationists toward the local population.

The common presumption, though rarely voiced this strongly in public, that local people are incapable of making intelligent, balanced decisions regarding land use results in an unethical and dangerous lack of equal

representation in the decision process. In addition, the different cultures and classes represent different worldviews of the human/nature relationship. Urban and suburban environmentalists, wealthy and otherwise, often see humans as completely distinct from the natural world, a cancer on the organism that should be removed from the wilderness as completely as possible. Rural people often see themselves as citizens of communities coexisting with the natural world; they live *with* the forest and feel that they have a right to be there and to use the resources that they need to survive. Both worldviews hold truths for their particular cultures; but when they meet head-on, the result has been confrontation and polarization.

Class in Democracy: Rights and Responsibilities

How real are the local people's perceptions of class inequalities? Class differences can be measured by, among other things, differences in incomes, attitudes, and levels of power in decision making. The following quotes and examples present a small sample of research on this subject.

Anthropologist Janet Fitchen writes in *Endangered Spaces, Enduring Places* (1991):

> Counties in the North Country have perennially been at or near the top of most indicators of economic distress in rural New York, often having the highest unemployment and poverty rates in the entire State. The region's desperate economic position was catapulted into national attention when Governor Mario Cuomo made a nominating speech in which he called attention to "the abject poor of Essex County in New York." . . . Undercount of unemployment is regarded as especially large in rural areas because they "contain disproportionately large numbers of both discouraged workers and involuntary part-time workers." And unemployment among young adults remains high. (Fitchen, 1991, pp. 54, 63)

The *Adirondack Daily Enterprise* reported in May 1990 that while New York State's overall jobless rate had dropped to 7.6 percent, Hamilton County (entirely within Park boundaries) had a jobless rate of 16 percent.

An Adirondack basket weaver, about forty years old, told me these details of her childhood:

"Daddy built guide boats for years, and we were caretakers' daughters. During the time I was growing up, caretakers' kids were not allowed to be

seen. You know, you stayed where the caretaker's quarters were. You *didn't* come down and mix with the people you were caretaking for, period. They brought their valets, their maids, and all their hired help with them from the city. It was unheard of for you to go down there. We didn't do a lot in the woods, and Daddy was gone all summer, from May until they left in September. We never went camping that I remember, overnight. I've only been in a guide boat twice in my lifetime. But I went hunting with him. I know what spruce gum is because he would pick it off the trees and chew it. When the nearest neighbors are miles and miles away, you get very self-reliant."

The Rockefellers and other wealthy families own estates of several thousand acres and summer houses, or "camps," many times larger than the year-round homes of most Adirondackers. The residents of the Adirondacks complain about acid rain. An upper-level executive of U.S. Steel, one of the companies responsible for sulphur dioxide emissions in the Midwest that drift to the Adirondacks and fall as acid rain, owns a seven-bedroom second home, complete with two-story boathouse, on Lake Placid; his house is decorated with loon carvings and pillows. He and his wife are active preservationists, hikers, and canoeists.

The Rockefellers made their money from the Standard Oil Company, one of the richest and most powerful holding companies in the world. The Standard Oil Company of New Jersey, which in 1972 changed its name to Exxon Corporation, has been responsible for some of the greatest environmental damage worldwide. And Exxon is just the largest of the old Standard Oil companies, which were forced to separate under antitrust laws; others are Mobil Corporation, Standard Oil of California, Standard Oil (Indiana), and the Atlantic Richfield Company. Oil interests have consistently pressured the government to allow drilling in environmentally sensitive areas, including the Arctic Wildlife Refuge. Exxon is also known to support the Wise Use movement. At the same time, the Rockefellers have been involved in most of the preservationist activity in the park, from the initial APA act to the Commission on the Adirondacks in the Twenty-First Century, as well as other preservation projects.

Another commissioner is Grumman CEO John Bierwirth. Grumman manufactures military and commercial aircraft, boats, canoes, truck and trailer bodies. Other commissioners work for large corporations which also impact the environment, including Pepsico and the Orange and Rockland Power Company. By some accounts, all the commissioners have second homes or retreats in the Adirondacks.

While several classes coexist in the Adirondacks, two constantly clash over the environment. One group has money, power, and influence; some of them are involved in prescribing regulations that they believe will preserve the Adirondacks, aesthetically and ecologically, as an appropriate place for what locals refer to as the "playground of the rich," as well as for many other, more ordinary New Yorkers and some tourists from out of state. Meanwhile, many who consider themselves Adirondackers, from home rule advocates to woodspeople to realtors, local government officials, and preservationists, scramble to make themselves heard, to voice their opinions, their concerns, and their own versions of aesthetics and conservation. These two vastly different classes seesaw in an uneasy relationship. Wall Street lawyer Peter Paine dresses like a logger when he comes to the Adirondacks. The caretakers and guides are both teachers and servants of the wealthy elites who spend their vacation in the Adirondacks. As Ralph Waldo Emerson wrote of his Adirondack visit:

> let men of cloth
> Bow to the stalwart churls in overalls:
> They are the doctors of the wilderness,
> And we the low-prized laymen.
>
> (Graham, 1978, p. 22)

Historian Philip G. Terrie writes, "Charles Dudley Warner expressed the elitist attitude with particular effectiveness; according to him, only 'those who are the most refined and most trained in intellectual fastidiousness,' only the 'most highly civilized' find 'the real enjoyment of camping and tramping in the woods.' These people, insisted Warner, were able to enjoy the spiritual features of the wilderness without abusing them, but the hoi polloi, whom Warner wished to keep out of the woods, were 'they who have strewn the Adirondacks with paper collars and tin cans' " (Terrie, 1985, p. 72).

What does it mean when people who have chosen to work for companies that have committed environmental damage on a scale of magnitude that outstrips anything that the whole Adirondack population could accomplish then participate in decisions to impose regulations on poorer people in order to preserve areas of recreational value and scenic beauty for their own enjoyment? Is it possible to separate ethically the spheres of responsiblity? Are the Rockefellers exonerated because they used some of the money they gained from oil refineries and supertankers, albeit in a different generation, to preserve the environment elsewhere, while regulating other people's choices down to where a footbridge may be placed or what color their houses should be painted? Is it possible to separate environmental good from political and socioeconomic reality?

The environmental movement has avoided this question for the most part so far, perhaps out of necessity. Although there are many preservationists who do not come from political, economic, or social elites, and who work hard through their jobs or during their spare time to fight for the environment, the environmental movement as a whole in the United States has lacked the kind of socioeconomic introspection and self-awareness that would permit the movement to reach out to other groups, including the disadvantaged, rural communities, and other marginalized people. Petra Kelly, one of the founders of the German Green Party, realized the importance of social factors years ago; many of the European environmental groups are more broadly based in the population, and address social as well as environmental concerns, well aware of their linkages.

In this country a growing movement of poor Hispanic and African-American communities is mobilizing against urban environmental hazards, as its members realize that a disproportionate number of hazardous waste sites are located in their communities (Bullard, 1990). The larger environmental special interest groups involved in the Adirondacks, such as the Sierra Club, the National Audubon Society, and the Wilderness Society, remain focused on areas of high recreational value to the middle and upper classes. The Sierra Club and a few others, however, have recently begun to look at issues of class and exclusivity. In an interesting reversal, some Earth First!ers have combined forces with loggers to halt log exports and destructive logging practices. But though many preservationists are not from wealthy elites, and devote their lives to protecting the natural environment, nevertheless, they may belong to and work for organizations that depend on the contributions of wealthy individuals, some of whom have gained their wealth at the expense of the environment.

Recognizing the responsibility of those who have gained wealth from polluting industries, and those who have enjoyed the amenities of urban living without attending to urban sprawl and pollution, must precede fair negotiation. Adirondackers must not bear all or most of the burden of providing pure air, pure water, and unsullied open space so that the rest of the state does not have to worry so much about the consequences of development elsewhere. Those who profit from polluting industries must recognize and address their responsibilities before they can blithely protect their vacation lands far from the smokestacks and environmental devastation that their work or investment produces. The biggest problem the Adirondacks faces in the twenty-first century may well be acid rain. In lower elevations, and in regions further south, we are facing an eastern forest health crisis due to ozone and other pollutants as well as exotic pests and diseases (Loucks, pers. comm.).

It seems appropriate to allow the preservationists a voice, as the state government has attempted to do. At the same time, the urban classes who have participated in the destruction of the environment to their socioeconomic benefit have to accept a more active role in rectifying the situation. Rural people, including Adirondackers living cheek by jowl with the very wealthy, have long recognized both the monetary advantages accrued by using the environment without long-term plans for maintaining ecological health, and the disjointed ethical system that allows the exploiters to regulate those who struggle to make a sustainable living from the land. Respect for the rights of an indigenous population to subsist on and enjoy their own property must be firmly in place before negotiation can succeed. And respect for the knowledge and decision-making ability of local people in land use issues has to precede any negotiation.

Inclusion, whether direct participation or democratic representation, is the central land use issue in the Adirondacks at this time, as well as in many other places. Knowledge cannot equal power for a group whose very existence is considered inferior. Until they are allowed to participate in the process of decision making on a fair representational basis, their knowledge will be ignored because they are ignored.

Fair representation, however, is a more complex issue than many locals recognize, and a deep-seated political problem as well. Environmentalists have a valid concern over local participation on regulatory boards such as the APA and planning commissions such as the Governor's Commission. Most regulatory boards that have failed in any sphere have done so because of infiltration by the very interests they were supposed to be regulating. According to the economist Milton Friedman: "every regulatory commission you can name, whatever may have been its origin, has sooner or later been taken over by the industry it is supposed to regulate and largely conducted in the interest of the industry" (Popper, 1981, p. 22). F. J. Popper, who quotes Friedman, adds: "Zoning and subdivision regulation have traditionally been the greatest single source of corruption in local government" (Popper, 1981, p. 52).

In the Adirondacks, many local government officials and prominent citizens involved in the land use issues at a political level are also developers.

While corruption has not been an issue, conflicts of interest have certainly arisen. Private groups negotiating for power in the process are also frequently involved in development. The Adirondack Fairness Coalition, which claims to represent the interests of Adirondackers, is run by real estate lawyers and others involved in development; its executive director is a realtor who is a recent arrival to the Adirondacks. Donald Gerdts of the Citizens' Council is also a small-time developer who moved to the Adirondacks not long ago. The question of who really represents the majority of local residents in land use decisions remains open. For example, some may have allowed Gertds to broker their position without accepting him as a representative of their values.

In the meantime, it appears that a majority are relatively silent politically and are virtually without a voice in land use decisions. Woodspeople, with their complex attitudes combining usufruct concerns, the need for long-term sustainability, and an appreciation and knowledge of forest ecology, as well as their cultural value for independence, may fall into this category. Local government officials, though elected by popular vote, are not usually elected just for their handling of land use issues. It is possible that a different mechanism to elicit fair representation other than using already elected local officials would raise fewer objections and represent local values for the forest more accurately.

Aesthetics, Ecology, and Zoning: Different Languages

Aesthetics and ecological health are two of the major values driving preservation efforts in the Park. These two values function very differently because of fundamental differences in their construction. Aesthetics is essentially an extrinsic value, applied by the observer according to his or her own subjective experience. Different groups involved in the Adirondack land use battles have different aesthetic preferences. Urban people, summer visitors and tourists, prefer the setting to include as few human structures as possible; anything such as camouflaging house color or screening vegetation which can help achieve this objective is to the good. The rural people who live in the Adirondacks do not like the looks of modern strip development either, but certain structures such as old houses and architecturally sophisticated boathouses are pleasing to many of them. In addition, among residents who know the territory, making houses less noticeable in wild areas may be a part of their own ethic, but many see it as a preference that should not be imposed by regulation.

The aesthetics of the first group may generally coincide with the preservation of ecological health, but not always. In some cases these aesthetic standards actually operate against ecological health. The generalized phrase "open space protection," which may be liberally interpreted as both an aesthetic and an ecological mandate, is actually a planning or zoning term that is not based on ecological standards. The Adirondack Council, the APA, and the Governor's Commission have all promoted farming as an acceptable and even preferred land use because it preserves open space in the form of vistas and bucolic landscapes; but farming has been labeled the number one source of surface water pollution in much of the United States.

Environmental aesthetics involves more than just appearances, however, and this is perhaps where the waters become murky. Wildlands, and specifically wilderness areas, are also "good to think." It has become important in this world of overgrown civilization and technology, as Adirondack resident Bill McKibben notes in *The End of Nature*, to be able to reflect on the wild earth in areas where nature is still in control, where something larger than human intellect, with its ethical shortcomings, has created the design — or lack of design. Nature is a mysteriously ordered chaos, in his view, from which our creativity and moral and mental health draw sustenance. So on an ethical level, there is more to this aesthetics than simply house color or plant screening or what kind of forest to maintain. It presents a philosophical and moral dilemma that the American people have to resolve before there is no longer a choice. Here the urbanites, who have seen more of the destruction that human beings can impose on the environment, have information about human relations with nature that rural citizens may not have. It is essential to share that information.

Valuing the health of the forest ecosystems also drives preservation in the Park. Ecological health is essentially an intrinsic value. While people can try to measure it, an ecosystem's successful reproduction of itself and its component species is the real measure of ecological health. Scientists monitor the health of different ecosystems at the Atmospheric Science Research Center, the Adirondack Ecological Center, and Paul Smith's College and Visitor Interpretive Center. But local people also monitor ecosystem health through anecdotal evidence that woodspeople and others involved in the forest collect and share with each other.

Indigenous knowledge and scientific knowledge may often agree about the state of an ecosystem, such as the devastation of the spruce forests on the upper slopes of the mountains. Yet policy makers and politicians probably do not pay enough attention to either of these sources of information, in part because the language they operate within is that of planning and zoning, not of ecology. Administrators must make decisions based on the generalized language of zoning, which mixes ecological and aesthetic concerns frequently without attempting to define them distinctly. Zoning thus creates generalized rules that often fit poorly with specific and localized ecological conditions.

For scientists such as Dick Sage, the results seem to miss the point. Worst of all, they may fail to protect the environment adequately. For local people, such decisions and regulations often appear arbitrary and undemocratic. When this happens, preserving their ownership and usufruct rights may become paramount.

Preservation interests, as incorporated by state agencies, reflect the agenda of a powerful elite and are not necessarily ecological but, rather, are often aesthetic and philosophical. Aesthetics are defined by zoning regulations that are designed to be oblique and open to interpretation, in phrases such as "open space character," "scenic vista," and "undue adverse impact." Typically, such language gives greatest powers of authority to the administrative boards that interpret them. Often, as on the APA, the majority of the board members are not scientists but lawyers and policy makers. Aesthetic concerns mingle with ecological considerations in the guise of inexact zoning language, adding up to a vague notion of wilderness and appropriate land uses that can be tested only in ad hoc cases. Ecological scientists may be as frequently ignored in the process as the local population, and scientific methods for determining ecologically sound regulations may take a low priority, as the example of the hamlet of Newcomb suggests.

The science of ecology would offer very different criteria for decision making, based on experiments and precise scientific language as the foundation for land use planning. Strictly scientific standards might be much more useful than aesthetics in protecting ecosystems. They would probably generate less hostility among local people. In addition, scientists could work with locals who are expert in indigenous knowledge of Adirondack ecosystems. As anthropologist Billie DeWalt notes, scientific knowledge and indigenous knowledge have their particular strengths and weaknesses. By working together and accepting their differences in approach, scientists and holders of indigenous knowledge could generate a more powerful understanding of local ecosystems than has yet been possible. But for this to happen, scientists must accept the validity of knowledge systems based on paradigms different from their own.

Yet divisions among scientists and interpretations of the data exist as surely as the current divisions. Pure objectivity remains difficult to attain; biases based on deeply held values are implicated in the very questions asked and methodologies chosen. In the end, when conflicts occur over values representing different worldviews, facts alone are not enough to solve the problems.

The language of community — the land community of Aldo Leopold, Native Americans, Wendell Berry, and others — could be installed as a unifying language of land management. This is the language of ecology, but it goes beyond natural science to an acceptance of human beings as part of the landscape. It recognizes that the boundaries of community are wide enough to encompass both the human and the natural community, so long as humans respect the functioning of the natural community. The language of community recognizes, in short, the possibility of a positive value for humans in the human/nature relationship.

Community and Conflict

Communities, human and wild, depend on a certain amount of conflict to generate the change that will permit a successful fit in the changing circumstances of the world. But how that conflict evolves can make all the difference between a successful fit and irreparable damage to the community and the relationships within it.

Each individual, each group, and each smaller community within the larger one brings to the conflict its own knowledge and its own worldview. Knowledge and worldview constitute the cornerstone of individuality and uniqueness, the sine qua non of identity, whether of an individual, a group, or a culture. Although factual information may be challenged, the construction of knowledge and the validity of a worldview taken as a whole must be accepted as legitimate before any conflict can be successfully resolved. Denial of the legitimacy of the knowledge, the worldview, and hence the claims and concerns of any party in a conflict results in that party's sense of the obliteration of its identity; at some level, whether that party is individual, group, culture, or community, it will find another way to assert its identity. If it does not, it faces extinguishment.

Labor relations specialist Sam Keltner lists several degrees of escalation of any conflict, ranging from the lowest-intensity levels of discussion and disagreement early in the process up through campaigning, litigation, and violent confrontations (Keltner, 1992). Why is it that the Adirondack land use conflict, like so many other conflicts, seems stuck at the last three levels? There seem to be at least three different answers.

The first concerns the process of the conflict. So far, although groups such as the Adirondack Planning Commission and others have attempted different kinds of negotiation, positional bargaining often characterizes the process on a parkwide level. Positional bargaining is negotiation that depends on successively taking — and then giving up — a sequence of positions. The clear dangers of positional bargaining include: (1) the negotiators tend to lock themselves into their positions; (2) as more attention is paid to positions, less attention is devoted to meeting the underlying concerns of the parties; (3) arguing over positions becomes a contest of will, endangering ongoing relationships; and (4) when there are many parties, positional bargaining becomes more problematic, leading to the formation of coalitions whose members may not really agree with one another (Fisher and Ury, 1991).

In the Adirondacks, positional bargaining over land use issues involves

Photo 16. James Latour, sawmill owner, Vermontville. Photo author

many different parties and interest groups, and often breaks down, resulting in standoffs, frozen positions, intensified campaigning, litigation, violent confrontations, and power struggles. Even when positional bargaining does seem to work, it often results in the fragmentation of whole systems: the ecology of the Adirondacks, and the human communities of the Adirondacks, are interdependent with the wild ecosystems. If some parts of a landscape or some community interests are traded away for other interests, and bargains are negotiated on an ad hoc, piecemeal basis, the logical and ecological integrity of the Adirondacks and its human communities is at risk.

Roger Fisher and William Ury of the Harvard Negotiation Project stress an alternative to positional bargaining called principled negotiation, or negotiation on the merits, which offers a way to produce a wise agreement that is efficient and does not damage the relationship between the parties. Principled negotiation is based on four basic points: (1) separating the people from the problem; (2) focusing on interests, not positions; (3) generating a variety of options; and (4) insisting that the result be based on some objective standard (Fisher and Ury, 1991, p. 13).

Photo 17. Sawmill, Vermontville. Photo author

But to reach a communication level where principled negotiating is possible means de-escalating the conflict to the point at which people can hear one another's voices — *all* the voices. And therein lies the second answer to the problem. The Adirondack land use conflict, like many others, involves many voices, some louder than others. But so long as some parties feel that their voices are not being listened to, or that the legitimacy of their worldview is being denied, or sense that the other parties characterize them as "ignorant," the conflict process will suffer breakdown or escalation. Parties who feel that their voices are being ignored may try violent tactics for reestablishing their identities within the process which only escalate the conflict. Other parties retaliate. The end result may be extreme polarization of positions even though the *interests* of the different parties may have much in common, as is often true in the Adirondacks. All the voices have to be heard and included before successful long-term negotiation can begin.

The third answer involves power, class, and culture, or the relative positions of the parties before the conflict began. Within the class-culture dynamic different values create underlying misunderstandings and confusion, which often intensify the conflict. To the extent that these differences remain unrecognized or suppressed, the conflict becomes charged with emotion as people interpret certain actions as threats to their values and come to fear that they have much to lose.

Fisher and Ury and other negotiators urge parties to focus on interests rather than positions and suggest that behind opposed positions lie shared and compatible interests as well as conflicting ones. But when power differentials exist, often the interests of the different sides have different levels of immediacy. For instance, Fisher and Ury list five basic human needs: security, economic well-being, a sense of belonging, recognition, and control over one's life (Fisher and Ury, 1991, p. 50). Many home rule advocates feel that most or all of these basic needs are threatened in some way by increased regulation in the park. Conversely, most of the preservationists' interests are of a wider, less personal kind: the health and well-being of the natural environment, long-term biological diversity, recreation, aesthetic integrity, and philosophical satisfaction. Because they feel that their basic needs are threatened, many Adirondackers believe that their best alternative to a negotiated agreement may be to move out of the Park, a drastic and undesirable option which leaves them in a vulnerable position in any negotiation. This is why stakeholder analysis and management fails to be equitable.

With less money to support their positions and interests, less access to political information systems, and less voting power as a political minority, Adirondackers, and citizens in rural areas in general, frequently have to fight hard to make themselves heard. Corporations looking for grassroots groups to support their own claims may capitalize on the feelings of personal and community vulnerability by appearing to offer a way to represent some of the concerns of rural people.

Different values for land use — for the forests as a "crop," a natural resource to be harvested sustainably, or a "campground" for the recreation of sportspeople, or a "cathedral" for the appreciation and wonder of small numbers of dedicated wilderness travelers — may stem from such different worldviews that real mutual understanding is precluded. In this case, as with different cultures when appreciation of one another's value systems is difficult, I would suggest a modification of discovering interests. Fisher and Ury suggest asking the question "Why?" in order to get behind stated positions (Fisher and Ury, 1991, p. 45). But when cultural and value differences run deep, the answer to that question may not make sense to the opposing party or parties. In this case it is important to *assume* a valid reason for the other's position, and then try to determine the specifics of what the position requires — in other words, the underlying practical interests.

Once it is accepted that the other party has a legitimate worldview that generates valid reasons for doing certain things or holding certain beliefs, whether or not the parties understand each other's views and the values, beliefs, and attitudes they generate, then the important questions shift to what, where, when, and how. Interests are still considered, but at a practical level, rather than at a level at which they can be discounted as differing too much from the questioner's own worldview. When any of the parties is a perceived minority, acceptance of the legitimacy of different worldviews is equally important in order for each party to be a positive element in a process leading to change.

At the same time, when value differences run so deep and worldviews differ so radically, the importance of using objective criteria in negotiation becomes even more critical. Otherwise, especially in decisions that are determined by power or force of will, one party will experience the decision as arbitrary and unpredictable. Hence the reactions of many Adirondackers to APA decisions based on vague and subjective aesthetic criteria. If aesthetic criteria have been predetermined without the participation of those affected, the situation becomes even worse. Now the subjective determinations of the aesthetic preferences of a coalition of one set of worldviews has been imposed on those with different worldviews and very different aesthetic preferences. Such decisions will be experienced as arbitrary, unpredictable, and unfair. Unless some kind of consensus can be reached on aesthetic criteria, the use of ecological criteria, as determined by scientists and local people with indigenous knowledge, seems a much clearer route to take. These ecological criteria should then be measured by field scientists and local indigenous knowledge holders working together as balanced teams.

The primary prerequisite for successful negotiation over land use management in the Adirondacks is representational local participation at the decision-making level, based on an ethic of respect for other citizens. It is equally important when the locals are perceived to be in a minority. This respect is not merely an attitude, but should be based on: (1) an appreciation of the indigenous Adirondacker's knowledge of the Adirondacks; (2) an appreciation of the ability of the local population to make informed decisions regarding land use; (3) an appreciation of the need for fairness in both responsibilities and privileges; (4) an appreciation of the rights of Adirondackers to the use and enjoyment of their own land, and the importance of these rights as a basis for the foundation of democratic principles; and (5) an appreciation of the value of different worldviews in constructing ideas of the human/nature relationship and the role of wilderness in it.

Alternative Options

Inventing options for mutual gain is also important. Many other land use planning alternatives have been applied in other parts of the United States and in other parts of the world. The Adirondack Park Agency, the Adirondack Council, and other groups have tried hard to make the Adirondacks a blueprint for the rest of the world. In taking this approach, however, these organizations may not have looked as hard as they might at other options in land use which could offer partial blueprints for the Adirondacks.

One of the major problems the Adirondacks faces in the next eight to ten years is the dilemma of the forest industry. Forest industry has traditionally supported a large number of Adirondackers and their families through logging and mill work; it also ensures open space on lands managed for timber production. Preservationists involved in Park planning have insisted that they support the forest industry and controlled logging; yet they have failed to address adequately the forest industry's primary concern — the lack of assurance that timberlands will remain available in the future. For these people "forever wild" has outlived its usefulness as a category for new land acquisitions by the state.

One alternative might be "timber reserves," or "forever working," as it is called by the timber companies. All new acquisitions on larger tracts suitable for timber management could be put into a state "forever working" timber reserve, on which stumpage could be sold for a fair market price. The monies would then go to the state to support management. Ceilings on percentages of reserves to be cut each decade could be set in advance, and fragile or vulnerable areas could be protected from cutting. Assurances would have to be made that endangered species considerations would not force closure of these lands to timber management (the "spotted owl" problem). Improvements in forest practices could be achieved through cooperation with Paul Smith's College and the Adirondack Ecological Center in Newcomb. International Paper approximated this idea, donating twenty thousand acres of valuable recreation land to the state while retaining timber rights.

Forest management is beginning to follow the Forest Service's commitment to ecosystem management in logging practices. But some preservationists and others see in this approach merely an excuse to cut more old growth. University of Washington forest ecologist Jerry Franklin, who is one of the leading spokespeople for "new forestry" in the West, says that scientists have learned that "we don't know how to create an old-growth ecosystem" once it is gone. "We can create complex forests . . . but we really can't create old-growth forests because there are a lot of things we don't know" (*Oregonian*, March 30, 1993, p. B4).

Yet in the Adirondacks, most of the forests were cut over in the last hundred years. Patches of true old growth are few and far between. Acquisition of the remaining private stands could be automatically granted "forever wild" status; but to classify second growth forest at the expense of the forest industry will increase hostility, escalate tensions, and in the end probably do more harm than good to the cause of ecological preservation.

One way to increase the benefits of timber work and create jobs is through value-added products. These increase the economic value of the product to the community by adding work (value) to the raw product before selling it outside the community. Thus, furniture is a value-added product; raw lumber is not. The Yellowwood consultancy strongly suggested this option to the APA in a 1990 report. Local people in hamlets such as Newcomb and Tupper Lake show high levels of interest in bringing in industries that would create products of this kind.

At the 1993 Forest Summit in the Pacific Northwest, where communities are facing many similar conflicts, value-added products made sense to many, from President Clinton to local community representatives to preservationists. Value-added products seem to provide a possible solution in which all sides gain. In addition, some potential products such as furniture and boats already have a base of expertise among the local population.

Extractive reserves, as they are used in the Amazon rain forest and elsewhere, provide an alternative for land classified as "wild forest," a classification that satisfies mainly recreational goals. Wild forest classification as it is currently applied ignores the usufruct rights of a population that has long met some of its economic needs through harvesting special forest products, as well as by hunting, trapping, and fishing. In addition, the production and use of these special forest products are part of what makes Adirondack cultures uniquely connected to their wild environment. Removing usufruct rights carries the same connotations of cultural dissolution here as it does in Third World countries, or among Native American populations, though the parallel is not widely recognized.

Many wild forest areas could be reclassified as "extractive reserves." Any new land acquired, especially smaller tracts or those near hamlets, could also be considered for extractive reserve status. These reserves would provide an opportunity for local people to meet some of their subsistence needs as well as develop home industries based on special forest products. A forest manager could establish and monitor a permit system similar to those available on Forest Service lands in the Smokies and parts of Oregon. A partial list of possible extracts includes firewood; maple sap; balsam boughs; herbs, medicines, and greens; seeds; spruce gum; cedar oil; mushrooms and fungi; and greenery for the floral industry. Access to the extractive reserve system could apply solely to full-time residents of twenty years or more, with priority given according to years of full-time residence and historic ties to the area. Permit fees should be kept to a minimum, with no permit fees charged to Mohawks, and the fees could be used to support management of the reserves.

Local ecological, economic, political, and cultural conditions have to be incorporated into decision making about extractive reserves. It is crucial to consider the density and seasonal availability of products, as well as product and ecosystem sustainability. Social infrastructure, such as middlemen and product demand, also determine the success of using extractive reserves.

While the extractive reserve system would allow harvesting from the forest, it would also preserve the basic integrity of the forest ecology while maintaining the integrity of the social system by permitting people to practice traditional subsistence and supplemental economies culturally tied to the bioregion.

Several regions, including the Pacific Northwest, northern New England, greater Yellowstone, and other areas, are simultaneously creating stakeholder partnerships or councils with representation from the widest range of stakeholder groups. The Northern Forest Lands Council was created in 1990 to seek ways to maintain the traditional patterns of land ownership and use of the northern forest in Maine, New Hampshire, New York, and Vermont. The council released its final report in September 1994 and formally disbanded. Its recommendations include greater participation of local people in the decision-making process and increased attention to economic factors in wildland conservation, including extraction where feasible and ecologically sustainable. As they disbanded, the governors appointed four people from each state to "Forest Roundtables" to convene regularly to work on forest issues. The Roundtable members were chosen to represent the broad spectrum of stakeholders in the northern forestlands, including government interests, industry, rural communities, and environmental groups.

At the same time, in the Pacific Northwest a similar need to achieve equality in decison making spawned the idea of Province Councils — stakeholder groups for each bioregion which would assist federal land managers with decisions about land management. Yet the membership of both of these groups, the Roundtables and the Province Councils, is determined by higher government officials. This represents a fundamental misunderstanding about grassroots communication and networking and presents a difficult task for managers. Almost inevitably, shadow groups with locally chosen representatives will spring up, as has happened in the Adirondacks with the creation of the Adirondack Association of Towns and Villages to counter the embattled Adirondack Park Agency, whose five "local" representatives are still selected by the governor.

Man and the Biosphere programs could look at supporting locally based grassroots stakeholder groups and at alternatives to "forever wild" and "wilderness" classifications in inhabited regions. The Lake Champlain–Adirondack area, as the fourth largest biosphere reserve in the United States and the most populated in the world, could provide the programs a chance to work with local governments to discover what sorts of options are best for indigenous populations in biosphere reserves, and to develop a mechanism to identify which land classifications best match local economic and ecological needs.

Indigenous knowledge and local participation in setting objectives and in research and decision making can ensure the usefulness of this approach. Although organizations such as Highlander in Tennessee in the southern Appalachian region have helped to organize local people facing industrial or environmental threats to their well-being, I believe that in the Adirondacks it may be more effective to make use of existing organizations, such as the sportspeople's organizations and their networks, the guide association, ANCA, and craft cooperatives to assist in the self-education and organization of woodspeople. These groups should have opportunities to work closely with scientists who respect their knowledge. In this way, woodspeople could help to integrate local indigenous knowledge and regional ecological perspectives with scientific findings.

❧ By recognizing the political history of the Adirondacks and other mountainous areas as natural resource colonies, it is possible to look to other areas which have been subject to colonialism, neocolonialism, or tourist colonialism to see their solutions.

Participatory rural appraisal offers a methodologically consistent approach to the inclusion of local people in research, agenda setting, and ultimately the development of plans for the communities' own management of their natural resources. An alternative to conventional top-down approaches, participatory rural appraisal "is based on village experiences where communities are working effectively to manage natural resources. ... The methodology assumes that popular participation is a fundamental ingredient in project planning; that locally maintained technologies as well as sustainable economic, political, and ecological systems are fundamental" (National Environment Secretariat, et al., 1991, p. 2).

Yet some people believe that this approach does not go far enough in empowering local communities to manage their natural resources and environment sustainably, since ultimately this process is initiated by scientists and regulatory agencies. Networks *among* pressured rural communities may offer the best alternative of all, as these communities share information about successful strategies and gain empowerment through a larger voice. Such networks are already in existence (Gupta, 1996); the planning and regulatory agencies and scientists should work to encourage rather than stifle this growing movement; although ultimately the growth of this grass-

roots movement will proceed independently of government initiatives, a   *277*
groundfire of the healthiest kind.

✤ If the recommendations of the commission report are passed in substantial form, special status and privileges and just compensation should be
accorded to the indigenous population in recognition of the fair distribution
of responsibilities and rights and substantial sacrifices in freedom, income,
and buying potential entailed by living within the boundaries of the Park.
This compensation would also underline the responsibilities of those outside
the Park to address their own communities' environmental problems,

Photo 18. Genevieve
Sutter, a local quilter,
creating images of the
forest, Tupper Lake.
Photo D. Kuklok

278   whether urban overgrowth, pollution, overconsumption, or transportation, and the demands for raw products including lumber and farm produce that are placed on these rural regions. Local challenges based on takings cases will continue to crop up here and elsewhere if these issues are not sufficiently addressed.

The ideas I have presented, generated from the suggestions of local people in interviews as well as from the solutions of local people in similar situations in other parts of the world, are based on the notion of community, but neither a human community nor a wild community. Instead, they are based on the idea that sustains woodspeople's lives and cultures, the idea that people can live *with* the forest, without the destruction or loss of integrity of either.

It is crucial that the woodspeople themselves make their voices heard above the battle, in the desolate pauses between confrontations, because in the end they are a part of the Adirondack land community. Because of their membership in this community and their role as the bearers of indigenous knowledge of the land, they are among the best potential mediators of the conflict — people who value the land and their deep connections to it.

Epilogue: Fire and Water

In 1995 a conservative assemblyman who votes consistently against environmental legislation created a plan to rid New York of acid rain pollution. His bill would establish stricter new acid rain standards and amend the Federal Clean Air Act to force upwind polluters into compliance (*Adirondack Daily Enterprise*, December 11, 1995). It would help many Adirondack lakes that once drew fishermen but now are crystal clear and devoid of most aquatic life. Environmentalists applauded the bill; it marked a moment of truce, a bridge between the different stakeholders, as each side recognized the dangers of acid rain, identified the industries causing the damage, and resolved to act together.

In that same year a windstorm damaged approximately 1 million acres of forested land in the park. But the Department of Environmental Conservation, under the constraints of the "forever wild" clause, debated for months whether to salvage some of the downed timber. The stumpage value of the state timber alone was estimated at between $120 million and $150 million. This money would have been generated in some of the poorest counties in New York State. But the state delayed making the decision for months. Meanwhile, the village of Tupper Lake was facing the prospect of one of its largest employers, Tupper Lake Hardwood, temporarily closing because of a shortage of logs. Many local people deplored the lack of a salvage plan for state lands and the additional waiting periods imposed by the APA for people to get permits to salvage wood on private lands. The logs were rotting.

Fire danger was another issue. After the 1950 blowdown, the attorney general of New York stated that timber could be salvaged on Forest Preserve land in the case of an emergency. Now, state officials were claiming that there was minimal forest fire danger. Local people contended that there was a danger; with forty to sixty tons of fuel on the ground per acre, they feared that fires could sweep out of control across the boundaries between public and private lands. Traditionally, the state and counties shared ex-

280   penses and responsibilities for fighting fires in the area. Because they perceived the state to be acting irresponsibly, by 1997 the county legislators
decided that they would stop paying money into the joint firefighting funds.
The specter of flames hangs in the space between the different groups —
preservationists, conservationists, Wise Use activists, developers, woodspeople, and others. The smoke that arises from these flames, if they come,
will be the smoke of battle.

Appendix

National and International
Examples of Regional
Land Use Planning

A CROSS NORTH AMERICA AND EVEN INTER-
nationally, the battles now are not just over whether to preserve
additional wildlands in parks, but over how to maintain wildlands
that have people living near them, who depend on these lands as a resource
base. The great wilderness parks such as Yellowstone and Yosemite are
preserves without people, though they are heavily affected by tourists. The
debate has moved to national and state forests and the rural lands scattered
among them, the lands that surround and buffer wilderness areas and connect one wild area to another, permitting the migration of wild species and
preventing genetic bottlenecks that could destroy them. But these are also
working lands that both permit the survival of rural Americans dependent
on the natural resource base and support the consumerist lifestyles of most
urban Americans.

The labels of ownership, public or private, mask the deeper issue of
who has the right to use the resources on these lands, or "usufruct." As
management of public lands becomes more restrictive and regulation of
private lands increases, rural people, including Native Americans, perceive
a loss of access to natural resources, whether on public or private land,

282 which in turn threatens their livelihoods and subsistence based on these resources. And in a country where democratic rights originated in land ownership and land use rights, for many rural people the problem goes deeper even than access to natural resources: it poses a threat to the fundamental principles of democracy.

In these areas there are many possibilities for creative management. Some reflect existing strategies; others struggle to pass various legislative and political barriers; still others are examples and ideas from the international sphere. These strategies offer hope; yet managers, interest groups, politicians, and local people must remain open-minded enough to consider the full range of possibilities, as well as insisting on the concurrent reclaiming of more damaged areas.

There is a growing realization among ecologists, wildland managers, and citizens of urban and rural communities that these remaining semi-populated wild areas should be managed based on watersheds, which carry water, soil, nutrients, and toxins across political and ownership boundaries. Watershed management and community management of natural resources offer possibilities in all these areas for avoiding onerous regulations on small landowners and small communities while conserving natural landscapes for many generations. Other possibilities include conservation easements on large private holdings, debated in the 1996 New York State legislature; extractive reserves on public holdings, such as those established in the Amazon rainforest; development of locally controlled forms of tourism that benefit communities directly, such as the CAMPFIRE program in Zimbabwe, which returns hunting profits to local communities; better development of value-added products where value is added to raw materials locally; and practical experimental areas based on equal interactions between recognized holders of local and indigenous knowledge in specific areas and field scientists working in those areas. A few examples from other areas facing problems similar to the Adirondacks follow here.

The Pacific Northwest

The Clinton administration's plan for managing the forests west of the Cascades affects forests that represent to different people giant moss-covered old growth that supports diverse species, including the endangered northern spotted owl and the marbled murrelet, and Douglas fir which provides the most productive timber stands in the United States, as well as homes for many farmers and ranchers. These temperate rainforests are among the richest timber producing lands in the world. Seventy percent of the private lands in the Oregon Coast Range is owned by ten large land-owners, most of them timber companies (Willer, 1995). In a diverse man-agement strategy that shifts management from the stand level to watersheds, scientists drew lines around riparian zones, late successional reserves (old growth) and adaptive management areas where scientists could experiment and implement new strategies immediately. In addition, social scientists involved in creating the plan suggested the establishment of councils, made up of stakeholders representing timber industry, preserva-tionists, natural resource dependent communities, Native Americans, and other interests. This idea derived from a stakeholder group, the Applegate Partnership, that developed at the grassroots level in southern Oregon.

Yet the administration missed a key lesson from the Adirondacks: the importance of involving local stakeholders in the process from the begin-ning. Grassroots movements cannot be legislated from the top or after the fact. In both the Adirondacks and the Pacific Northwest, participation of local stakeholders was left until the end of the planning process and rele-gated to public hearings. In Salem, Oregon, the Assistant Secretary of the Interior listened to public commentary in two hearings on the plan for the Pacific Northwest forests. He left the room for forty-five minutes while comments were being offered and at another point made several phone calls, facing away from the audience. The room was only one quarter full —a silent indication of the reputation for meaninglessness that public hear-ings have acquired. "They listen to our comments and then do exactly what they were going to do anyway," one landowner commented. Many others echoed his sentiments.

In 1995 a lawsuit (brought by timber and environmental interests to-gether) based on the Federal Advisory Committee Act threatened the ability of the grassroots coalitions of diverse stakeholders to influence Forest Ser-vice and Bureau of Land Management decision-making, unless the coali-tions allowed their membership to be determined by the federal government. The Forest Service was to choose preferred interest group representatives out of a pool of volunteer candidates, and then allow Wash-ington, D.C. staff to make the final decisions on which interest groups were to be represented, and which candidates were to participate in "Province Advisory Councils." The meaning of representation is keenly threatened when "representatives" are chosen from the top rather than by the commu-nities they claim to represent. When a citizen observer of the Siuslaw Province Advisory Council suggested a subcommittee be formed to address participation issues, the Forest Service staff readily agreed and took the lead in organizing it. But the staff did not convene any meetings of the subcommittee until the summer of 1997, two years later, when it was reconstructed as a media subcommittee. At the same time, the Forest Service began logging in my own rural community which had worked closely with their staff two years earlier. Without warning, we woke to the sounds of log trucks driving through private land on easements granted decades earlier, and to the sound of saws cutting the forest on the ridges above us. This lack of attention to local participation can only weaken the relationship of the Forest Service with rural communities.

Watershed Councils organized by volunteer local citizens and facilitators paid by the state seem to work better. These councils address both ecological and economic issues in the communities located in these watersheds, through meetings and practical projects. State support enables projects such as "Jobs in the Woods" and "Hire the Fisher" which offer retraining in ecosystem reparation projects. While this retraining at best offers shaky hope for future jobs for former loggers and fishers, it has been locally conceived and implemented, and benefits local watersheds and their communities.

Appalachia

Diverse groups in Appalachia are coming together to fight for both their environment and the heritage and survival of the communities dependent upon it. Timber workers, small farming communities, Cherokees, mining townspeople, and back-to-the-landers are all stakeholders, along with the tourists who come to see the dogwoods in the spring and the pink haze of rhododendrons on the mountaintops. The Great Smoky Mountains National Park includes the highest peaks. Cherokee National Forest covers tens of thousands of acres of adjacent forest land. There, too, local people have been shut out of some traditional uses of wild forest; when the creation of the National Forest forced some people from their homes, they left the family cemeteries. Local tradition has long celebrated the annual Decoration Day when family members gather at the cemeteries. Recent road closures in the National Forest have severely limited access to these areas, particularly for the elderly, while improving the aesthetics of these parts for tourists.

At the same time paper mills pollute the rivers, slag heaps from the most productive coal mines in the United States still smoke in places, and pollution from industrial and urban centers blows over the mountains on the wind. Now Appalachian woodsmen and some scientists believe that the most biologically diverse forest in North America is dying. Working together, Appalachian woodsmen relying on their indigenous knowledge of the area and scientists relying on their understanding of ecology unravel the patterns of change they are witnessing. Biologist Orie Loucks of the zoology department at Miami University in Ohio has found a proliferation of standing tree skeletons of more than twenty species. He believes that ozone pollution and excess nitrogen deposition from the air are responsible, as well as exotic pests and diseases. He has found that the annual mortality rate for forest tree species has doubled and then tripled in the past few years. Multiplied out, the eastern forests could be facing 50 percent mortality in the next century (Loucks, pers. comm., 1997). Many of the human communities in the area go back generations; some families have been there for hundreds of years. They have noted the changes in the landscape. Their knowledge of the area is unique, dense, specific. So is their dependence on the land. Local cultures intertwined with the forest ecosystems on which they depend are at stake. Orie Loucks has worked with anthropologists and local people to get local representation on scientific boards and regional panels. He listens to local people and recruits them as guides and co-researchers in the field. Yet Orie Loucks's work with local people is an exception to decision-making processes that leave local participation to the last.

The New Jersey Pinelands

In one of the regional land use planning organizations structurally most similar to the Adirondack Park Agency, the New Jersey Pinelands Commission works to manage the Pinelands National Reserve created in 1979. The Preservation Area includes 368,000 acres of semi-wilderness. The Protection Area, whose boundaries are also defined by New Jersey's Pinelands Protection Act, includes 565,000 acres that surround the Preservation Area, and is divided into six different management areas. This region, also a biosphere reserve, is thus managed in zoning patterns similar to those of the Adirondack Park. The Pinelands Commission includes six state representatives, six local elected officials, and one federal official, in an attempt to balance local, regional, and national interests. It seems more evenly balanced than the Adirondack Park Commission, yet local people often complain about being left out of the decision-making process (Collins and Russell, 1988).

The Northern Forest Lands

The Northern Forest Lands cover areas in four states: New York, Maine, New Hampshire and Vermont, and include all of the Adirondack Park. Efforts to plan for the future of this area began with the Northern Forest Lands Study in 1988, and the Governors' Task Force on Northern Forest Lands. The Northern Forest Lands Council, appointed by the governors, attempted to work both with local stakeholders who are well respected in their communities and with the timber industries that dominate private land ownership in the region. New York members included Newcomb Councilwoman and citizen activist Barbara Sweet, Robert Stegeman of the Empire State Forest Products Association and International Paper Company, legal counsel for the Adirondack Mountain Club Neil Woodworth, and Robert Bendick, the Deputy Commissioner of Natural Resources for the Department of Environmental Conservation. The Council's report, which breaks recommendations into four categories, fostering stewardship of private land, protecting exceptional resources, strengthening economies of rural communities, and promoting more informed decisions, indicates broader-based interests than the more preservationist Governor's Commission on the Adirondacks in the Twenty-First Century. In a more practical and informed approach, the Northern Forest Lands Council spent much time on incentives for private landowners and reviewing federal and state tax policies, sustainable forest management, government regulations, and community development. Their additional focus on promoting more informed decisions and continued dialogue among the four states is an innovative approach that could be mirrored in regions facing similar problems. The efforts of the Northern Forest Lands Council, though widely contested — perhaps because of past experiences as much as what the Council itself did or did not do — have moved the discussion beyond the prevailing stalemate of preservationists versus industry and development.

The International Level

Almost everywhere that wildlands intermingle with human communities, grassroots movements involving a wide range of stakeholders are springing up. In the Greater Yellowstone Ecosystem, as scientists and environmentalists call it, ranchers alternately battle and work with environmentalists over forest management, the reintroduction of wolves, and the loosening of fire controls after the great fires of 1988. In British Columbia, whole communities are fighting the clear-cutting of their forests by international timber companies. In eastern Canada, the Cree Indians and environmentalists battled for new public involvement processes to prevent a huge hydroelectric dam planned for James Bay, which would have affected the traditional hunting and fishing grounds of the Cree.

The World Wildlife Fund, realizing the interdependence of healthy wildlife populations and the surrounding human communities, has developed a program called "Integrated Conservation and Development" which is designed to promote both direct and indirect benefits to local communities combined with conservation of local wildlife and their habitats. This approach would make sense in much of rural United States, where even hunting licenses and tags are becoming prohibitively expensive for rural people, who may suffer economically from reduced development regionally. Unfortunately, functionally integrated programs such as this seem to be reserved for other people in other countries.

If we look to the future, two international examples that I have some personal experience with come to mind. The first, the Bafing Faunal Reserve in Mali, West Africa, where I lived for nearly four years, represents a kind of barely managed Adirondack region of West Africa, complete with the same constellation of resource dependent hamlets, skilled woodspeople, hill country, and poachers of the resources from outside the region. Yet there, a Malian-born Frenchman who spoke the local dialect discovered through months of interviewing and living in the local hamlets, that the local people really preferred greater management of the area, if it would help control outside poaching, which in several cases was threatening wildlife populations, including elands and chimpanzees. Local leaders had in place a sophisticated system for monitoring and controlling their own harvest of the wildlife, which the external poaching was disrupting. Unfortunately, the World Bank did not fund a continuation of the project, and it has continued only under national support for two foresters in one of the poorest countries of the world, whose efforts in this direction must be considered heroic given the pressing demands on national funds (Pavy, 1993).

Finally, in the sublimely beautiful island country of São Tomé y Principe, off the coast of West Africa, where pure sand beaches and pristine cloud rainforest combine with endemic bird species in one of the best potential ecotourism sites in the world, I witnessed the beginning of either the best or the worst of all possible situations for local people. Under immense pressure from the International Monetary Fund and the World Bank, this small country with the same population as the Adirondacks had begun to privatize government holdings in 1994 when I worked there briefly as a consultant. Poor advice from specialists from these international giants had resulted in a privatization plan that encouraged wholesale clear-cutting of the steep slopes and discouraged reforestation because land tenure was only granted for five years initially. At the same time, the United States Agency for International Development was encouraging the production of coffee and cacao for export on the best agricultural lands, rather than promoting food self-sufficiency (at less than 50 percent in this tropical Eden in 1994). The European Economic Community's ecological education and management branch was designing an ecotourism reserve without the benefit of much local input, to have a cloud forest high peak preserve and several buffer zones where extractive uses were not permitted, although recreation would be. Italian, Portuguese, and French restaurant and resort owners were moving in quickly. At that critical juncture, there was a window of time in which São Toméans could possibly wrest control of their future from the international army descending on it. It was possible to become food self-sufficient if they so desired, and to have a locally-based ecotourism operation, if they wished, where São Toméans could own the businesses, instead of working as poorly paid waiters and waitresses, maids and bellhops. Yet international and national literature on the subject of conservation and development still fails to address the issue of who has control and who benefits. The power dynamic is treated almost as if it didn't exist. Even economist Thomas Michael Power, whose 1996 book, *Lost Landscapes and Failed Economies*, has been gathered up by crusading environmentalists as demonstration that preservation and ecotourism boosts local communities, cannot say whether the populations of these communities are made up of the same people who have lived there for generations, or newcomers from urban areas who have displaced fragmented and endangered communities of place. The situation is similar to the one we have examined at length in this book: along the main street of Lake Placid, most of the businesses are owned by people who have lived in the Adirondacks for less than fifteen years, and some who have lived there less than five.

Bibliography

Abbey, E. 1975. *The Monkey Wrench Gang.* New York: Avon Books.

Adirondack Park Agency. 1982. Adirondack Park Agency Rules and Regulations. Raybrook, N.Y.: APA.

———. 1985. *Adirondack Goals Program: Final Report on the Community Workshops: A Summary of Public Comment and Discussion.* Raybrook, N.Y.: APA.

Adirondack Park Agency Act as amended to July 15, 1981. Executive Law, Article 27.

Adirondack Park Agency Staff. 1983. *Economic Development Needs of the Adirondack Park.* Staff draft. Raybrook, N.Y.: Adirondack Park Agency.

Anderson, L., ed. 1991. *Sisters of the Earth: Women's Prose and Poetry about Nature.* New York: Random House.

Awa, N. E. 1989. "Participation and Indigenous Knowledge in Rural Development." *Knowledge: Creation, Diffusion, Utilization* 10 (4):304–316.

———. 1992. "The Indigenous Farmer and the Scientific Researcher: Issues in Participatory Research in Africa." Paper presented to the Working Group Session on Participatory Communication Research of the International Association of Mass Communication Research, Sao Paulo, Brazil.

Barrett, J. W. 1980. "The Northeastern Region." In *Regional Silviculture of the United States.* J. W. Barrett, ed. New York: John Wiley and Sons.

290 Batteau, A., ed. 1983. *Appalachia and America: Autonomy and Regional Dependence.* Lexington: University Press of Kentucky.

Beaver, P. D. 1986. *Rural Community in the Appalachian South.* Lexington: University Press of Kentucky.

Belanger, D. O. 1988. *Managing American Wildlife: A History of the International Association of Fish and Wildlife Agencies.* Amherst: University of Massachusetts Press.

Bennett, B. C. 1992. "Plants and People of the Amazonian Rainforests: The Role of Ethnobotany in Sustainable Development." *BioScience* 42 (8):599–607.

Berlin, B., D. R. Breedlove, and P. H. Raven. 1974. *Principals of Tzeltal Plant Classification: An Introduction to the Botanical Ethnography of a Mayan-Speaking People of Highland Chiapas.* New York: Academic Press.

Berry, W. 1993. *Sex, Economy, Freedom, and Community.* New York: Pantheon Books.

Bethke, R. D. 1981. *Adirondack Voices: Woodsmen and Woodslore.* Chicago: University of Illinois Press.

Bird, B. K. 1952. *Caulked Shoes: Life in Adirondack Lumber Camps.* Prospect, N.Y.: Prospect Books.

Blackburn, J. W., and W. M. Bruce, eds. 1995. *Mediating Environmental Conflicts: Theory and Practice.* Westport, Conn.: Quorum Books.

Blumer, H. 1969. *Symbolic Interactionism.* Englewood Cliffs, N.J.: Prentice-Hall.

Boag, P. G. 1992. *Environment and Experience: Settlement Culture in Nineteenth-Century Oregon.* Berkeley: University of California Press.

Boster, J., B. Berlin, and J. O'Neill. 1986. "The Correspondance of Jivaroan to Scientific Ornithology." *American Anthropologist* 88: 569–583.

Brody, H. 1981. *Maps and Dreams.* New York: Pantheon Books.

Brokensha, D., D. Warren, and O. Werner, eds. 1980. *Indigenous Knowledge Systems and Development.* Lanham, Md.: University Press of America.

Browder, J. O. 1992. "The Limits of Extractivism: Tropical Forest Strategies beyond Extractive Reserves." *BioScience* 42 (3):174–182.

Brown, B. A. 1995. *In Timber Country: Working People's Stories of Environmental Conflict and Urban Flight.* Philadelphia: Temple University Press.

——. 1996. "Fencing the Northwest Forests: Decline of Public Access and Accustomed Rights." *Cultural Survival Quarterly* 20 (1):50–53.

Brown, C. H. 1985. "Mode of Subsistence and Folk Biological Taxonomy." *Current Anthropology* 26 (1):43–63.

Brown, E. 1985. *The Forest Preserve of New York State: A Handbook for Conservationists.* Glens Falls, N.Y.: Adirondack Mountain Club.

Brush, S. B. 1986. "Genetic Diversity and Conservation in Traditional Farming Systems." *Journal of Ethnobiology* 6 (1):151–167.

——. 1992. "Ethnoecology, Biodiversity, and Modernization in Andean Potato Agriculture. Journal of Ethnobiology 12 (2):161–185.

Brush, S. B. and D. Stabinsky, eds. 1996. *Valuing Local Knowledge: Indigenous People and Intellectual Property Rights.* Washington, D.C.: Island Press.

Bullard, R. D. 1990. *Dumping in Dixie: Race, Class, and Environmental Quality.* Boulder: 291 Westview Press.

Callicott, J. B. 1987. *Companion to "A Sand Almanac:" Interpretive and Critical Essays.* Madison: University of Wisconsin Press.

Campbell, R. D. 1985. *The People of the Land of Flint.* New York: University Press of America.

Carr, J. H., and E. E. Duensing, eds. 1983. *Land Use Issues of the 1980s.* New Brunswick, N.J.: Center for Urban Policy Research.

Carroll, M. S., and R. G. Lee. 1990. "Occupational Community and Identity among Pacific Northwestern Loggers: Implications for Adapting to Economic Changes." In R. G. Lee, D. R. Field, and W. R. Burch, eds. *Community and Forestry: Continuities in the Sociology of Natural Resources.* Boulder: Westview Press.

Chambers, R. 1983. *Rural Development: Putting the Last First.* London: Longman.

Chambers, R. 1992. "Methods for Analysis by Farmers: The Professional Challenge." Paper for the Association for Farming Systems Research/Extension 1991–1992 Symposium, Michigan State University.

Chambers, R., A. Pacey, and L. A. Thrupp, eds. 1989. *Farmer First: Farmer Innovation and Agricultural Innovation.* London: Intermediate Technology Publications.

Cheney, J. 1989a. "Postmodern Environmental Ethics: Ethics as Bioregional Narrative." *Environmental Ethics* 11 (2):117–134.

Cheney, J. 1989b. "The Neo-Stoicism of Radical Environmentalism." *Environmental Ethics* 11 (4):293–325.

Cohen, A. P. 1985. *The Symbolic Construction of Community.* New York: Tavistock.

Collins, B. R. and E. W. B. Russell, eds. 1988. *Protecting the New Jersey Pinelands: A New Direction in Land-Use Management.* New Brunswick, N.J.: Rutgers University Press.

Commission on the Adirondacks in the Twenty-First Century. 1990. *The Adirondack Park in the Twenty-First Century.* Albany: State of New York.

Cronon, W. 1983. *Changes in the Land: Indians, Colonists, and the Ecology of New England.* New York: Farrar, Straus and Giroux.

Cronon, W., ed. 1996. *Uncommon Ground: Rethinking the Human Place in Nature.* New York: W. W. Norton and Company.

Crowfoot, J. E., and J. M. Wondolleck. 1990. *Environmental Disputes: Community Involvement in Conflict Resolution.* Covelo, Calif.: Island Press.

Culhane, P. J., H. P. Friesema, and J. A. Beecher. 1987. *Forecasts and Environmental Decisionmaking: The Content and Predictive Accuracy of Environmental Impact Statements.* Boulder: Westview Press.

Cuomo, M. M. 1991. *Governor Mario M. Cuomo's Proposals for the Adirondacks.* Albany. New York State Government.

Daly, D. 1990. "Extractive Reserves: A Great New Hope." *Garden* November–December 1990: 14:21 and 32.

292   Danielson, M. N. 1995. *Profits and Politics in Paradise: The Development of Hilton Head Island.* Columbia: University of South Carolina Press.

Decker, D. J., and G. R. Goff, eds. 1987. *Valuing Wildlife: Economic and Social Perspectives.* Boulder: Westview Press.

D'Elia, A. N. 1979. *The Adirondack Rebellion.* Onchiota, N.Y.: Onchiota Books.

Denzin, N. K., and Y. S. Lincoln, eds. 1994. *Handbook of Qualitative Research.* London: Sage Publications, Inc.

Department of Environmental Conservation. 1979. State Land Master Plan.

———. 1987. Draft Environmental Impact Statement.

———. 1989. "Planning the Management of New York's Wildlife: Preliminary Assessment of Wildlife Management Needs." Draft for Public Review and Comment. Division of Fish and Wildlife.

———. 1990. Directory of Primary Wood-Using Industries in New York State.

Devall, B., and G. Sessions. 1985. *Deep Ecology: Living as if Nature Mattered.* Salt Lake City: Peregrine Smith Books.

DeWalt, B. R. 1994. "Using Indigenous Knowledge to Improve Agriculture and Natural Resource Management." *Human Organization* 53 (2):123–131.

Diamond, I., and G. F. Orenstein, eds. 1990. *Reweaving the World: The Emergence of Ecofeminism.* San Francisco: Sierra Club Books.

Dietrich, W. 1992. *The Final Forest: The Battle for the Last Great Trees of the Pacific Northwest.* New York: Penguin Books.

Diffenderfer, M., and D. Birch. 1997. Bioregionalism: A Comparative Study of the Adirondacks and the Sierra Nevada." *Society and Natural Resources* 10:3–16.

Dillman, D. A., and D. J. Hobbs, eds. 1982. *Rural Society in the United States: Issues for the 1980's.* Boulder: Westview Press.

Dobbs, D., and R. Ober. 1995. *The Northern Forest.* White River Junction, Vt.: Chelsea Green Publishing Company.

Donaldson, A. L. 1921. *A History of the Adirondacks.* New York: The Century Co.

Donnelly, M. 1993. "Dominion Theology and 'Wise' Use." *Wild Oregon* 19 (1):15.

Draper, D., and H. G. Kariel. 1990. "Metatourism: Dealing Critically with the Future of Tourism Environments." *Journal of Cultural Geography* 11 (1):139–155.

Dunham, H. L. 1952. "Adirondack French Louie: Early Life in the North Woods." Utica, N.Y.

Duryea, M. L., and K. A. Kainer. 1992. "Tapping Women's Knowledge: Plant Resource Use in Extractive Reserves, Acre, Brazil." *Economic Botany* 46 (4):408–425.

Eckersley, R. 1989. "Divining Evolution: The Ecological Ethics of Murray Bookchin." *Environmental Ethics* 11 (1):99–116.

Emerson, R. W. 1867. *The Adirondacks: A Journal Dedicated to My Fellow Travellers in August 1858: May Day and Other Poems.* Boston: Ticknor and Fields.

Empire State Forest Products Association. 1991. *New York Forest Policy Summary.*   *293*
Albany: Empire State Forest Products Association.

Erichsen-Brown, C. 1979. *Medicinal and Other Uses of North American Plants: A Historical Survey with Special Reference to the Eastern Indian Tribes.* New York: Dover Publications.

Faulkner, W. 1940. *Go Down Moses.* New York: Random House.

Fennessy, L. 1988. "The History of Newcomb." Newcomb, N.Y.

Fisher, R. and W. Ury. 1991. *Getting to Yes: Negotiating Agreement without Giving In,* 2d ed. New York: Penguin Books.

Fisher, S. L., ed. 1993. *Fighting Back in Appalachia: Traditions of Resistance and Change.* Philadelphia: Temple University Press.

Fitchen, J. M. 1980. *Poverty in Rural America.* Boulder: Westview Press.

———. 1991. *Endangered Spaces, Enduring Places: Change, Identity, and Survival in Rural America.* Boulder: Westview Press.

Foreman, D. 1991. *Confessions of an Eco Warrior.* New York: Harmony Books.

Fortmann, L. 1988. "Predicting Natural Resource Micro-Protest." *Rural Sociology* 53 (3):357–367.

———. 1996. "Bonanza! The Unasked Questions: Domestic Land Tenure through International Lenses." *Society and Natural Resources* 9:537–547.

Fortmann, L., and J. Kusel. 1990. "New Voices, Old Beliefs: Forest Environmentalism among New and Long-Standing Rural Residents." *Rural Sociology* 55 (2):214–232.

Foster, M. K., J. Campisi, and M. Mithun, eds. 1984. *Extending the Rafters: Interdisciplinary Approaches to Iroquoian Studies.* Albany: State University of New York Press.

Fowler, A., ed. 1968. *Cranberry Lake from Wilderness to Adirondack Park.* Syracuse: Syracuse University Press.

Fowler, B. 1974. *Adirondack Album.* Volume 2. Schenectady: Outdoor Associates.

———. 1982. *Adirondack Album.* Volume 3. Schenectady: Outdoor Associates.

Fox, W. 1989. "The Deep Ecology–Ecofeminism Debate and Its Parallels." *Environmental Ethics* 11 (1):5–25.

Freemuth, John. 1996. "The Emergence of Ecosystem Management: Reinterpreting the Gospel?" *Society and Natural Resources* 9:411–417.

Garrow, R. G., and B. Barnes, ed. 1984. *Legends of Our Nations.* Cornwall Island, Ontario: North American Indian Travelling College.

Geertz, C. 1973. *The Interpretation of Cultures.* New York: Basic Books.

———. 1983. *Local Knowledge: Further Essays in Interpretive Anthropology.* New York: Basic Books.

———. 1988. *Works and Lives: The Anthropologist as Author.* Stanford: Stanford University Press.

Geisler, C. 1983. "Introduction: The New Lay of the Land." In *Who Owns Appalachia?*

294   *Landownership and Its Impact."* The Appalachia Land Ownership Task Force. Lexington: University Press of Kentucky.

Geisler, C., and F. J. Popper, eds. 1984. *Land Reform, American Style.* Rowman & Allanheld.

Gleick, J. 1987. *Chaos.* New York: Viking.

Godoy, R., and R. Lubowski. 1992. "Guidelines for the Economic Valuation of Nontimber Tropical Forest Products." *Current Anthropology* 33 (4):423–432.

Graham, F., Jr. 1978. *The Adirondack Park: A Political History.* Syracuse: Syracuse University Press.

Grayson, T. 1990. Research notes on pesticides used on blackflies. Unpublished.

Greaves, T., ed. 1994. *Intellectual Property Rights for Indigenous Peoples: A Sourcebook.* Oklahoma City: Society for Applied Anthropology.

Greenhouse, C. J. 1985. "Anthropology at Home: Whose Home?" *Human Organization* 44 (3):261–264.

Greider, W. 1992. *Who Will Tell the People: The Betrayal of American Democracy.* New York: Simon and Schuster.

Guba, E. G., and Y. S. Lincoln. 1989. *Fourth Generation Evaluation.* London: Sage Publications.

Guha, R. 1989. "Radical American Environmentalism and Wilderness Preservation: A Third World Critique." *Environmental Ethics* 11 (1):71–83.

Gupta, A. K. 1996. "The Honey Bee Network: Voices from Grassroots Innovators." *Cultural Survival Quarterly* 20 (1):57–60.

Guss, D. M., ed. 1985. *The Language of the Birds: Tales, Texts, and Poems of Interspecies Communication.* San Francisco: North Point Press.

Haeuber, R. 1996. "Setting the Environmental Policy Agenda: The Case of Ecosystem Management." *Natural Resources Journal* 36:1–26.

Hallowell, C. 1992. "Save Our School." *Harrowsmith's Country Life* 41:24–29.

Halpern, D., ed. 1987. *On Nature: Nature, Landscape, and Natural History.* San Francisco: North Point Press.

Harmon, D. 1987. "Cultural Diversity, Human Subsistence, and the National Park Ideal." *Environmental Ethics* 9:147–158.

Hays, S. P. 1987. *Beauty, Health, and Permanence: Environmental Politics in the United States, 1955–1985.* New York: Cambridge University Press.

Healy, R. 1979. *Land Use and the States.* Baltimore: Johns Hopkins University Press.

Hecht, S., and A. Cockburn. 1989. *The Fate of the Forest.* London: Verso.

Heller, M. 1989. *Call Me Adirondack: Names and Their Stories.* Saranac Lake: Chauncy Press.

Hobart, M., ed. 1993. *An Anthropological Critique of Development: The Growth of Ignorance.* New York: Routledge.

Hochschild, H. K. 1962a. *An Adirondack Resort in the Nineteenth Century: Blue Mountain Lake, 1870–1900: Stagecoaches and Luxury Hotels.* Blue Mountain Lake, N.Y.: Adirondack Museum.

——. 1962b. *Life and Leisure in the Adirondack Backwoods.* Blue Mountain Lake, N.Y.: 295
Adirondack Museum.

——. 1962c. *Lumberjacks and Rivermen in the Central Adirondacks, 1850–1950.* Blue
Mountain Lake, N.Y.: Adirondack Museum.

Holmes, T. P. 1990. *The Future of the Adirondacks: A Survey of Attitudes.* Prepared for
the Adirondack Museum. Saranac Lake, N.Y.: Timothy Holmes and Associates.

Horton, M., and P. Freire. 1990. *We Make the Road by Walking: Conversations on
Education and Social Change.* Philadelphia: Temple University Press.

Hostetler, J. A, 1993. *Amish Society,* 4th ed. Baltimore: Johns Hopkins University
Press.

Hughes, D. M. 1996. "When Parks Encroach upon People: Expanding National
Parks in the Rusitu Valley, Zimbabwe." *Cultural Survival Quarterly* 20 (1):36–40.

Hunn, E. 1982. "The Utilitarian Factor in Folk Biological Classification." *American
Anthropologist* 84:830–847.

Irland, L. C. 1982. *Wildlands and Woodlots: The Story of New England's Forests.* Hanover,
N.H.: University Press of New England.

Jamieson, P., ed. 1982. *The Adirondack Reader.* Glens Falls, N.Y.: The Adirondack
Mountain Club.

——. 1986. *Adirondack Pilgrimage.* Glens Falls, N.Y.: Adirondack Mountain Club.

Keller, J. E. 1980. *Adirondack Wilderness: A Story of Man and Nature.* Syracuse: Syracuse University Press.

Kellert, S. R. 1974. *From Kinship to Mastery: A Study of American Attitudes toward
Animals.*

——. 1985. "Conflict and Communications in Wildlife Resource Management."
Keynote Address. Transactions of the Northeast Section of the Wildlife Society.

——. 1986. "Public Understanding and Appreciation of the Biosphere Reserve
Concept." *Environmental Conservation* 13 (2):101–105.

——. 1987. "The Contributions of Wildlife to Human Quality of Life." In *Valuing
Wildlife: Economic and Social Perspectives.* D. J. Decker and G. R. Goff, eds.
Boulder: Westview Press.

——. 1989. "Perceptions of Animals in America." In *Perceptions of Animals in American
Culture* R. J. Hoage, ed. Washington, D.C.: Smithsonian Institution Press.

Kellert, S. R., and J. K. Berry. 1987. "Attitudes, Knowledge, and Behaviors toward
Wildlife as Affected by Gender." *Wildlife Society Bulletin.* 15:363–371.

Kellert, S. R., and E. O. Wilson, eds. 1993. *The Biophilia Hypothesis.* Covelo, Calif.:
Island Press.

Keltner, S. 1992. "Lincoln County Peaceworks Conference on Mediation." Lincoln
City, Oregon.

Kenney, S. M. 1985. "The Adirondack Park Private Land Use and Development
Plan: Has There Been a Taking?" Master's thesis, Cornell University.

Ketchledge, E. H. 1967. *Trees of the Adirondack High Peak Region.* Glens Falls, N.Y.:
Adirondack Mountain Club.

296 Ketchledge, E. H. 1990. "Alpine Flora." Lecture at Heart Lake.

Kidder, C. 1992. "Return of the Red Wolf." *Nature Conservancy* September–October 1992:10–15.

King, Y. 1990. "Healing the Wounds: Feminism, Ecology, and the Nature, Culture Dualism." In *Reweaving the World: The Emergence of Ecofeminism*. Irene Diamond and Gloria Feman Orenstein, eds. San Francisco: Sierra Club Books.

Kingsolver, A. E. 1992. "Contested Livelihoods: 'Placing' One Another in 'Cedar,' Kentucky." *Anthropological Quarterly* 65 (3):128–135.

Kirby, J. T. 1987. *Rural Worlds Lost: The American South*, 1920–1960. Baton Rouge: Louisiana State University Press.

Kohm, K. A., and J. F. Franklin, eds. 1997. *Creating a Forestry for the Twenty-First Century: The Science of Ecosystem Management*. Covelo, Calif.: Island Press.

Kuhn, T. S. 1962. *The Structure of Scientific Revolutions*. Chicago: University of Chicago Press.

LaBastille, A. 1987. *Beyond Black Bear Lake*. New York: W. W. Norton & Co.

Lakoff, G., and M. Johnson. 1980. *Metaphors We Live By*. Chicago: University of Chicago Press.

Lee, R. G. 1994. *Broken Trust, Broken Land: Freeing Ourselves from the War over the Environment*. Wilsonville, Ore.: Bookpartners.

Lee, R. G., D. R. Field, and W. R. Burch, Jr., eds. 1990. *Community and Forestry: Continuities in the Sociology of Natural Resources*. Boulder: Westview Press.

Leopold, A. 1966. *A Sand County Almanac: With Essays on Conservation from Round River*. New York: Ballantine Books.

———. 1991. *The River of the Mother of God and Other Essays*. Ed. S. L. Flader and J. B. Callicott. Madison: University of Wisconsin Press.

Lester, J. P., ed. 1995. *Environmental Politics and Policy: Theories and Evidence*. Durham: Duke University Press.

Lévi-Strauss, C. 1962. *The Savage Mind*. Chicago: University of Chicago Press.

Liroff, R. A., and G. G. Davis. 1981. *Protecting Open Space: Land Use Control in the Adirondack Park*. Cambridge: Ballinger.

Longstreth, T. M. 1917. *The Adirondacks*. New York: Century Company.

Lopez, B. 1989. *Crossing Open Ground*. New York: Random House.

Loucks, O. L. 1992. "Forest Response Research in NAPAP: Potentially Successful Linkage of Policy and Science." *Ecological Applications* 2 (2):117–123.

Lovelock, J. 1988. *The Ages of Gaia: A Biography of Our Living Earth*. New York: W. W. Norton and Co.

———. 1991. *Healing Gaia: Practical Medicine for the Planet*. New York: Harmony Books.

Lyon, T. J., and P. Stine, eds. 1992. *On Nature's Terms*. Texas A & M University Press.

Mahmood, C. K. 1992. "Do Ethnic Groups Exist?: A Cognitive Perspective on the Concept of Cultures." *Ethnology* 30 (1):1–14.

Manning, R. E. 1985. "Crowding Norms in Backcountry Settings: A Review and Synthesis." *Journal of Leisure Research* 17 (2):75–89.

Marden, P. G., and A. M. Schwartz. 1980. "Comparative Regional Issues: Land Use and Environmental Planning in the Adirondacks and Appalachians." In *Appalachia/America*. W. Somerville, ed., Proceedings of the 1980 Appalachian Studies Conference. East Tennessee State University: Appalachian Consortium Press.

Marleau, W. R. 1986. *Big Moose Station*. Old Forge, N.Y.: Marleau Family Publishing Company.

Matthews, A. 1990. "The Poppers and the Plains." *New York Times Magazine*. June 24.

Matthews, E. M. 1965. *Neighbor and Kin: Life in a Tennessee Ridge Community*. Nashville: Vanderbilt University Press.

McKibben, B. 1989. *The End of Nature*. New York: Random House.

McMartin, B. 1990. *Realizing the Recreational Potential of the Adirondack Wild Forests*. Volume 3 of *20/20 Vision*. Elizabethtown, N.Y.: Adirondack Council.

———. 1994. *The Great Forest of the Adirondacks*. Utica, N.Y.: North Country Books.

Medeiros, P. 1992. "A Proposal for an Adirondack Primeval." *Wild Earth*, Special Issue: 32–43.

Meine, C. 1987. "Aldo Leopold's Early Years." In *Companion to "A Sand County Almanac": Interpretive and Critical Essays*. J. Baird Callicott, ed. Madison: University of Wisconsin Press.

Mello, R. A. 1987. *Last Stand of the Red Spruce*. Washington, D.C.: Island Press.

Merchant, C. 1983. *The Death of Nature: Women, Ecology, and the Scientific Revolution*. San Francisco: Harper and Row.

Miedzian, M. 1991. *Boys Will Be Boys: Breaking the Link between Masculinity and Violence*. New York: Doubleday.

Miller, M. L., R. P. Gale, and P. J. Brown, eds. 1987. *Social Science in Natural Resource Management Systems*. Boulder: Westview Press.

Mitchell, M. K., J. K. Thompson, and B. K. Barnes, eds. 1984. *Traditional Teachings*. Cornwall Island, Ontario: North American Indian Travelling College.

Moran, E. F. 1991. "Human Adaptive Strategies in Amazonian Blackwater Ecosystems." *American Anthropologist* 93 (2):361–382.

Moran, E. F., ed. 1990. *The Ecosystem Approach in Anthropology: From Concept to Practice*. Ann Arbor: University of Michigan Press.

Muir, J. 1961. *The Mountains of California*. Garden City, N.Y.: Anchor Books/Doubleday.

Murray, W. H. H. 1869. *Adventures in the Wilderness, or Camp Life in the Adirondacks*. Boston: Fields, Osgood and Co.

Nabhan, G. 1985. *Gathering the Desert*. Tucson: University of Arizona Press.

Nabhan, G., and S. St. Antoine. 1993. "The Loss of Floral and Faunal Story: The Extinction of Experience." In *The Biophilia Hypothesis*, S. R. Kellert and E. O. Wilson, eds. Covelo, Calif.: Island Press.

298   Nash, R. F. 1982. *Wilderness and the American Mind*. New Haven: Yale University Press.

———. 1989. *The Rights of Nature: A History of Environmental Ethics*. Madison: University of Wisconsin Press.

National Environment Secretariat, Clark University, Egerton University, and The Center for International Development and Environment of the World Resources Institute. 1991. Participatory Rural Appraisal Handbook. Clark University, Worcester, Mass.

Nollman, J. 1990. *Spiritual Ecology: A Guide for Reconnecting with Nature*. New York: Bantam Books.

Norton, B. G., ed. 1986. *The Preservation of Species: The Value of Biological Diversity*. Princeton: Princeton University Press.

O'Callaghan, K. 1993. "The Wise Use Movement: Whose Agenda?" *Wild Oregon* 19 (1):12–14.

Oelschlager, M. 1991. *The Idea of Wilderness: From Prehistory to the Age of Ecology*. New Haven: Yale University Press.

Oldfield, M. L., and J. B. Alcorn. 1991. *Biodiversity: Culture, Conservation, and Ecodevelopment*. Boulder: Westview Press.

Parker, A. C. 1968. *Parker on the Iroquois: Iroquois Uses of Maize and Other Food Plants, The Code of Handsome Lake, the Seneca Prophet, The Constitution of the Five Nations*. Syracuse: Syracuse University Press.

Pavy, J.-M. 1993. Mali Bafing Faunal Reserve: Biodiversity and Human Resource Survey and Recommendations. Draft.

Peck, J. G. 1987. *Night Camp: Tales of the Adirondacks*. Utica, N.Y.: North Country Books.

Pendley, W. P. 1994. *It Takes a Hero: The Grassroots Battle against Environmental Oppression*. Bellevue, Wash.: Free Enterprise Press.

Perlin, J. 1991. *A Forest Journey: The Role of Wood in the Development of Civilization*. Cambridge: Harvard University Press.

Platt, R. H. 1991. *Land Use Control: Geography, Law, and Public Policy*. Englewood Cliffs, N.J.: Prentice-Hall.

Plumwood, V. 1996. "Has Democracy Failed Ecology? An Ecofeminist Perspective." In *Ecology and Democracy*, F. Mathews, ed. Portland, Ore.: Frank Cass.

Pollan, M. 1990. "Beyond the Wilderness." *Harper's Magazine* April:38–48.

———. 1991. *Second Nature*. New York: Atlantic Monthly Press.

Popper, F. J. 1981. *The Politics of Land-Use Reform*. Madison: University of Wisconsin Press.

Power, T. M. 1996. *Lost Landscapes and Failed Economics: The Search for a Value of Place*. Covelo, Calif.: Island Press.

Prance, G. T. 1989. "Economic Prospects from Tropical Rainforest Ethnobotany." In *Fragile Lands of Latin America: Strategies for Sustainable Development*. J. O. Browder, ed. Boulder: Westview Press.

Price, M. F. 1996. "People in Biosphere Reserves: An Evolving Concept." *Society*   *299*
and Natural Resources, 9:645–654.

Ratner, S. E. 1984. "Diversified Household Survival Strategies and Natural Resource Use in the Adirondacks." Master's thesis, Cornell University.

———. 1990. "Report to the Adirondack Park Agency." Draft, Yellowwood Consulting Group.

Ratner, S. E., and P. Ide. 1985. "Strategies for Community Economic Development
through Natural Resource Use in Northern New York." Ithaca: Cornell University Department of Agricultural Economics.

Reason, P. 1994. "Three Approaches to Participative Inquiry." In *Handbook of Qualitative Research,* N. K. Denzin and Y. S. Lincoln, eds. London: Sage Publications.

Redclift, M. 1991. "The Multiple Dimensions of Sustainable Development." *Geography* 76 (1):36–42.

Reed, P. 1989. "Man Apart: An Alternative to the Self-Realization Approach."
Environmental Ethics 11 (1):53–69.

Rehfus, R. O. 1985. "Conflict Resolution and Dispute Management Techniques in
Fishery Management: An Unexplored Potential." Transactions of the Northeast
Section of the Wildlife Society, Hartford, Conn.

Renn, O., T. Webler, and P. Wiedemann, eds. 1995. *Fairness and Competence in
Citizen Participation: Evaluating Models for Environmental Discourse.* Boston: Kluwer
Academic Publishers.

Richards, K. B., ed. 1985. "Strategic Plan for Forest Resources in New York State."
Albany: Forest Resources Planning, New York State Department of Environmental Conservation.

Richards, P., L. J. Slikkerveer, and A. O. Phillips. 1985. *Indigenous Agricultural
Revolution: Ecology and Food Production in West Africa.* London: Hutchinson and
Co.

———. 1989. "Indigenous Knowledge Systems for Agriculture and Rural Development: The CIKARD Inaugural Lectures." Iowa State University Research
Foundation, Technology and Social Change Program.

Rodale, R. 1986. "Extension in Reverse: Farmers Lecture Experts." *New Farm* September–October:26–28.

Rolston, H. III. 1987. "Beauty and the Beast: Aesthetic Experience of Wildlife." In
Valuing Wildlife: Economic and Social Perspectives. D. J. Decker and G. R. Goff,
eds. Boulder: Westview Press.

Rushforth, S. 1992. "The Legitimation of Beliefs in a Hunter-Gatherer Society:
Bearlake Athapaskan Knowledge and Authority." *American Ethnologist* 19
(3):483–500.

Ryan, J. C. 1992. "Goods from the Woods: Managing Tropical Forests for Preservation and Profit." *Journal of Forestry* 90 (4):25–28.

Sale, K. 1985. *Dwellers in the Land: The Bioregional Vision.* San Francisco: Sierra Club
Books.

300   Scarce, R. 1990. *Eco-Warriors: Understanding the Radical Environmental Movement.* Chicago: Noble Press.

Schaefer, P. 1989. *Defending the Wilderness: The Adirondack Writings of Paul Schaefer.* Syracuse: Syracuse University Press.

Schenkel, A. F. 1995. *The Rich Man and the Kingdom.* Minneapolis: Fortress Press.

Schon, D. A. 1983. *The Reflective Practitioner: How Professionals Think in Action.* New York: Basic Books.

Schwartzman, S. 1989. "Extractive Reserves: The Rubber Tappers' Strategy for Sustainable Use of the Amazon Rainforest." In *Fragile Lands of Latin America: Strategies for Sustainable Development.* J. Browder, ed. Boulder: Westview Press.

Sedjo, R. A., ed. 1985. *Investments in Forestry: Resources, Land Use, and Public Policy.* Boulder: Westview Press.

Seitz, V. R. 1995. *Women, Development, and Communities for Empowerment in Appalachia.* Albany: State University of New York Press.

Shafer, C. L. 1990. *Nature Reserves: Island Theory and Conservation Practice.* Washington, D.C.: Smithsonian Institution Press.

Shannon, M. A. 1990. "Building Trust: The Formation of a Social Contract." In *Community and Forestry: Continuities in the Sociology of Natural Resources.* R. G. Lee, D. R. Field, and W. R. Burch, eds. Boulder: Westview Press.

Sheffer, R. 1988. *Lost River.* Boonville, N.Y.: Night Tree Press.

Shepard, P. 1985. *Totemic Culture.* In *The Language of the Birds: Tales, Texts, and Poems of Interspecies Communications.* D. M. Guss, ed. San Francisco: North Point Press.

Siccama, T. G., M. Bliss, and H. W. Vogelmann. 1982. "Decline of Red Spruce in the Green Mountains of Vermont." *Bulletin of the Torrey Botanical Club* 109:165.

Simmons, L. J. 1976. *Mostly Spruce and Hemlock.* Vail-Ballou Press.

Skiffington, K. K. 1991. "Noblesse Oblige: A Strategy for Local Boundary Making." *Ethnology* 30 (3):265–277.

Society of American Foresters. 1989. *Report of the Society of American Foresters National Task Force on Community Stability.* Bethesda, Md.: Society of American Foresters, SAF Resource Policy Series.

Spretnak, C. 1990. "Ecofeminism: Our Roots and Flowering." In *Reweaving the World: The Emergence of Ecofeminism.* Irene Diamond and Gloria Feman Orenstein, eds. San Francisco: Sierra Club Books.

Stapleton, R. M. 1993. "A Call to Action." *National Parks* 67 (3–4):37–40.

Stevens, W. K. 1992. "Novel Strategy Puts People at Heart of Texas Preserve." *New York Times* March 31: B5.

Street, A. B. 1860. *Woods and Waters, or the Saranacs and Racket.* New York: M. Doolady.

Sylvester, N. 1989. *Historical Sketches of Northern New York and the Adirondack Wilderness.* Mamaroneck, N.Y.: Harbor Hill Books.

Terrie, P. G. 1985. *Forever Wild: Environmental Aesthetics and the Adirondack Forest Preserve.* Philadelphia: Temple University Press.

Tobias, M., ed. 1985. *Deep Ecology.* San Diego: Avant Books.   *301*

Todd, J. 1983. *Long Lake: A Facsimile of the 1845 Edition.* Mamaroneck, N.Y.: Harbor Hill Books.

Tucker, C. K. and G. F. Tucker. 1989. "Critical Characteristics of New York State Maple Syrup Producers: Socio-economics, Tradition, and Personal Expertise." Parts I and II, *Maple Syrup Digest* 1A(2):24–25, 1A(3):26–27.

Tyler, H. E. 1969. *Log Cabin Days: Folk Tales of the Adirondacks.* Saranac Lake, N.Y.: Currier Press.

Ury, W. 1993. *Getting Past No: Negotiating Your Way From Confrontation to Cooperation.* New York: Bantam Books.

VanValkenburgh, N. J. 1985. *Land Acquisition for New York State: An Historical Perspective.* Arkville, N.Y.: Catskill Center.

Walker, G. B., and S. E. Daniels. 1996. "The Clinton Administration, the Northwest Forest Conference, and Managing Conflict: When Talk and Structure Collide." *Society and Natural Resources* 9:77–91.

Ward, V., ed. 1990. *I Always Tell the Truth (Even If I Have to Lie to Do It!): Stories from the Adirondack Liars' Club.* Greenfield Center, N.Y.: Greenfield Review Press.

Watkins, T. H. 1992. "Father of the Forests." *Journal of Forestry* 90 (1):12–15.

Welch, F. 1968. "The Making of a Woodsman." In *Cranberry Lake from Wilderness to Adirondack Park.* A. Fowler, ed. Syracuse: Syracuse University Press.

Western, D., R. M. Wright, and S. C. Strum, eds. 1994. *Natural Connections: Perspectives in Community-Based Conservation.* Covelo, Calif.: Island Press.

Whisnant, D.E . 1983. *All That Is Native and Fine: The Politics of Culture in an American Region.* Chapel Hill: University of North Carolina Press.

White, W. C. 1985. *Adirondack Country.* Syracuse, N.Y.: Syracuse University Press.

Whittaker, R. H., F. H. Bormann, G. E. Likens, and T. G. Siccama. 1974. "The Hubbard Brook Ecosystem Study: Forest Biomass and Production." *Ecological Monographs* 44(2).

Whyte, W. F., ed. 1991. *Participatory Action Research.* London: Sage Publications.

Wild Earth Winter 1996/1997. 6(4):36–83.

Wilkinson, C. F., and H. M. Anderson. 1987. *Land and Resource Planning in the National Forests.* Washington, D.C.: Island Press.

Willer, C. 1995. *Gated Lands: A Report on the Ownership of Oregon's Private Coast Range Forests.* Newport, Ore.: Coast Range Association.

Williams, D. R., M. E. Patterson, and J. R. Roggenbuck. 1992. "Beyond the Commodity Metaphor: Examining Emotional and Symbolic Attachment to Place." *Leisure Sciences* 14:29–46.

Wilson, E. O., ed. 1988. *Biodiversity.* Washington, D.C.: National Academy Press.

Young, I. M. 1990. *Justice and the Politics of Difference.* Princeton: Princeton University Press.

Zinser, C. I. 1980. *The Economic Impact of the Adirondack Park Private Land Use and Development Plan.* Albany: State University of New York Press.

Index

Catherine Henshaw Knott is Director of Women in International Development and Adjunct Assistant Professor of Anthropology at Oregon State University.